New Perspectives on the Social Aspects of Digital Gaming

T0298540

This is a timely addition to Game Studies, especially in the way it addresses issues at the heart of gaming communities at present. A strong body of complimentary chapters produce a well-rounded picture of gaming communities and the issues they face.

—*Esther MacCallum-Stewart, University of the West of England, UK*

As with the previous volume, this book brings together an interesting and enlightening sampler of the latest original research on social aspects of digital games from talented new scholars and established leaders in the field. An excellent survey on where research on digital games is going, and where it should go.

—*James D. Ivory, Virginia Tech, USA*

Expanding on the work in the volume Multiplayer, this new book explores several other areas related to social gaming in detail. The aim is to go beyond a typical "edited book" concept, and offer a very concise volume with several focal points that are most relevant for the current debate about multiplayer games, both in academia and society. As a result, the volume offers the latest research findings on online gaming, social forms of gaming, identification, gender issues and games for change, primarily applying a social-scientific approach.

Rachel Kowert recently completed a Postdoctoral Fellowship at the University of Münster, Germany.

Thorsten Quandt holds the chair of Online Communication at the University of Münster, Germany.

Routledge Advances in Game Studies

1 Video Games and Social Competence
Rachel Kowert

2 Sexuality in Role-Playing Games
Ashley ML Brown

3 Gender, Age, and Digital Games in the Domestic Context
Alison Harvey

4 The Dark Side of Game Play
Controversial Issues in Playful Environments
*Edited by Torill Elvira Mortensen, Jonas Linderoth,
and Ashley ML Brown*

5 Understanding Counterplay in Video Games
Alan F. Meades

6 Video Game Policy
Production, Distribution, and Consumption
Edited by Steven Conway and Jennifer deWinter

7 Digital Games as History
How Videogames Represent the Past and Offer Access to
Historical Practice
Adam Chapman

8 New Perspectives on the Social Aspects of Digital Gaming
Multiplayer 2
Edited by Rachel Kowert and Thorsten Quandt

New Perspectives on the Social Aspects of Digital Gaming

Multiplayer 2

Edited by Rachel Kowert and Thorsten Quandt

Routledge
Taylor & Francis Group

LONDON AND NEW YORK

First published 2017
by Routledge

2 Park Square, Milton Park, Abingdon, Oxfordshire OX14 4RN
52 Vanderbilt Avenue, New York, NY 10017

Routledge is an imprint of the Taylor & Francis Group, an informa business

First issued in paperback 2019

Library of Congress Cataloging-in-Publication Data
CIP data has been applied for.

ISBN: 978-1-138-64363-5 (hbk)
ISBN: 978-0-367-87723-1 (pbk)

Typeset in Sabon
by codeMantra

Contents

List of Figures and Tables   vii

1 *Multiplayer* and Beyond: Witnessing the Evolution
   of Gaming   1
   THORSTEN QUANDT AND RACHEL KOWERT

PART I
Social Forms of Gaming

2 From Social Play to Social Games and Back: The
   Emergence and Development of Social Network Games   11
   FRANS MÄYRÄ, JAAKKO STENROS, JANNE PAAVILAINEN,
   AND ANNAKAISA KULTIMA

3 Identifying Social Forms of Flow in Multiuser
   Video Games   32
   JOCERAN BORDERIE AND NICOLAS MICHINOV

4 Envisioning the Other: A Grounded Exploration of
   Social Roles in Digital Game Play   46
   JASMIEN VERVAEKE, FREDERIK DE GROVE, AND JAN VAN LOOY

PART II
Online Gaming

5 Multiplayer Games as the Ultimate Communication
   Lab and Incubator: A Multimedia Study   67
   JOHN L. SHERRY, ANDY BOYAN, KENDRA KNIGHT,
   CHERYLANN EDWARDS, AND QI HAO

6 The MMORPG Designer's Journey: Casualization
and its Consequences for Social Interactions   82
DANIEL PIETSCHMANN, BENNY LIEBOLD, AND GEORG VALTIN

7 Multiplayer Features and Game Success   97
ANDRÉ MARCHAND

PART III
Gender Issues in Gaming Communities

8 Sexism in Video Games and the Gaming Community   115
JESSE FOX AND WAI YEN TANG

9 Women Are From *FarmVille*, Men Are From
ViceCity: The Cycle of Exclusion and Sexism in
Video Game Content and Culture   136
RACHEL KOWERT, JOHANNES BREUER, AND
THORSTEN QUANDT

PART IV
Games for Change

10 The Key Features of Persuasive Games: A Model
and Case Analysis   153
RUUD S. JACOBS, JEROEN JANSZ, AND TERESA DE LA HERA
CONDE-PUMPIDO

11 "Resist the Dictatorship of Malygos on Coldarra
Island!": Evidence of MMOG Culture in Taiwan's
Sunflower Social Movement   172
HOLIN LIN AND CHUEN-TSAI SUN

12 Between Drudgery and "Promesse du Bonheur":
Games and Gamification   185
MATHIAS FUCHS

List of Contributors   201
Index   209

Figures and Tables

Figures

3.1   Team profiles showing solitary, group, and team flow
      episodes.   39
5.1   Distribution of speech acts across groups.   75
7.1   Slopes for moderating effects (total performance model).   108
9.1   Proposed theoretical model of exclusion and sexism in
      video game content and culture.   144
10.1 Model of persuasive dimensions employed in
      persuasive games.   155
12.1 Poster announcing co-working spaces in the streets
      of Berlin.   188

Tables

2.1   Player relations in games   22
3.1   Subtypes of positive interdependence and their definitions 34
3.2   Coding scheme   37
3.3   Interdependence subtypes in each experimental condition   38
4.1   Four properties of social play settings   49
4.2   Overview of the four emerging roles and their properties   52
5.1   Study corpus by group size and discursive flexibility
      constraints   72
5.2   Examples of illocutionary acts from the study corpus   73
5.3   Shannon entropy Searle codes   75
5.4   Sequence analysis: Identity between interactions
      within group for Searle codes   76
5.5   Sequence analysis: Identity between interactions
      between group for Searle codes   76
7.1   Descriptive statistics   101
7.2   Software regression results   105
10.1 Emphasis on persuasive elements of the games studied   158

1 *Multiplayer* and Beyond

Witnessing the Evolution of Gaming

Thorsten Quandt and Rachel Kowert

When the first *Multiplayer* volume was published some years ago, it was primarily looking at the social aspects of digital gaming – with a strong focus on online (computer) games, virtual worlds, and, to some extent, console games. The core message of the book was a very simple one and beyond the depth and variation of the individual articles: Modern gaming is mostly a social form of mainstream media entertainment. In that sense, the book elucidated that the stereotypical image of the solitary, reclusive, and socially inept gaming geek – in popular culture often equated with exaggerated and condescending depictions of pubescent, male 'nerds' – was just echoing a radically reduced caricature of computer gamers from earlier phases in the evolution of gaming.

The evolution of gaming has not stopped. In fact, even in the few years since the first *Multiplayer* volume, there have been many crucial developments and changes in the industry. For example, there has been a differentiation of distribution channels, with a decline in boxed products and a rise in online distribution. Mobile gaming on smartphones has also become a dynamic market, social (network) games have been on the rise (and the decline again), and virtual reality head-mounted displays have come to be touted as the 'next big thing' to revolutionise (not only) gaming. These are just a few of the notable developments in a very short time, and, as editors, we felt that a new *Multiplayer* book was necessary to fill some of the research gaps that were becoming all too obvious with the many innovations in the field.

The current book is not meant to replace the older one, but rather should be seen as complementary to the previous one, by adding new and innovative aspects. It can be argued that any edited volume in such a dynamic environment will always remain incomplete, especially when relying on concrete and current research. Technological developments and social changes will lead to new phenomena that were unknown at the time of writing. And these are not only peripheral fluctuation in the material objects of analysis, but changes to the very essence of the phenomenon per se. So gaming itself does not remain the same!

The evolutionary metaphor (despite some obvious limitations) may be a helpful for a moment, in understanding this statement better: Gaming, as a social phenomenon, can be regarded as being coevolving with society and its communication and media technologies. Even the use of basic technologies that may look like static 'devices' at first sight (a console, a computer, a smartphone, etc.) becomes embedded and shaped in our social environments until they are superseded by new generations of superior devices with improved capabilities and functions. With the 'software' side, the evolutionary character is probably even more obvious – games are updated and 'patched', extended with download content, adapted to new situations and demands, socially embedded in day-to-day practices, and sometimes even used in ways beyond the imagination of the developers and designers. And when regarding gaming as a social 'collectivity', its evolutionary character, with ongoing changes and differentiation, is more than apparent – and again, this sequel of *Multiplayer* is a reaction to this.

For us as scientific observers, the fast differentiation of the field poses many problems, though. As noted previously, our work always remains incomplete, and often we are even slower than the developments in the field. Studies need to be prepared, ethically approved, and conducted, often with limited resources. Analyses need considerable time as well, and the writing and publishing process delays the public circulation of innovative scientific findings considerably (and to be frank, editors sometimes also delay the process by imposing stressful rewriting procedures on their esteemed authors!). As a result, and probably also in principle, our work is just a snapshot of a social reality that has already evolved in a different direction. When reading older texts on gaming and gamer culture, we are often surprised how 'ancient' these descriptions read – sometimes like ethnographic depictions of exotic tribes from colonial times. Without any doubt, much of the excellent work in this book will probably make a similar impression to future generations of games researchers.

The work in this book is current and many of the authors are on the forefront of cutting-edge research in digital games. However, it is important to note that some of the work contained within this volume has a more general applicability to the field and future researchers will likely relate to it as a valid analysis of core qualities of gaming for many years to come. They touch upon the very essence of gaming and their work will pass the test of time. However, other articles focus on aspects that are currently relevant, but may lose their importance in the future. Their objects of analysis will change, disappear, or be replaced by other modes of gaming. Still, there is value to this in depicting specific evolutionary phases of development, or specific branches of gaming that are relevant at a given point of time (and that lead to subsequent developments). Much like solo gaming was, at a certain point, the main and leading mode of use, it is still echoed by the lingering stereotypes mentioned before.

In that sense, the articles in this book are current, and mostly based on up-to-date research, but they are also a reflection of a specific status quo, representing gaming as of now. We are witnessing the evolution of gaming while it happens! Gaming is not a fixed and finished, static object of analysis, but something much more organic. Recently discovered social aspects – or recently evolved aspects – of gaming are in the focus of *Multiplayer 2*; but some articles also refer to its rich (pre) history and speculate on potential futures that are most likely even more social than what we see now (and most likely beyond our current imagination).

As with other forms of evolutionary analysis, looking back can also be instructive in learning about the roots of developments, general principles and potential future paths. Indeed, the social side of gaming can be traced back to the very roots of the field: Frans Mäyrä, Jaako Stenros, Janne Paavilainen, and Annakaisa Kultima argue in their piece on social network games that the very DNA of gaming already had a social component in it. They note that early experimental electronic games and some early arcade video games were meant to be played by two players, or they were played in the social context of arcades. In their further analysis, Mäyrä and colleagues focus on social network games (including *Facebook* games, like *Farmville,* etc.) – their (short) history, their characteristics, and their potential for social play. Interestingly, despite their name, 'social' games can be argued to be not so social after all. Still, they had a key influence on the development of the gaming market and its (re)financing structures. In that respect, they already have left their very own mark in the genetic heritage of gaming – although their future is currently not that clear, given the notable decline of social games (at the time of writing), as also described in the article by Mäyrä and colleagues.

Despite the wealth of current research acknowledging the social side of gaming (much more than it was the case some years ago), many basic concepts of use and effects research are still rooted in a single-player perspective. That is, they implicitly treat the gamer as somebody who is playing against an automated or computer controlled character, in total social isolation. As argued by Joceran Borderie and Nicolas Michinov in their piece, this kind of reduction unnecessarily places the focus on individual perceptions and processes within a closed system. By focusing on Cszikszentmihalyi's seminal concept of flow and discussing it in the context of multiuser video games, Borderie and Michinov outline findings from a lab study on *League of Legends* players. Perhaps surprisingly, they argue that flow can be conceptualised and measured as a social phenomenon in-group situations rather than being be limited to a self-referring, inward-looking state in mind. Their work demonstrates the need to rethink our base categories when discussing the social aspects of digital gaming.

The subsequent piece by Jasmien Vervaeke, Frederik De Grove, and Jan Van Looy follows a similar pattern, by reflecting and testing some base ideas of gaming and gamers in a social context. However, whereas Borderie and Michinov take an arguably 'individualistic' concept and transfer it into a social context, Vervaeke and colleagues can show that inherently 'social' concepts can also have a rather nonsocial component. In their empirical study on experiences with other people while gaming, they discover four archetypes of interactions with, and constructions of, the 'other'. Not all of these are social, at least in a common-sense meaning: Although the 'others' in gaming can be coplayers or even companions in meaningful social relationships, they can also serve as sole witnesses of the player's actions and progress, or even as purely functional tools for playing the game. These findings challenge us to think about our conceptualization of interactions with others as being inherently and automatically social and meaningful. For example, as indicated by their 'tool' archetype, interactions with humans in gaming can sometimes be reduced to a merely instrumental relation. On the other hand, the 'companion' archetype shows that gaming can also be much more than a superficial, solitary activity that relies on 'beating' game mechanics or breaking high scores (as it is still often depicted in the public debate). Vervaeke and colleagues also note that there can be deep relationships with others, with the game simply serving as an environment for being together.

Such a meaningful social interaction is certainly impossible without forms of communication. Not all of them need to be verbal, but many games offer forms of direct textual and oral utterances via embedded chat channels. Furthermore, team speak can be added to games that do not offer such options, and considerably enhance the social experience. The study by John Sherry, Andy Boyan, Kendar Knight, Cherylann Edwards, and Qui Hao focusses on communication as a core element of social interaction in multiplayer games. Using Searle's speech act categories as a conceptual basis, and applying innovative methods of analysis (partially derived from bioinformatics), they look for recurring patterns and predictable sequences in the flow of utterances. As Sherry and colleagues argue, human communication, by definition, is not random, because it is at least partially rule-based, logical, and therefore predictable. However, they also note that there may be some flexibility in the flow of communication, depending on its circumstances, underlying tasks, and discursive restraints. So human communication can be analysed and categorised according to its deep structure. Sherry and colleagues compare various types of communication in their study, from *World of Warcraft* (WoW) raids to film scripts, and find striking differences – that may be helpful for the development of base categories for future analyses of in-game communication, and comparisons with other nongaming activities. In that sense, the work by Sherry and colleagues give us a glimpse at future analyses of gaming that make it comparable to other forms of meaningful communicative interaction.

Interactions are also a central element to the work of Daniel Pietschmann, Benny Liebold, and Georg Valtin. They pick up the evolutionary metaphor introduced previously, and apply this idea to the analysis of MMORPGs (Massively Multiplayer Online Role Playing Games) as a genre. In essence, they argue that genres are not fixed and can develop over time, and in sync with these changes, the gameplay characteristics and social interactions in the respective games can change. They discuss this for several cases, with *WoW* being the most prominent one. As they show, interaction in early MMORPGs was a necessity due to the difficult mechanics and harsh conditions of the in-game-world – so social aspects were a result of a 'need to cooperate' to succeed. However, as they further argue, this lead to frustrations of gamers outside the hardcore group, and the industry reacted by making the games more accessible, easy and 'casual', partially removing the need to cooperate. Pietschmann and colleagues note that some modern MMORPGs do not even allow cooperation in some of their parts (as is the case with the introduction of phasing in *WoW*, or a pure single player expansion of the popular MMORPG *Star Wars: The Old Republic*). They argue that this process of casualization actually reduces meaningful social interaction in the genre, making the games more of a single player experience. Their analyses serve as a reminder for observers and researchers to test and rethink their ideas of gaming and adapt them to the changes of gaming as an organic, evolving object of analysis.

Indeed, a temporal and evolutionary way of thinking is also essential for the subsequent study by André Marchand. He analyses the success of games depending on the inclusion of multiplayer features, but also in connection to the lifecycles of console generations. As noted previously, even the hardware side of gaming should not be thought of as something static: The respective console systems form dynamically changing environments for specific games, with some types of games being more successful in earlier stages of market presence than in later ones. In addition to this, the consoles are also competing against each other, amplifying, dampening, accelerating, or slowing down sales in other console environments. Naturally, there are some very strong, general effects of sales being high (shortly after a console's introduction and directly after the release of games), which are relatively independent from the environment and the competition. However, as Marchand notes in his article, the market success of multiplayer games in such dynamic environments is strongly connected to the user base: He finds that online multiplayer games are especially successful in later stages of a console's lifecycle, as the user base is higher and allows for attractive and easy online gaming with many coplayers being available. So this can counter the decline of sales in later stages of a console's lifecycle, and 'breathe new life' into older system's sales.

The composition and development of the user base is not only relevant for economic questions, but it also has a strong influence on player experiences. As games are social in so many ways – played with others or in social contexts, embedded in player communities, released, promoted, and debated in societal contexts – they are also dependent on who the 'others' in gaming are, how they behave in interactions, and how we perceive them ourselves. As Jesse Fox and Wai Yen Tang note in their article, there are many myths regarding the user base. In the public, there is still a prevailing stereotype of gaming being a predominantly male hobby, despite numerous studies indicating a much more balanced gamer population that is nearing the gender distribution in the societal base population. The notion of gaming being a 'male thing' may be explained by public perceptions developing slower than the social reality (and even scientific studies!), but it may also be explained by gaming experiences still being gendered in many ways. Unfortunately, inequalities and even harassment are still part of gaming, and this is especially the case with multiplayer games, where, unfortunately, sexist attitudes and behaviour are common. Fox and Tang give a lucid overview of the literature on sexism in video games and the gaming community, and as they can show, there are multiple forms and fields of sexism in gaming that are well documented. They further argue that there is a need to react and actively work against toxic gamer culture (that not only affects women, but also other groups of gamers) as this would not only benefit society, but also the industry and game sales. In their chapter, Rachel Kowert, Johannes Breuer, and Thorsten Quandt also focus on sexism in video game content and culture by identifying and outlining a 'cycle (model) of exclusion' for female game players. According to Kowert and colleagues, there are three central components that drive the cycle: (1) early media and gender socialization, (2) the video game industry, and (3) player communities. They propose to observe these three in sync, as the components and their interplay cannot be fully separated, and they argue that joint efforts on all levels are needed to break the cycle of exclusion. Indeed, thinking about gaming and the user base as organically evolving is also helpful in this context: Such a perspective fosters the hope that toxic, antisocial forms of exclusion can be reduced over time, and indeed, that gaming can become a more friendly environment for social experience.

Such a positive attitude towards change also lies at the heart of the next piece by Ruud S. Jacobs, Jeroen Jansz, and De la Hera, as they focus on persuasive games. Theis specific type of serious game is meant to change or reinforce (positively connoted) attitudes, and in essence, also subsequent behaviour. In their case analysis of 11 persuasive games, Jacobs, Jansz and De la Hera identify three major themes: (1) poverty and hardship, (2) lived experience and suffering from disorders, (3) violence and politics. They further analyse to what degree specific persuasive dimensions are used in these games, and find a high reliance on procedural, linguistic, and – to some extent – narrative persuasion, whereas other strategies are used rarely. Based on their analysis, they come to the conclusion that persuasive games are in many ways different from mainstream titles, as they do not necessarily appeal to large audiences. In that sense, Jacobs and colleagues deem (at least some) persuasive games as a form of 'digital pamphlet'. So although these games are typically not 'multiplayer' titles, they are still social, in the sense that their aim is to positively influence and change society. As we can learn from this work, we see that the role of games can go beyond pure 'entertainment' and even solo gaming can have an inherently social meaning.

The role of video games in society is further emphasised in the subsequent article by Lin and Sun. In their case analysis of the Sunflower movement in Taiwan, they show that the skills and knowledge acquired in MMOGs can be transferred from a gaming environment to political actions in the real world. They argue that the Sunflower student protest movement against a Taiwanese trade agreement with China had four characteristics that were directly influenced by MMOG culture, based on the notable experience with these games by many of the protesters: (1) game-like organization and collaboration; (2) ease of collaboration with strangers; (3) 'game tip' creation, usage, and distribution; (4) game culture as a reference to understand situations and take action. As argued by the authors, these aspects of gaming found their way into day-to-day behaviour and tangibly contributed the Sunflower social movement that had a notable impact society! Interestingly, Lin and Sun model MMOGs as a part of participatory culture argues that gaming is a segment of a larger, ongoing development towards participation that is fostered by new technologies and online communication. This is an interesting thought, as it doesn't regard gaming as something that is unique and detached from societal trends and changes but deeply embedded into them and, as a consequence, the influence goes in both directions, from gaming to societies and vice versa.

The final piece of the book returns the focus to the impact of games on society and everyday life, but from a very different perspective. The chapter by Mathias Fuchs focusses the concept of gamification that has been controversially debated in recent times. He argues that the transfer of gameplay characteristics into other areas of life, like health and self-improvement, learning, behavioural change, and work, can be used for the (seemingly) good and the bad. Although some people have regard gamification as a useful and effective form of incentivising desirable forms of behaviour, others have deemed it a form of mental conditioning and manipulation or as a rather empty marketing hype. Fuchs critically analyses the potential forms, uses, and effects of gamification, and concludes that gamification may actually be an ideology (i.e. the unification of work and play is a 'necessary false consciousness'). Although this may sound radical at first, it is a reminder that social aspects of gaming do not necessarily equate beneficial or desirable phenomena. We have to take this reminder seriously – if gaming is a deeply social phenomenon these days, we have to move beyond shallow analyses of 'obvious' risks of direct effects, and turn to more complex analyses of indirect social effects and developments.

The articles in this book give some hints at such developments. The authors observed various 'social' aspects of digital games from surprising angles. Naturally, on a rather mundane level, modern video games are often played with others, so there is a natural social component to multiplayer gaming. However, the articles go much further than that. As we learn from the analyses, we are reminded that games are deeply embedded into society. They are used for pleasure and joy, learning, and change. They are loved, hated, controversial, discussed, and their meaning often transgresses the boundaries of pure entertainment.

We also learn from the work in this book that gaming is not static – it's changing, evolving, and rather 'organic' as a part of an ongoing evolution. For the scientific observer, this is a fantastic opportunity! We may analyse processes while they happen, and phenomena while they develop, always learning something new and exciting. This book is a collection of such observations and we hope that the reader is equally excited by the explorations of many new social aspects of gaming that evolved in recent times.

Part I
Social Forms of Gaming

2 From Social Play to Social Games and Back

The Emergence and Development of Social Network Games

Frans Mäyrä, Jaakko Stenros, Janne Paavilainen, and Annakaisa Kultima

Games have been studied for well over a century, and the academic interest in play stretches back to antiquity. Yet contemporary game studies coalesced as a field around the turn of the millennium. As a field, game studies has been organised around a (rather deceptively) singular object of scrutiny: 'games'. However, as a social construct the category of 'games' is a moving target – and there are multiple social and discursive contexts and communities that have a stake in how games and play are defined. Gaming communities, fans, casual gamers, designers, scholars as well as academic fandom ('aca-fans'), different parts of the game industry, hobbyists, legislators, educators, and artists all have diverse yet partially overlapping stakes in this discussion. Questions such as "What is a game?", "Who is a gamer?", and "Are games art?" are all part of this discussion on how to understand and properly position games. Obviously, the conceptualization of games has direct implications on the characterisation of game studies as a field.

Against this background, it is hardly surprising that when a new breed of relatively simple games emerged in 2007[1], played by people who did not identify as gamers, who at times had limited contact with canonical digital games, and played those games for free in a new context, namely *Facebook*, that these games tended to be dismissed by traditional gamers and game media. Games developed for services such as *MySpace* and later particularly *Facebook*, which are commonly discussed under the terms *social games* or *social network games*, were at the time only the latest incarnation of *casual games* (see Kultima, 2015; Kuittinen et al., 2007), and were cast in the same lowly regarded category as early mobile phone games and browser-based games.

The term itself – social games – was contested right from the start because arguably game play has always been social and *Facebook* games were not considered particularly social. They did introduce, broadly speaking, a new type of mediated sociability in games by using social network connections as an integrated part of the game mechanics. From the developer perspective, such aims were probably primarily aligned with advertising the games to new players, whereas social interaction can in many services also unintentionally lead into formation of friendships or online communities (Malinen, 2016).

In this chapter, we document the rise of *Facebook* social games, explore the sociability they fostered, and discuss how social games are positioned in the wide field of games – and what they reveal and reflect about games and game studies. We start with a historical overview into the origins and development of social games, and then move to discuss how various examples of social games, with social, monetization, and distribution-related key features that have shaped these games and their operation. The advantages and downsides of such features are then discussed in more detail, making use of a series of studies that have included both game developer as well as social game player perspectives, while also analysing the games themselves in detail. The conclusions of this chapter will reflect upon the impact of social games for the direction game business and game culture is taking, including the free-to-play games developed for mobile devices and 'app ecosystems'. Social games are contextualised within a wider move of gaming to the mainstream of society – and the ludification of culture.

This chapter is grounded in multiple overlapping frames of research, broadly situated within the multidisciplinary field of games and player studies. The authors have carried out studies in this area in the University of Tampere Game Research Lab, an interdisciplinary research unit, since the turn of the millennium, and much of this chapter benefits from these years of research, situated at the interstices of multiple disciplines and scholarly orientations. Multi- and interdisciplinary research work has genuine transformative and innovative potential, but it also carries built-in, fruitful tension: in this case, there was a push towards (humanities-based) theory formation about the ontology of games and play and the research was from the start both held (in social sciences style) societally and ethically accountable as well as be practical and create contributions with application value (in the spirit of much design research and experimental human computer interaction [HCI] traditions). When funding for emerging game and play forms has been coming from technology or innovation funds, the work in this area has also been required to closely link with the industry interests. Such divergent goals are possible to fit together when game and player research is carried out under a dual strategy: for example, many research projects in this area have been carried out by using at first design research strategies and methods, then moving on to observe, interview, and survey players when the game form has reached wider popularity. The analytical and theoretical dimensions of these design-oriented and empirical studies have simultaneously been aimed to identify and produce interpretations about what these emerging phenomena in the field of gaming and game design are and what they mean.

Short History of Social Play and Social Games

Play is considered to be one of primal activities, and it is not only re-stricted to humans. According to the scholars of animal play, most vertebrates engage in at least some play activities (Burghardt, 2005). Commonly play is divided into three categories, play with the body, play with objects, and play with others (i.e. social play) (Bekoff & Byers, 1998; Burghardt, 2005, 81–110). Of the three, social play is the most complex, and likely to have emerged latest in evolution. Correspond-ingly, in human children social play develops after locomotor play and object play, but before the understanding of rule-based play fully deve-lops. As play is so widespread in the animal kingdom and there is a cost to playing (playtime is away from gathering food, it exposes one to harm and predators), according to evolutionary theories it must have a benefit. However, although numerous theories about the function and purpose of play were put forward during the 20th century, all remain contested in light of evidence (Burghardt, 2005).

In research, play has been perceived as instrumental for developing skills, social play includes learning by imitation and adaptation into complex, social environments (e.g., Piaget, 1951). However, rather early on, the more diverse perspectives to play have also been articulated. Notable is, for example, Brian Sutton-Smith's critique of Piaget (1966), where he maintains that play is not only a tool for adaptive learning, otherwise increasing intelligence would lessen the popularity of play, which appears clearly to be untrue. Play, and also social play, is thus more ambiguous phenomenon than its straightforward reduction to evolutionary benefits would suggest (Sutton-Smith, 1966; Pellegrini, Dupuis, & Smith, 2007).

Although the historical perspective in studies of social digital games is typically rather short, it is important to emphasise that social play as an underlying phenomenon predates not only games, but humans alto-gether. All playing of games is enactment of social play, in some sense (Stenros, Paavilainen, & Mäyrä, 2011a). Solitary game play is obviously possible, but it is more of an exception (for a contrary view of digital play, see Myers, 2010). Single-player digital games are mostly character-ised by being founded on solitary play, more precisely play with an ob-ject, although obviously there are elements of play with the body, and it is important to note that the player is not an abstraction but an embodied being. Also, in digital game play, sociability is a key element in many of the so-called single player games, most obviously through players com-peting with others through high scores, but also via the multiple roles that games have in building social capital (Bourdieu, 1986; Consalvo, 2007). It would be an exaggeration to characterise digital play as mostly solitary activity or one dominated by single-player gaming. From the very beginning, digital games have had a strong social component.

The first video game patent, titled "Cathode Ray-Tube Amusement Device" acknowledged the significance of spectators and suggested game design features accordingly (Goldsmith & Mann, 1948). Two years after a tic-tac-toe game *Bertie the Brain* was demonstrated for the audience during the 1950 Canadian National Exhibition and can be considered as the first arcade game as exhibition attendees lined up to play against artificial intelligence. Early experimental electronic games, such as *Tennis for Two* (1958) and *SpaceWar!* (1962), were actually often two-player games. *Pong* (1972), arguably the beginning of commercially successful arcade and home console games, could be played either by two people or against the computer. However, the classic coin-operated arcade video game and early computer games moved the technical emphasis towards single-player games. Yet they were often played in a social setting in arcades and at homes, with an audience and with competing with scores, later aided by incorporated score boards. For example, Ian Bogost (2004) observes that the introduction of a high score list[2] in arcade game *Asteroids* (1979) "transformed the game from a solitary challenge – man against rock – to a social challenge – man against man". Furthermore, even if a game was implemented as a single-player game, it could be played by alternating players (known as *hot seat gaming*). Indeed, early advertisements for digital games and consoles often feature multiple people engaged with the fun activity (Young, 2007).

The sociability around a game is the building block of various gaming cultures. Having knowledge about games, achieved either through playing or other sources has lent the players status, and has been characterised as *gaming capital* (Consalvo, 2007; Malaby, 2006; Walsh & Apperley, 2008). Earlier such knowledge and expertise was expressed through anecdotes and expert play, it later has been rendered more visible though walkthroughs and "Let's Play" videos shared online. The expertise gained in game play has also become more openly shared and even gamified with the help of 'achievements' that many online game services provide for excellence in play. Although media specializing in digital games targeting players has existed at least since the early 1980s, the spread of the Internet has taken the discourse on a different level. Not only was there access to discussions on varied topics which enabled gaming communities to gather around specific, even obscure interest, but these subcultures were rendered visible.

Multiplayer games have existed alongside single-player games throughout the history of digital games, from two-player games to games set in multi-user environments. Even so, around the turn of the millennium it was possible to perceive digital game play as mainly a solitary experience. Zagal et al. (2000) sum this sentiment up: "Whereas the vast majority of games played all over the world are collective in nature (that is, they involve the participation of more than one person), practically all electronic games are individual." At the time, the

stereotypical image of the gamer in the media was also often an iso-
lated, antisocial male.

As Internet connections started to become more common and faster
in the Western world, multiplayer games were moving from LAN parties
to the Internet. The popularity and visibility of massively multiplayer
online games and other online worlds was rising fast in the early years of
the new millennium. Although it is certainly possible to play these games
alone together (Ducheneaut, Yee, Nickell, & Moore, 2006), just using
the other players as a backdrop, the social aspect of play was undeniable
and integral to game play. Midway through the first decade of the new
century, numerous party games for consoles started to pick up traction.
In *SingStar* (2004), *Guitar Hero* (2005), and *Dance Dance Revolution*
(released for PlayStation 2 in the United States and Europe in 2007), the
performativity and socializing played important roles. When *Facebook*
games emerged in 2007, 'social' was a hype word in games, and 'social
media' was starting to be all the rage in digital culture. Not surprisingly,
these games were dubbed *social games* by the game industry, which was
a shorter version for *social network games* that emphasised the platform
for play – the social network service.

We find it helpful to divide the social games on *Facebook* into five
generations. The division is done based on a combination of factors. Key
elements include the shifting opportunities and restrictions of *Facebook*
as a technical platform, developments in game design features and monetization models taking advantage the underlying social network site,
and the changes in usage and attitudes of the people playing – and not
playing – games on *Facebook*.

Facebook games appeared in 2007 after the launch of application
programming interface (API) that allowed third-party developers to
create content for the service. However, there had been social games
in *Facebook* before, and also *MySpace* had featured some earlier gaming content. Apparently, one of the first social games was a *Catch 21*
card game tournament organised by WorldWinner in 2005 that ran
in *Facebook* from September 1 to September 15, with a PlayStation 2
as a grand prise[3]. In 2006, *Facebook* employee Bob Trahan developed
Friend Game where the user was quizzed about her friends[4]. In addition, it is safe to assume that *Facebook* users used the platform in various playful activities though it had no official support for games per se.
These proto-social games on *Facebook* appear today mostly as historical
curiosities.

The first generation of social games on *Facebook* started after the
API was launched in 2007. *Facebook* was soon filled with games – some
using more social game play features than others. The early social games
were often unofficial clones or versions of classic arcade titles, digitised
versions from card and board games, quiz games, and also casual games
which had gained popularity earlier. For example, there was a *PacMan*

(2007), a *Risk* clone called *Attack!* (2007), and a *Scrabble* clone called *Scrabulous* (2007). Some of these games allowed player-to-player interaction, whereas others were single-player games using very little social design features, apart from posting high-scores to users' profile. In this first phase, the games barely used the social network, nor did they monetise the users effectively. In hindsight, the first generation was manifesting more as a testing ground for the social network games and springboard for the future, more fully developed social game design models.

The second generation of social games is marked by aggressive spread of games. Another ongoing trend was the gradual development of more capable interactive web technologies and *Facebook* API features to open up possibilities for browser-based games to be more graphical and have more game play features. Although initially social games of this generation still had little actual gaming content, they were designed to function as viral marketing for themselves. Games such as *Zombies* (2007) were released that used the social network and virality with a pyramid scheme mechanic (Losh, 2008). New players were invited into the game as they got 'bitten' (by a mouse click) by their zombie friends. Zombie players could now recruit more players by 'biting' nonparticipants, thus recruiting players into their expanding zombie army. Zombie armies could then fight each other in a simple zero-sum game where the results were virally broadcast inside the network. In these games, the viral nature of the social network was a strong component in game play and such games were used for transmedial marketing purposes as well (Losh, 2008). The same basic model was applied into multiple variations, such as *Friends for Sale* (2007), where one could 'buy' *Facebook* friends as pets and have popularity contests that were run within the social network. The typical second-generation social game design was still rather simplistic, but the designers had started to identify some of the features specific to the *Facebook* platform.

In the third generation, the popularity of social games skyrocketed. Game design was becoming more sophisticated, as *Facebook* as a gaming platform was becoming powerful enough to handle more complex game designs. Simultaneously, the aggressive marketing though viral spread in the social media network ensured that maximal numbers of possible players heard about the games. The games being free to play, the developers had to come up with mechanics that restricted free play and drove the player towards in-app purchases to gain revenue. These *offline progress mechanics* were time-based like the *appointment* and/ or *energy* mechanics (Paavilainen, Hamari, Stenros, & Kinnunen, 2013), which forced the player to wait a certain amount of time before the game could progress – or the players could open their wallets for instant progression. Farm simulators like *Happy Farm* (2008) and *FarmVille* (2009) gained tens of millions of users who enjoyed easy game play in a friendly setting. Such games were cooperative in their nature, being later defined as *massively single-player games* (Stenros et al., 2011a).

During this time some game companies, such as Zynga, were becoming not only successful, but even infamous. Both viral features of the network and new monetization methods were used – sometimes in overly aggressive manner, which caused a lot of stir among players and game industry. One peculiar phenomenon was third party offers (i.e. lead-generation offers), which led into scamming accusations. Offer walls allowed players to gain in-game currency by buying software online, subscribe to shady mobile services, or participate in various quizzes with hidden fees. Because of the hidden fees it would have been often cheaper for the player to buy in-game currency directly from the game instead.

Development of social games was also changing. It became common to launch beta versions games as soon as there was something to play, called Minimum Viable Product in the industry. Development would go on while the game was live, and a game might change drastically overnight. The games would never be finalised, finished products, but would linger in "perpetual beta" (Nummenmaa, Kultima, & Alha, 2011). As time passed, this became the expected development practice: the game would be an evolving service (Nummenmaa, Kultima, Alha, & Mikkonen, 2013).

Due to excessive growth of game related posts, *Facebook* was forced to change its policy for applications to reduce the message spam. This marks the beginning of the fourth generation in the history of social games. As these games continued to become more sophisticated and fitting for the *Facebook* context, the aggressive viral marketing had burned through all the goodwill their users had with their friends. Some users had got completely fed up with spammy games and friend requirements for advancing in game. Indeed, these have been considered as major playability problems in social games (Paavilainen et al., 2012; 2013; 2015a). This change forced the developers to emphasise player retention instead of viral spreading of games, and thus the playable content became more important than epidemic growth in use numbers. Meanwhile, monetization strategies were developed further and took many new forms. In the fourth generation, the social game ecosystem started to stabilise as the cost of acquiring new users again required real investments from the game distributor. As advertising became more central, also aggressive cross promotion of games in ad banners became a standard practice in social network games.

Although social games became very successful and found their own format of casual game play in a viral network with in-game monetization, a debate focussed on a view that these games were not actually social – or maybe not even games. Players, developers, and researchers (Paavilainen et al., forthcoming) expressed their disdain against social games that were considered something less than 'real games'. At the time, there was also certain evolutionary hope that social games would become more social in the future, though not all developers agreed that it would be necessary (Järvinen, 2010). The casual game design values that strongly informed the ways in which social network games were developed, emphasised such social features were *acceptability*, *accessibility*, *simplicity*, and *flexibility* were the leading principles; for example, real-time interaction, and even active engagement in play with one's real-world friends did not develop into a key aspect of successful social game design. Rather, the sociability that social network games provided was strong in the "alone together" (Ducheneaut et al., 2006; cf. Kultima, 2009) style of casual social contacts.

Over the years, social games maintained this focus, while becoming more versatile in providing also 'traditional' game experiences in the forms familiar from massively multiplayer online role-playing games, real-time strategy games, and first-person shooters. The key differentiating factors remained in the ways of how these games emphasise synchronous game play and direct interaction between players.

At the time of writing, in 2016, social games in *Facebook* have declined a bit in popularity as play has moved from desktop to mobile iOS and Android platforms. There are still though many successful games in *Facebook* like *Candy Crush Saga* (2012), but there are also many popular social games that feature just a landing page in *Facebook* with a link to mobile version. This is the fifth generation: social games that function on numerous platforms. The service platform that was once the most popular environment for playing games has gained another role as a user acquisition channel for mobile gamers. The relevance of social network services nevertheless remains, and many standalone computer games today feature different sharing options to *Facebook* and other social network services.

Characteristics of Social Network Games

The years 2006 to 2008 have been discussed as period for the *casual turn* (Kultima, 2009; 2015) or the *casual revolution* (Juul, 2009). From the perspectives of game industry and game studies alike, this is when the pull of simpler, more approachable digital games could no longer be ignored. Small downloadable games, browser-based games, games with mimetic interfaces (like that of Nintendo Wii), party games where challenge or competition was not primary, games played on mobile phones, and social network games were all part of this reemergence of digital games that are easier to pick up. These games were widening the gamer demographics. They used new distribution models and new monetization models – and as these casual games started to make considerable profit, the casual turn influenced not only the cultural conception of what is a game, but what was considered as a successful and influential game.

This casual turn was neither revolutionary, nor completely unexpected. Juul (2009) points out that casual games allowed numerous lapsed gamers who had grown up with arcade games and early console games to reconnect with games after they had been alienated by the increasingly specialised digital games of the 1990s. Kultima (2009; cf. Enevold, 2014) identifies an even wider cultural context for this change and sees the change as unsurprising – rather than revolution, the development should more properly be addressed as the *normalization* of digital play. The casual turn is revolutionary only if it is examined through the prism of enthusiastic video gamers, meaning those game fans that buy and play AAA console games, support the traditional gamer press, and strongly identify themselves as gamers. Yet when the same events are approached with a wider conception of games and gamers, it just seems that playing digital games – and digital play in general – have become widely accepted, even a transparent parts of the everyday life.

This normalization of digital play cast earlier research on digital games in a new light. Although previously *immersion* has been seen as a key ingredient in game experiences with complex games featuring elaborate story-worlds and role-play (Brown & Cairns, 2004; Ermi & Mäyrä, 2005) and a *flow* state has been seen as pivotal in balancing skill and absorption in gripping game play (Sweetser & Wyeth, 2005), now alternative game design values and ideals have been identified. Play culture is no longer necessarily dominated by dedicated subcultures, but games can be found not only in easy to pick-up browser-based games, but there is casual digital play happening on online services such as Flickr and Twitter (Mäyrä, 2011). Kultima (2009) has argued that casual digital play needs to take two things into consideration, first that there are new and more heterogeneous user groups, and that games are no longer necessarily an absorbing primary activity, but that they are played for numerous reasons in numerous contexts. They can be a secondary activity – and played for instrumental reasons; derived from this context and culture of play, such games can be seen to embody the aforementioned four key casual game design values: acceptability, accessibility, simplicity, and flexibility. In another, large-scale player interview and survey study, the major portion of players approached games with a casual mindset, primarily aiming to use them for killing time, filling gaps, or for relaxing – thus not primarily because of their interest in the actual contents of games themselves (Kallio, Mäyrä, & Kaipainen, 2011). Also, Paavilainen et al. (2013) found that such casual motivations are often the driving force behind playing games in *Facebook*.

Such analysis of player motivations can then be applied into design, and Paavilainen (2010) has provided the key elements for social games in a form of high-level heuristics which can be used for designing or evaluating social games (Paavilainen, 2010). The design research can also be based on detailed studies of how popular and successful social games operate. Tyni, Sotamaa, and Toivonen (2011) present such a close reading of the western pioneer simulation game *FrontierVille* (2010) that provides an overview how social games operated during their heyday. Using the free-to-play revenue model in a clever way, the game accommodates for both paying and nonpaying players while rhythm design allows the players to play either casually or intensively depending on their motivation. These rhythms of game play can be seen to build up from day-to-day and weekly periods towards longer cycles, a structure drawing inspiration from seasons in television series. Sociability is rather shallow, but it provides the feeling of playing together with friends (cf. Ducheneaut et al., 2006; Stenros et al., 2011a).

The broadening of perspectives to how digital games and game playing are qualitatively perceived as a phenomena, and changing understanding of who game players (or 'gamers') are, coincides in academia with the commercial restructuration of game industry. In intellectual terms, it is possible to connect the normalization of digital play to wider cultural and societal developments. For example, as casual turn entered the agenda of experts working both in academia and industry, there was also rise in the scholarly discussion that aimed to identify a more general *rise of ludus in society* (e.g. Stenros, Montola, & Mäyrä, 2007). This discourse that focussed on these developments called them 'ludification of culture' (Raessens, 2006) or 'ludification of society' (Walz, 2006), and aimed to make sense about the perceived proliferation of game-related thinking and game elements outside of games proper. The concept and phenomena related to *gamification* (Deterding, Dixon, Khaled, & Nacke, 2011; Huotari & Hamari, 2012) has in media and public discussions grown to become the most visible part of this trend, but there has also been discussion of a 'ludic turn in media theory' (Raessens, 2012), and even manifestos advocating that we have entered into a *Ludic Century* where not only games, but game design and design thinking will rule (Zimmerman, 2015). It is possible to think of this change as a combination of the ludification of culture (games influencing culture) and the 'cultivation of ludus' (games changing as they migrate to new territories), as Walz and Deterding (2015) have argued. New game design values are needed as games have entered the cultural mainstream, and as they are being adopted in new contexts. The practices and aims of game development are thus increasingly based on 'design value pluralism' rather than reducing the design principles within the game design practice into a homogenous value set.

Although social network games with their advertisement and micropayment-based revenue models transformed game industry, also researchers became interested in the social element of these so-called social games (Consalvo, 2011; Paavilainen, forthcoming). Before online gaming, the social contact needed to exist before engagement in joint game play session. The era of early Internet gaming in the late 1990s made it possible to find friends online through the games. Later, with social games, this situation changed again as now the player already had the social network which can be used for playful purposes.

To account how this broader frame of developments operates in practice, more detailed understanding about social games is needed. As one response, a series of research projects were carried out by the University of Tampere research team in 2006–2016, involving the use of multiple research methodologies that were used for gathering information about social play, including using both surveys and interviews, targeting both players as well as developers, and also conducting expert evaluations into the actual game play of social games (e.g. Paavilainen et al., 2012, 2013; Stenros et al., 2011a).

After studies that outlined the casual game cultures, related discussions and identified the casual game design values (Kuittinen et al., 2007; Kultima, 2009) one line of our research moved on to create a more inclusive and comprehensive typology of how the social interaction is linked with game play in different types of games. Under closer analysis, it has become clear that there is not only social interaction within games, but also around them, and there might be important social reasons that influence play also in single-player games. The social games of *Facebook* emerged as a category of their own, dominantly categorised as 'massively single player games' where one's social network's copresence acts as the context of game play (see Table 2.1). According to this analysis, it is important to pay attention to how it is not only the number of players engaged directly with playing of games that has an effect on what kind sociability informs social game play. Also what kinds of player relationships are involved is crucial to take into account, and how player interactions are related to games, or with other players.

The interviews carried out among the users of social games provided also many other useful insights. It was, for example, evident that social media like *Facebook* are managed in increasingly careful manner by its users (cf. Stenros, Paavilainen, & Kinnunen, 2011b). Game play is modified with the use of friend listings, and privacy settings are used to frame particular activities or comments as directed towards certain audiences. The social networks of typical users do not only consist of game players, but there are several diverse and overlapping groups where they belong, and in some of their social networks game play might be disapproved (Paavilainen et al., 2013).

By using the *Playful Experiences* (PLEX) framework (Arrasvuori et al., 2011; Korhonen, Montola, & Arrasvuori, 2009) we have found that social games provide a wide spectrum of different experiences (Paavilainen, Koskinen, Korhonen, & Alha, 2015b). Completion, Competition, and Challenge were the most common PLEX categories in social games, whereas the next experience cluster included Exploration,

Fellowship, Control, Discovery, and Relaxation. Interestingly, from the aforementioned categories only Fellowship is explicitly social experience, as Competition can also have a nonsocial relationship towards oneself or the game – not necessarily to friends (Paavilainen et al., 2015b). As social games are getting more diverse, also the spectrum of experiences is expanding.

In addition to actual entertainment games, *playful communication* is one of the informal games or play behaviours that many people engage with in these services. In the daily flows of social communication, invites, or virtual gifts related to games can serve as *phatic* or *poetic* communication, as games are used as ways of social self-expression (Mäyrä, 2012; Rao, 2008). Not all social interplay, or even playfulness that involves the use of fun or humour, is actually mutually enjoyable or well-meaning, though. It is important to recognise that social play sometimes has elements of playful teasing, disparaging humour, or fierce competition that can be experienced as aggression, as well (Mäyrä, 2012). The players themselves have reported that sociability in social games can also be "hellish annoyance" (Paavilainen et al., 2013); this was something of an issue particularly while playing the second and third generation of social network games.

Table 2.1 Player relations in games

Players		Players' Relationship	Description
	Single Player	Reflective, Competitive*	• Knowledge of others playing the same game makes the game more social • Social media have made single player gaming more transparent • Play increases gaming capital, made visible through reward mechanisms such as achievements and trophies • Single player gaming can be strongly performative
	Two Players	Reflective, Competitive, Collaborative	• Two-player gaming has many forms in relation to time, place and system • Communication channels include face-to-face, in-game channel(s) or 3rd party channel(s) • Competition is often tiered

Players	Players' Relationship	Description
Multiplayer	Reflective, Competitive, Co-operative, Collaborative	• All players have direct effect on each other • Numerous communication channels (e.g. global, team, zone, one-on-one) • External communication channels such as discussion forums and wikis
Massively Multiplayer	Reflective, Competitive, Co-operative, Collaborative, Neutral	• Macro-communities, micro-communities, friends • Complex communication channel hierarchy (e.g. global, groups, sub-groups, one-on-one) • Neutral players, players as tokens or props, playing "alone together"
Massively Single Player	Reflective, Competitive, Co-operative, (Collaborative,) Neutral	• Content sharing between players • Little or no real in-game interaction between players

*Single-player competes only via mechanics that are not part of the core game play experience.

Social games can be played in many different ways. Instead of playing the game according to the developer-intended patterns, it is possible to *play the system* – or even 'play the other players' (Stenros, 2010). Indeed, if one starts to play social games competitively, they appear to reward playing the system. In our player interviews, reverse-engineering the most profitable play patterns were a common interest amongst the more devoted players of social games such as *FarmVille*, and adding new people as friends on *Facebook* has been a strategy in gaining an advantage in the game. In a sense, the *Facebook* games that encourage sociability to advertise themselves do not frame people so much as individual human beings, but as numbers or in-game resources. Such design solutions can also lead to some players also to treat their friends, other people, simply as tokens. Focusing on this aspect, it can be argued that engagement in such social games is not social play, but object play where other people are treated as objects. Even if the argumentation was not taken that far, it is easy to find comparisons to other kinds of playings of system or of other players, from 'Google bombing' and 'Wikipedia edit warring' to grief play (cf. Stenros, 2015). This is a further example of how games and game-like systems are being used for different purposes in social contexts. Not all, and not always even the most important, social engagements taking place within these games appear to be primarily design driven, but rather emergent social phenomena, derived from the affordances of the social networks.

Although social motivations are central for many game players, there are several other important game player motivations as well (e.g. Kallio et al., 2011; Yee, 2007). It is also worth noting that social motivations can operate in negative or antisocial modes, too, while informing game play. Anecdotal evidence in our player interviews suggests that for some people a single-player 'social game' can factually work as a respite or antidote against the (real-world) social contacts, responsibilities and stress that they can be associated with. One example of this is a parent who both at work and at home is bombarded by communication and requests from colleagues and family members alike – a social game can for such a user be the safe haven of social isolation, where direct communication and presence of others can be blocked out for a moment.

Whereas social game players are typically driven by motives that relate to pleasures, challenges and other experiences of gaming content on the one hand, or social motivations on the other, the commercial development of social network services and social games is more typically driven by financial, commercial interests. In advertisement-based business models, the key customers for a gaming company are advertising businesses, and in financial terms, game is a means to create ad displays and clicks. The human attention is from an economic perspective a scarce resource, and social games are an attractive means for focusing and controlling this attention, for financial gain (cf. Davenport & Beck, 2001). On the other hand, the rise of free-to-play revenue model and micropayments has meant that the game design is being reconceived with the monetization incentives as a key priority: although it is important that playing a game is fun and engaging to a certain degree, there also needs to be artificial obstacles or disturbances for the player experience, so that game players become motivated to purchase in-game, virtual tools and goods, or power-ups that are necessary for removing such obstacles.

Social games have been at the forefront of transfer from the off-the-shelf software product model into digital distribution models and service paradigm (cf. Stenros & Sotamaa, 2009) that have also meant comprehensive changes in the underlying game industry operational logistics and business models. From the perspective of the player, this transformation of gaming scene has on the other hand meant explosive growth of freely available gaming entertainment in the Internet, but also increasing requirements to develop new gaming literacy. The new required skills also include understanding and ability to make sensible use of games that operate under the new monetization strategies. Although the initial reactions to free-to-play games in game enthusiast and hobbyist forums have often been strongly negative (Alha et al., 2014), the easily accessible social and casual games have also attracted new audiences, growing the player base in some cases into hundreds of millions. The economic growth of the game industry and the growing maturity of the field has made it easier to gain acceptance to game development as a real work and force in society. Although seemingly simple, contemporary social and casual games have been developed to include sometimes rather complex systems of distinctive virtual currencies, and time investment into in-game resource harvesting and other activities that many games require can also be seen to function as certain kinds of currency systems.

The perceived value, time, and money interact in complex ways in contemporary social, online game play. Also gambling games have in some forms intermingle with entertainment games in social media from the very start, and chat or other social features have been implemented into real-money gambling services – of which the enduring popularity of Zynga's *Facebook* version of *Texas Hold'em Poker* is just one example. Investments of real money, play money, time, and social reputation or gaming capital all combine to form new configurations, where both games and money can hold multiple, both serious and playful forms (Kinnunen, 2010). Furthermore, also social sharing of links to games, view-to-pay style interactions with game trailers and other advertisement for games, as well as actual in-game as well as pre- and postgame activities all contribute to the more comprehensive phenomenon that we have called Expanded Game Experience (Kultima & Stenros, 2010). As digital distribution and service design holds increasing significance to how players experience and interact with games, such approach has been necessary step in the analysis of contemporary (social) games to take into account the manner of how entering, reentering or leaving the game has an influence on games' significances to the players. In the current practice of commercial game productions, the business model cannot be treated as a separate layer of design, as it is intertwined with the very core of game play design, making it even more important to consider game design from a more holistic and comprehensive point of view.

Conclusions and Future Directions

As a conclusion, our research of social network games suggests that the developments that have taken place as this form of designing, distributing, and playing games has become increasingly common are indicative of the directions for game business and game culture more generally.

The most visible sign of this change is how *pay-to-play* services and retail games have been accompanied and sometimes also replaced by the *free-to-play* versions of games developed and distributed first inside *Facebook*, then into mobile devices and their 'app ecosystems'. It also appears important to consider how 'attention economy' opens up perspectives into the ways how social games are designed, and how they operate. In the age of information overflow, human attention is a scarce resource and 'free' games like those distributed in social media aim to attract, manipulate, and monetise such attention in various ways – providing particular kinds of experiences to the online, socially networked player in return. Social play and sociability themselves have appeared as so multidimensional and varied phenomena, that both the design of 'social games' as well as research into the forms of social (game) play have hardly yet exhausted the potentials in this field. The competencies of game playing as well as design characteristics have during the 'casual turn' and social games growth become an increasingly visible part of late modern culture, daily lives, and service design more generally. From this perspective, social games have been one popular element in the 'ludification of culture' that is still an ongoing process.

More specifically, within the field of commercial game development and distribution, social network game features have become increasingly common in services such as *Steam*, which have expanded from game distribution channels into game-specific social networks of their own. All major digital game industry players have their own versions of such services that add multiplayer and social networking functionalities into their computer and video games today, including *PlayStation Network*, *Xbox Live*, and *Nintendo Network*. Similarly, the mobile counterparts of such services reach hundreds of millions users, most notably those of Apple iOS (Game Center) and Google's Android (Google Play). As these environments, technologies, and ecosystems have gained in the attention economy, *Facebook* has changed from being primarily a gaming platform to user acquisition and information synchronization platform. With its more than a billion daily active users (as of December 2015), *Facebook* is still an attractive environment for game application developers to use in tandem with the mobile app stores, to do research and experimentation to reach their optimal user base, do 'soft launches' in limited geographical areas, and then to target marketing campaigns to reach more users. With *Facebook* acquiring Oculus, the developers of Rift Virtual Reality device for $2 billion in 2014, the service might yet also transform into a new kind of gaming and entertainment platform in the future. Social play and interaction in immersive alternative realities are most likely an element in such a future strategy for a social network provider.

The key lessons from research into the social play and social games are hard to summarise shortly, but it is clear that studying a techno-social configuration such as games in *Facebook* and other social networking services requires multiple competencies and will benefit from multidisciplinary research team collaboration. Typically, the studies to social games combine perspectives drawn from sociology, media studies, political economy, HCI, philosophy, design research, and textual analysis – as well as from the native tradition of game studies itself. A mixed method approach, and openness towards theoretical dialogue is beneficial for grasping the complexity and wide reach of a phenomenon like social play and social games. In the case of University of Tampere social games research projects, we have particularly made use of triangulation where the perspectives of critical game analysis, player experience studies, and game industry economics are used in combination. This has helped us to understand better both the motivations of game developers for implementing certain features into these games, the reasons for players to play (or not play) them with various strategies, and also how these games function in multiple cultural and social contexts.

The potential weakness of such diverse approach is that it might lead to somewhat fragmented view: case studies that are closely observant of empirical phenomena and developments at the micro-level of individual game industry products, and game player subgroups do not easily provide any consistent and macro-historical theories that would organise research into a unified whole. However, we feel that the benefits outweigh the limitations: only with such multi- and interdisciplinary approach can we produce the rich data and interesting combinations of research approaches. For example, the popularity and limitations of social games can at least partially be explained with both technical (e.g. game usability, distribution, platform), psychological (play motivations), commercial (e.g. marketing) and cultural factors (e.g. changes in games' societal role).

This chapter has identified and discussed the evolution of social games within a certain cultural, technical, and commercial context, including some important differences in the ways five generations of social games have been implemented and interacted with. The sociability of social play that these games are associated with has emerged in analysis both to include very broad-ranging dimensions such as the casual turn and ludification of culture and society, as well as very narrow and specific ones – including individual social functions such as invite or gift mechanisms, that have been introduced in social games as a genre.

As the social network games continue to be developed into new forms in mobile platforms, and potentially in virtual or augmented reality, and beyond, it is interesting also to reflect on the future directions of research in this field. Although it is futile to try to hypothesise the future steps in information and communication technologies that will be made relevant for gaming, it nevertheless remains clear that social play will be one important element also in such future gaming landscape, and that there will be need for multidisciplinary and multiperspectival studies into the design, experiences, practices, and significances of social games also in the future.

Notes

1 2007 was the year when *Facebook* gave third-party developers access to create and distribute games in the service, by opening up the *Facebook* API (Application Programming Interface). Social games grew to utilise this opportunity.
2 The first arcade game to feature a high-score list was *Star Fire* and the feature was copied to *Asteroids* according to the game designer Ed Logg (Retro Gamer, 2009).
3 See: https://www.worldwinner.com/cgi/news/in_the_news.html?year=2005& article=09_08_2005_Facebook.html&item=pr.
4 See: https://www. *Facebook*.com/notes/*Facebook*/musings-of-a-*Facebook*-engineer/2209542130/.

References

Alha, K., Koskinen, E., Paavilainen, J., Hamari, J., & Kinnunen, J. (2014). Free-to-Play games: Professionals' perspectives. In *Proceedings of the 2014 International DiGRA Nordic Conference*. Retrieved from http://www.digra.org/digital-library/publications/free-to-play-games-professionals-perspectives/.

Arrasvuori, J., Boberg M., Holopainen J., Korhonen H., Lucero A., & Montola M. (2011) Applying the PLEX framework in designing for playfulness. In *Proceedings of the 2011 Conference on Designing Pleasurable Products and Interfaces*. New York: ACM.

Bekoff, M., & Byers, J. A. (Eds.), (1998). *Animal play: Evolutionary, comparative and ecological perspectives*. Cambridge: Cambridge University Press.

Bogost, I. (2004). Asynchronous multiplay: Futures for casual multiplayer experience. Paper presented at the *Other Players Conference on Multiplayer Phenomena*. Copenhagen, Denmark, December 1– 3 2004.

Bourdieu, P. (1986). The forms of capital. In J. Richardson (Ed.), *Handbook of theory and research for the sociology of education* (pp. 46–58). New York: Greenwood.

Brown, E., & Cairns, P. (2004). A grounded investigation of game immersion. In *CHI '04 Extended Abstracts on Human Factors in Computing Systems* (pp. 1297–1300). New York: ACM. http://doi.org/10.1145/985921.986048.

Burghardt, G. M. (2005). *The genesis of animal play. Testing the limits*. Cambridge, MA: The MIT Press.

Consalvo, M. (2007). *Cheating: Gaining advantage in videogames*. Cambridge, MA: The MIT Press.

Consalvo, M. (2011). Using your friends: Social mechanics in social games. In *Proceedings of the 6th International Conference on Foundations of Digital Games (FDG '11)*. New York: ACM.

Davenport, T. H. & Beck, J. C. (2001). *The attention economy: Understanding the new currency of business*. Boston, MA: Harvard Business School Press.

Deterding, S., Dixon, D., Khaled, R., & Nacke, L. (2011). From game design elements to gamefulness: Defining "gamification." In *Proceedings of the 15th International Academic MindTrek Conference: Envisioning Future Media Environments* (pp. 9–15). New York: ACM. http://doi.org/10.1145/2181037.2181040.

Ducheneaut, N., Yee, N., Nickell, E., & Moore, R. J. (2006). "Alone together?": Exploring the social dynamics of massively multiplayer online games. In *Proceedings of the SIGCHI Conference on Human Factors in Computing Systems* (pp. 407–416). New York: ACM. http://doi.org/10.1145/1124772.1124834.

Enevold, J. (2014). Digital materialities and family practices: The gendered, practical, aesthetical and technological domestication of play. *ToDiGRA*, *1*(2).

Ermi, L., & Mäyrä, F. (2005). Fundamental components of the gameplay experience: Analysing immersion. In *Proceedings of DiGRA 2005*. Vancouver: University of Vancouver. Retrieved from http://www.digra.org/dl/db/06276.41516.pdf.

Goldsmith, T.T. Jr., & Mann, E. R. (1948). Cathode-ray tube amusement device. U.S Patent no. 2,455,992. Retrieved from http://www.pong-story.com/2455992.pdf.

Huotari, K., & Hamari, J. (2012). Defining gamification: A service marketing perspective. In *Proceeding of the 16th International Academic MindTrek Conference* (pp. 17–22). Tampere: ACM Press. Retrieved from http://dl.acm.org/citation.cfm?id=2393137.

Järvinen, A. (2010). The state of social in social games. Gamasutra, October 19, 2010. Retrieved from http://www.gamasutra.com/view/feature/134548/the_state_of_social_in_social_games.php.

Juul, J. (2009). *Casual revolution: Reinventing video games and their players.* Cambridge, MA: The MIT Press.

Kallio, K. P., Mäyrä, F., & Kaipainen, K. (2011). At least nine ways to play: Approaching gamer mentalities. *Games and Culture*, *6*(4), 327–353. http://doi.org/10.1177/1555412010391089.

Kinnunen, J. (2010). Leikkisä Raha Peleissä. In: Suominen, J., et al (Eds.) *Pelitutkimuksen vuosikirja*, 42–57. Tampere: Tampereen yliopisto.

Korhonen, H., Montola, M., & Arrasvuori, J. (2009). Understanding playful user experience through digital games. In *Proceedings of the DPPI*, Université de Technologie de Compiègne (pp. 274–285).

Kultima, A. (2009). Casual game design values. In *Proceedings of MindTrek 2009* (pp. 58–65). Tampere: ACM. Retrieved from http://portal.acm.org/citation.cfm?doid=1621841.1621854.

Kultima, A. (2015). Online games, casual. In *The International Encyclopedia of Digital Communication and Society*. Retrieved from http://onlinelibrary.wiley.com/doi/10.1002/9781118767771.wbiedcs107/abstract.

Kultima, A., & Stenros, J. (2010). Designing games for everyone: The expanded game experience model. In: *Proceedings of the International Academic Conference on the Future of Game Design and Technology* (pp. 66–73). Futureplay '10. New York: ACM.

Kuittinen, J., Kultima, A., Niemelä, J., & Paavilainen, J. (2007). Casual games discussion. In *Proceedings of the 2007 Conference on Future*

Play: Research, Play Share (pp. 105–112). Toronto, Canada: ACM. http://doi.org/10.1145/1328202.1328221.

Losh, E. (2008). In polite company: Rules of play in five Facebook games. In *Proceedings of Advances in Computer Entertainment Technology* (pp. 345–351). New York: ACM.

Malaby, T. (2006). Parlaying Value capital in and beyond virtual worlds. *Games and Culture, 1*(2), 141–162. http://doi.org/10.1177/1555412006286688.

Malinen, S. (2016). *Sociability and sense of community among users of online services.* Acta Universitatis Tamperensis: 2125. Tampere: Tampere University Press. http://tampub.uta.fi/handle/10024/98292.

Mäyrä, F. (2011). Games in the mobile Internet: Towards contextual play. In G. Crawford, V. Gosling, & B. Light (Eds.), *Online gaming in context: The social and cultural significance of online games* (pp. 108–129). New York: Routledge.

Mäyrä, F. (2012). Playful mobile communication – services supporting the culture of play. *Interactions: Studies in Communication & Culture, 3*(1) (30 October), 55–70.

Myers, D. (2010). *Play redux: The form of computer games.* Ann Arbor: The University of Michigan Press: The University of Michigan Library.

Nummenmaa T., Kultima, A., & Alha, K. (2011). Change in change: Designing game evolution. In Kultima A., Alha, K. (Eds.), *Changing faces of game innovation: GaIn and GIIP research project report.* TRIM Research Reports 4. Tampere: University of Tampere, 91–101.

Nummenmaa, T., Kultima A., Alha, K., & Mikkonen, T. (2013). Applying Lehman's laws to game evolution. In Robbes R., Robles G. (Eds.), *Proceedings of the 2013 International Workshop on Principles of Software Evolution* (pp. 11–17). New York: ACM.

Paavilainen, J. (2010). Critical review on video game evaluation heuristics: Social games perspective. In *Proceedings of the International Academic Conference on the Future of Game Design and Technology* (pp. 56–65). New York: ACM.

Paavilainen, J., Alha, K., & Korhonen, H. (2012). Exploring playability of social network games. In *Proceedings of the 9th International Conference on Advances in Computer Entertainment (ACE '12)* (pp. 336–351). Heidelberg: Springer-Verlag Berlin.

Paavilainen, J., Alha, K., & Korhonen, H. (2015a). Domain-specific playability problems in social network games. *International Journal of Arts and Technology, 8*, 4. http://dx.doi.org/10.1504/IJART.2015.073579.

Paavilainen, J., Alha, K., & Korhonen, H. (forthcoming). Review of social features in social network games.

Paavilainen, J., Hamari, J., Stenros, J. & Kinnunen, J. (2013). Social network games players' perspectives. *Simulation & Gaming 44*(6), 794–820.

Paavilainen, J., Koskinen, E., Korhonen, H., & Alha, K. (2015b). Exploring playful experiences in social network games. In *Proceedings of the 2015 DiGRA International Conference.* Retrieved from: http://www.digra.org/digital-library/publications/exploring-playful-experiences-in-social-network-games/.

Pellegrini, A. D., Dupuis D., & Smith, P. K. (2007). Play in evolution and development. *Developmental Review 27*(2 June), 261–276.

Piaget, J. (1951). *The child's conception of the world.* Lanham, MD: Rowman & Littlefield.

Raessens, J. (2006). Playful identities, or the ludification of culture. *Games and Culture, 1*(1), 52–57. http://doi.org/10.1177/1555412005281779.

Raessens, J. F. F. (2012). Homo ludens 2.0 The ludic turn in media theory. Universiteit Utrecht, Faculteit Geesteswetenschappen. Retrieved from http://dspace.library.uu.nl/handle/1874/255181.

Rao, V. (2008). Facebook applications and playful mood: The construction of Facebook as a "third place". In *Proceedings of the 12th International MindTrek Conference on Entertainment and Media in the Ubiquitous Era* (pp. 8–12). New York: ACM Press.

Stenros, J. (2010). Playing the system: Using frame analysis to understand online play. In *Proceedings of Futureplay '10* (pp. 9–16). New York: ACM.

Stenros, J. (2015). *Playfulness, play, and games: A Constructionist ludology approach*. Acta Universitatis Tamperensis: 2049. Tampere: University of Tampere.

Stenros, J., Montola, M., & Mäyrä, F. (2007). Pervasive games in ludic society. In *Proceedings of the 2007 Conference on Future Play* (pp. 30–37). Toronto, Canada: ACM. http://dx.doi.org/10.1145/1328202.1328209.

Stenros, J., Paavilainen, J., & Mäyrä, F. (2011a). Social interaction in games. *International Journal of Arts and Technology*, 4(3), 342–358. http://doi.org/10.1504/IJART.2011.041486.

Stenros, J., Paavilainen, J. & Kinnunen, J. (2011b). "Giving good 'face': Playful performances of self in Facebook". *Proceedings of MindTrek 2011*. New York: ACM.

Stenros, J. & Sotamaa, O. (2009). Commoditization of helping players play: Rise of the service paradigm. *Proceedings of DiGRA 2009 Conference, Breaking New Ground: Innovation in Games, Play, Practice and Theory*.

Sutton-Smith, B. (1966). Piaget on play: A critique. *Psychological Review* 73(1 January):104–110.

Sweetser, P., & Wyeth, P. (2005). GameFlow: A Model for Evaluating Player Enjoyment in Games. *Computers in Entertainment (CIE)*, 3(3):1–24. http://doi.org/10.1145/1077246.1077253.

Tyni, H., Sotamaa, O., & Toivonen, S. (2011). Howdy pardner!: On free-to-play, sociability and rhythm design in FrontierVille. In *Proceedings of the 15th International Academic MindTrek Conference: Envisioning Future Media Environments* (pp. 22–29). New York: ACM Press.

Walsh, C., & Apperley, T. (2008). Researching digital game players: Gameplay and gaming capital. In *Proceedings of IADIS 2008* (pp. 99–102). Amsterdam, The Netherlands: IADIS. Retrieved from http://oro.open.ac.uk/19578/1/200815c013.pdf.

Walz, S. P. (2006). Welcome to my playce! Retrieved from http://spw.playbe.com.

Walz, S. P., & Deterding, S. (Eds.), (2015). *The gameful world: approaches, issues, applications*. Cambridge, MA: The MIT Press.

Yee, N. (2007). Motivations for play in online games. *CyberPsychology and Behavior*, 9, 772–775.

Young, B.-M. (2007). The disappearance and reappearance and disappearance of the player in videogame advertising. *Situated Play, Proceedings of DiGRA 2007 Conference*.

Zagal, J., Nussbaum, M., & Rosas, R. (2000). A model to support the design of multiplayer games. *Presence*, 9(5), 448–462.

Zimmerman, E. (2015). Manifesto for a ludic century. In S. P. Walz & S. Deterding (Eds.), *The gameful world: Approaches, issues, applications* (pp. 19–22). Cambridge, MA: The MIT Press.

3 Identifying Social Forms of Flow in Multiuser Video Games

Joceran Borderie and Nicolas Michinov

Today, gaming is a social activity for a great number of people. According to recent statistics, 62% of gamers play with others, either in person or online (Entertainment Software Association, 2015). Paradoxically, although the number of studies on gaming is increasing (e.g. Chou & Ting, 2003; Nacke & Lindley, 2009; Wan & Chiou, 2006), there is a lack of empirical evidence concerning team functioning in multiuser videogames and its impact on social and psychological outcomes, such as flow experience among online team players.

At an individual level, Flow Theory (Csikszentmihalyi, 1993) has been suggested as a coherent means of explaining some of the psychological processes at stake during gaming activities. According to this theory, flow (also called optimal experience) is a mental state that can occur while carrying out activities perceived as autotelic (i.e. intrinsically re-warding). The optimal experience is likely to emerge when activities are steered toward a precise goal and give clear performance feedback. They must also challenge the player's skills while remaining feasible. The individual, totally focussed and immersed, may then feel a loss of self-perception, a strong sense of control, and altered time perception (for more about flow theory, see Csikszentmihalyi, 1990).

Apart from flow, immersion and presence are the most widely discussed concepts in the videogame context (Nacke & Lindley, 2008). Although these concepts overlap in some aspects, they are distinct. Immersion has been defined as a process comprising three consecutive steps: engagement, engrossment and total immersion (Brown & Cairns, 2004). Based on interviews, authors have identified contextual, human and computer factors that prevent progression from one step to the next. In terms of user experience, total immersion is very close to what Slater (2002) defined as presence: the sense of being in a virtual world. However, presence is possible without immersion, and vice versa. Ermi and Mayra (2005) proposed a different approach. In their SCI model, they defined immersion as having three different forms: sensory immersion (S), challenge-based immersion (C), and imaginative perception (I). Flow state could imply a sense of fusion between the totally focussed individual and the task at hand. In the light of this approach, challenge-based immersion could thus be closely related to flow. In conclusion, immersion, presence and flow share some dimensions, but they also have their own specific features.

In the literature, video game studies have mostly focussed on the emergence of flow as a mental state, an individual subjective experience (Chen, 2006; Nacke & Lindley, 2009; Reese, 2010, 2015; Sweetser & Wyeth, 2005). However, it is important to investigate whether flow state can exist in a group, whether there are social forms of flow, and whether a team can experience a cooperative optimal state. Indeed, as optimal experience have been identified as determinant for performances and well-being, knowing more about ways these states could be shared within groups and teams would open up a wealth of perspectives about team management in multiple fields, including e-sports, sports, defense, and occupational organizations.

Recently, some researchers have explored the social forms of flow state, shared within a group or team (Borderie, 2015; Borderie & Michinov, 2014; Sawyer, 2007; Walker, 2010). However, today, there are few studies about the emergence conditions and the nature of the social form of flow (Léger, Sénécal, Aubé, Cameron, & Ortiz de Guinea, 2013; Nakamura & Csikszentmihalyi, 2002).

Walker (2010), in a study on the enjoyable nature of the optimal experience, investigated the role of positive interdependence among tympanic ball players. This research aimed to determine whether performing a pleasant task is more pleasurable alone, in a group, or in a team. To this end, after the game, participants in each condition were invited to self-rate how they experienced the activity. In addition, trained observers rated the joy displayed by the participants during the game. Findings revealed that players and observers gave similar ratings. Although this research was not directly focussed on social forms of flow, it raised interesting issues about the relationship between positive interdependence and the expression of optimal experiences in multiplayer contexts.

In line with Walker's study (2010), the aim of the present research was to further understand the role of positive interdependence in the emergence of social forms of flow. In this context, positive interdependence is defined as the perception of group members that they and their actions are linked in such a way that they cannot succeed without each other (Johnson & Johnson, 1999, 2002). This concept is one of the founding principles of every cooperation initiative (Johnson & Johnson, 1999, 2002) and can be differentiated by subtype (see Table 3.1).

Positive interdependence has mostly been used and studied in educational settings where tasks can be long and complex. By contrast, digital games players often perform a large number of actions per minute making gameplay input multiple and fast. Accordingly, 'action interdependence'

Table 3.1 Subtypes of positive interdependence and their definitions

Subtype	Definition
Goal interdependence	Members of the group share common target goals
Resource interdependence	Members share resources they have to exchange
Role interdependence	Members have different roles that can be combined to achieve synergy
Reward interdependence	The extent to which the goal reward is linked to global or individual performance
Task interdependence	The extent to which task progression (i.e., initiation, progression, conclusion) of team members are bound

has been suggested as a more appropriate denomination to grasp game-play in its micro wealth (Borderie & Michinov, 2014). Positive interdependence is also central in the definition of a team: "a distinguishable set of two or more people who interact, dynamically, interdependently, and adaptively toward a common and valued goal, who have each been assigned specific roles or functions to perform, and who have a limited life-span of membership" (Salas, Dickinson, Converse, & Tannenbaum, 1992, p. 4).

From this perspective, some authors have suggested a distinction between co-active and interactive forms of social flow. Coactive social flow, also called 'group flow', may emerge when individuals perform an activity together without interacting. By contrast, interactive social flow, also called 'team flow', may emerge when team members are bound by a more constraining positive interdependence (Borderie, 2015; Borderie & Michinov, 2014; Walker, 2015).

Because very little is known about the emergence and functioning of social forms of flow and there remains a need to study how this complex mental state could be experienced and shared in groups and teams, that is the aim of the current study. More specifically, this study aims to identify social forms of flow within teams using an experimental design varying the level of interdependence between players (high vs low interdependence). It was hypothesised that a high positive interdependence relationship between teammates in a multiplayer game would facilitate the emergence of social forms of flow (i.e. group flow and team flow). In view of the current lack of theoretical or empirical information about social forms of flow, it is difficult to make accurate predictions about group and team flow. To test our hypothesis, we measured social flow states using a new observation method based on players' facial, postural, and verbal behaviours.

Materials and Methods

Participants

Sixty-nine male players, aged 20 to 35, were recruited to play *League of Legends* (also called *LoL*, Riot Games, 2009) in groups of three in a laboratory setting. All of them regularly played digital games, from 1 to 50 hours per week; 37 (53.62%) played online multiplayer games at least once a week, and all of them had already played at least once. Participants knew their teammates, but were not familiar with the game.

Rationale for Selecting League of Legends

League of Legends was chosen as the experimental task for several reasons. First, it is free to play a large part of its content. Second, we could easily modify the game rules by adding specific instructions. Third, a preliminary analysis of the game design (see the following section) confirmed that it is a relevant flow vector as it promotes immersion and concentration (through the game's fast pace and immersive virtual world), has clear goals (that can be broken down into subgoals), provides immediate feedback to the players about their actions, and provides players with a sense of control (through specific, methodical in-game actions allowing for the development of a sense of mastery).

Description of the League of Legends

League of Legends is a Multiplayer Online Battle Arena (MOBA) type game. As in most MOBAs, the goal is to destroy the Nexus (base camp) of the opposing team. Each player controls a virtual character called a 'champion'. Champions have different skills (some are experts in combat but incompetent as magicians, other are experts in magic but physically weak, etc.) and specific powers (shooting ice arrows, hitting the ground to stun opponents, etc.). As they progress, champions earn experience points, improving their skills and powers. They also earn gold, which can be spent to buy items granting bonuses. The gameplay of each champion is therefore closely linked to his characteristics and skills and to the items he has at a given time. Additionally, in LoL, the teamplay ('collective gameplay' or 'all collective actions undertaken by the players') is central, and champions have complementary profiles. Morgana, Ashe, and Malphite, the three champions chosen in our study, have simple cooperative skills: slowing down or immobilizing enemies, ability to use defensive spells on teammates, etc.

The champions fight on three lanes, making progressive breaks, which ultimately lead to the destruction of the enemy Nexus. Defensive towers belonging to each camp are arranged along the lanes. These towers are autonomous and attack all enemies within range, projecting a destructive energy ball on the targeted unit.

Apparatus

League of Legends was run on computers using Windows 7 and connected to the Internet. We filmed each player with a webcam and merged the video channels using Evocam software to have the three players' behaviours on a single record. Match replays were recorded using LoLreplay.

Coding Scheme

As suggested by several researchers, there is a crucial need to develop qualitative measures of flow to capture the essence of this complex state while being experienced (Cosma, 1999; Csikszentmihalyi, 1992; Lazarovitz, 2003). Consequently, a new observation method of flow identification was used in the present study. Based on the definition of flow (Csikszentmihalyi, 1990) and its conceptual dimensions (clear goal, accurate feedback, concentration, sense of control, loss of self-consciousness, alteration of time perception, autotelic experience, balance challenge/skills), we identified a pattern, theoretically reflecting a flow state: a concentration phase followed by a certain degree of satisfaction (see Borderie, 2015). This two-phase pattern was supported by two arguments advanced in the literature about the mental states involved in the flow experience: (1) flow state is characterised by a high level of concentration (Csikszentmihalyi, 1990), and (2) happiness or elation are emotions likely to be signatures of flow (Csikszentmihalyi, 1990; Csikszentmihalyi & Larson, 1987). Next, we developed a coding scheme (see Table 3.2) breaking down these two mental states into observable facial, postural, and verbal behaviours. As we wished to classify players' mental states in mutually exclusive categories, we identified two additional states: *discomfort* (including all psychic entropy states such as apathy, boredom, anxiety, etc.) and *others* (all observable behaviours not included in the discomfort, joy, and concentration categories). To complete the coding scheme, we also consulted previous observational coding tools such as the Facial Action Coding System (Ekman, Friesen, & Hager, 2002) and the Specific Affect Coding System (Coan & Gottman, 2007).

The same method was used to identify group and team flow episodes. To detect these social optimal experiences, we looked for episodes during which the specific behaviour was simultaneously expressed by at least two teammates. In order to distinguish 'group flow' from 'team flow',

Table 3.2 Coding scheme

Player's mental state	Postural and Facial clues	Verbal clues
Concentration	Approaches the screen or is close to the screen, fixed gaze, grimace, overall tension	Silence interrupting a sentence, repetition of a verbal chunk ("go! go! go!")
Joy	Smiles, grins, laughs, raises arms or fists as a sign of victory	Verbalization expressing joy ("Yes!", "Nice!")
Discomfort (Psychic Entropy states: Boredom, Anxiety, Apathy)	Sighs, mumbles, pouts, sprawls in chair, hits the desktop, mouse or keyboard	Expresses anger, swears, utters insults; Expresses boredom or difficulty
Other secondary behaviors	Uses mobile phone	Communication between players, asks the experimenter a question

the game replays were also analysed to determine to what extent players had actually interacted while performing team actions. Thus, when real interaction occurred between players (i.e. combining skills, planning spatial strategies, task- or team-oriented communication), we labeled it as a team flow episode, whereas when the players' characters were only in copresence and there was no underlying cooperative intention (i.e. only being present in the same space, incoherent use of skills), we labeled it as a group flow episode. We also used behavioural records to obtain additional information about the participants' verbal communication. We do not distinguish between 'players' and 'characters' because the evidence of interaction we sought could be found at either level of analysis.

Experimental Protocol

For each experimental condition, we modified the game rules by giving different instructions to the players about how they had to play together.

For the low interdependence condition, participants were instructed as follows: "Within the allotted time, you must get as many points as possible by destroying enemy towers (3 points) and/or champions (1 point) on your lane. Every tower you lose will cost you 2 points. Among all the teams taking part in this study, the one that scores most points will earn a bonus voucher of 15 euros for each of its members".

Thus, in this condition, players had individual responsibility and better had to play separately (while being on the same map).

In the high interdependence condition, participants received the following instruction: "Within the allotted time, you must earn as many points as possible *together* by destroying enemy towers (3 points) and/or champions

Table 3.3 Interdependence subtypes in each experimental condition

Interdependence subtype	Description	Present in the low interdependence condition	Present in the high interdependence condition
Task	Each player is assigned a task linked to that of his partners.	No	Yes
Goal	Goals and performance defined in collective terms.	No	Yes
Resources	Players have to share their resources.	No	No
Role	Combination of actions specific to each character essential for the team's efficiency.	No	No, but strong complementarity
Rewards	If the team wins, every player receives the same reward.	Yes	Yes

(1 point). *Points will be earned only if at least two of you achieve the objectives.* Every tower you lose will cost you 2 points. The team that scores most points will earn a bonus voucher of 15 euros for each of its members". In this condition, players had to stay together to earn points. The interdependence subtypes for each experimental condition are summarised in Table 3.3.

Procedure

Overall, the test lasted about one hour and spanned three phases. First, the participants were prepared and familiarised with the game and the test conditions (phase 1, 30 minutes). Thus, when they arrived at the laboratory, participants were welcomed and thanked. The experimenter made sure of their free and informed consent, ensuring them that they could stop their participation at any time without any negative consequences. Players were randomly assigned a seat and the role of one of the three champions (Malphite, Ashe, or Morgana). As they were in separate cubicles, participants could not see their teammates and could only communicate verbally.

Then, the familiarization phase began. It lasted 20 minutes and involved playing two games of 10 minutes each under the experimental conditions. It enabled players to get used to the game controls, their champions and to ignore the presence of the webcam.

Next, the participants played the game during 15 minutes under the experimental condition (phase 2, 15 min). This phase also included the video capture of the game session. During the game, the experimenter was in a cubicle similar to those of the players, out of sight, but accessible in case of need. After 15 minutes, the experimenter stopped the game.

Finally, at the end of the game session, a debriefing took place (phase 3, about 10 min) this included the experimenter told the players about the purpose of the study, answered any questions and took notes of any comments about the game and the participants experience. The players were thanked again for their participation.

Results

For each group of players, we obtained a timeline showing their behavioural profile over time. Illustration of these timelines is shown on Figure 3.1.

In accordance with our predictions, the Mann-Whitney U test (or Wilcoxon rank-sum test) revealed a significant effect between the two interdependence conditions on the number of group flow episodes. There were significantly more episodes in the high interdependence than low interdependence condition, $U = 20$, $p < .01$. Regarding team flow episodes, the same test revealed no significant effect between the two conditions. Overall, 13 episodes of group flow were detected (and only four episodes of team flow), all in the 'high interdependence' condition.

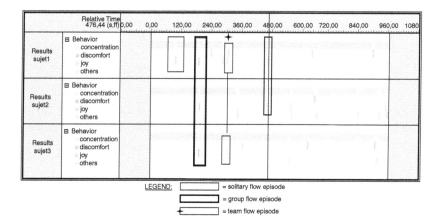

Figure 3.1 Team profiles showing solitary, group, and team flow episodes.

Additional Results From Behavioural Records

Analysis of behavioural records revealed that players' facial expressions were often insufficient to detect team flow episodes. For group flow episodes, we only had to look for occurrence of the pattern we had defined (simultaneous episodes of concentration followed by satisfaction) while characters played the game coactively. By contrast, to identify team flow episodes, we also had to be sure that players truly interacted, which could be hard to determine solely on the basis of game replays or facial expression recordings.

Thus, audio data were very important to detect sequences during which players organised and put into practice their cooperative plans. It also helped to confirm whether there was a concomitant flow pattern.

For example, in one of the four-team flow episodes (group 22, 54 s), team flow was noted when player 1 and player 2 were pursuing each other. They were playing cat and mouse using the level design to hide from each other:

PLAYER 1: *"Find me! You can't find me! Where am I?"*
PLAYER 2: *"Boo, there! You're the cat now!"*

Another team flow episode was identified during a fight in which two players of group 22 (2 min 9 s) set up a cooperative plan to attack the opponent champion:

PLAYER 1: *"Yeah! I rooted (immobilised) him, attack him!"*
PLAYER 2: *"Yeah!"*

The same group experienced a third team flow episode during another fight (group 22, 12 min 42 s):

PLAYER 1: *"Wait! I'll root him! And put a shield on you".*
PLAYER 2: *"What is it?"*
PLAYER 1: *"It protects you from magic attacks!"*
PLAYER 2: *"Yeah!! Thanks".*

The fourth team flow episode (group 8, 7 min 49 s) also occurred during a fight. A player immobilised the enemy champion, and his mates took advantage of that action:

PLAYER 1: *"I rooted him!"*
PLAYER 2: *"The champion, the champion, again, again".*
PLAYER 3: *"Niiice!"*
PLAYER 2: *"Ah-ha!"* (Satisfied)
PLAYER 1: *"Yes! We got him!!"*

Discussion

The purpose of this study was to explore the role of positive interdependence in the functioning of social forms of flow. More specifically, we aimed to investigate how different degrees of positive interdependence could promote the emergence of team flow and group flow. Notably, this study used a new method to detect optimal experiences through observation of the players' behaviours. Although the observation tool was not directly validated, it fulfilled the primary goal of identifying social flow episodes experienced by the players. So it served its purpose to establish the relationship between optimal experiences and the positive interdependence brought about by the teamplay.

Our results revealed that group flow states were more often experienced in the 'high interdependence' condition than in the 'low interdependence' condition. These results are consistent with Walker's (2010) findings, suggesting the importance of positive interdependence in the emergence of social forms of flow. Game replay analysis extended the interpretation of this result, notably revealing that players in the 'low interdependence' condition rarely came together, and then only briefly; they said that they were afraid of losing their towers and therefore decided to split up and share the responsibility, each of them taking care of one lane, protecting its towers and trying to advance to the opponent's camp alone. In other words, the three players did similar tasks (defeating enemy towers and champions) but individually. Thus, they met rarely or briefly before returning to their lane. That these players carried a heavy, individual responsibility limited their opportunities to meet and interact. At a functional level, we assume that it was specifically the goal and task subtypes of positive interdependence that had the greatest impact on the development of these simultaneous and shared optimal experience episodes. Indeed, game replays also revealed that the avatars of players in the 'high interdependence' condition were often with their mates, increasing the likelihood of experiencing a group flow state when engaging coactively in a fight. Thus, the players were not only 'theoretically' linked by a common goal (to eliminate the maximum number of towers and enemy champions) that they could have achieved independently, but also by a task prerequisite whose achievement required the support of all the players (for the team to earn points, avatars had to be together). This led them to meet, to focus on common subgoals (pack together, locate enemy units, collectively engage in a fight, etc.), thus creating the conditions for group flow.

Regarding team flow states, although four episodes have been identified when the interdependence induced between teammates was high, statistical analyses did not reveal a significant difference in occurrence of this state between the two experimental conditions. In the 'low interdependence' condition, players did not experience any team flow episode, which seems to be related to the fact that their avatars rarely met in the game, making it difficult for the players to cooperate (see group flow). In the 'high interdependence' condition, that only four episodes of team flow were identified raises the question of what prevented the players from experiencing the cooperative optimal experience more often. Indeed, in this condition, 13 episodes of group flow were identified, compared with only four team flow episodes. This means that players, despite sharing many game situations (including 13 that could have enabled them to experience group flow), were rarely able to really cooperate. Game replays revealed that players often took part in team fights together, but at the heart of the action, acted completely independently.

The first explanation of this phenomenon is related to the fact that players did not master the game sufficiently to make use of the complementarity of their champions. The videos showed that players used their powers separately, unable to benefit from collaboration possibilities. This is partly supported by the fact that members of only one group (group 22, whose members experienced three episodes of team flow) referred to opportunities for their champions to collaborate. They were thus the only players to have expressed their willingness to develop and put into action a form of shared mental model allowing them to organise their collective actions (Cannon-Bower, Salas & Converse, 1993). Mental models are meta-cognitive structures allowing individuals to share information. Players use them to memorise empirical knowledge about the game, its gameplay, etc., as well as for shared action scripts, which describe sequentially the actions to be taken in a specific situation during the game (Richter & Lechner, 2009). The dialogues quoted previously clearly highlight a form of these team action models: players communicate to build a sequential script describing the actions each of them has to take (First, I immobilise him, then both of you attack, etc.).

Thus, most of the participants were limited by their own lack of knowledge about how their avatars could collaborate, and their subsequent inability to organise effective collective action. Furthermore, at a basic level, players encountered great gameplay difficulty mastering the controls required to perform certain actions. To be effective, certain characters' abilities require a subtle mastery of the controls (e.g. Morgana's cage requires aiming and clicking with great accuracy while anticipating the target's movements). Again, this is confirmed by game replays, as players were frequently observed to use their abilities inappropriately, clicking frenetically on power icons without really understanding how they worked. In future studies, it would therefore be interesting to explore how experienced players build up and use their collective tactics.

The second reason that may explain the rarity of team flow episodes in the 'high interdependence' condition is not related to the way the participants played, but to the absence of a genuine interdependence role between the characters of the game. Thus, champions have complementary powers, probably allowing a team flow state to be reached when used collaboratively, but, strictly speaking, this does not allow real operational dependence between players. Indeed, although much less effective, basic fights may well be carried out without interacting with other avatars. It is therefore the teamplay mechanics of the game, which feature complementarities between avatars, rather than real interdependence of roles and tasks that could explain this result.

Regarding limitations of this study, it should be noted that the observation tool used was not thoroughly tested. Indeed, although this detection method was pretested to ensure it allowed to detect group and team flow experiences, future studies should test its validity by varying gameplay types encountered by the players and through direct comparison of behaviour observation and players' reported feelings. However, authors recently validated the usability of this flow detection tool in single player conditions (Borderie & Michinov, *in press*) and call to extend its application to multiplayer settings. Another limitation of this study is that participants were beginners. Although it allowed greater control on experimental conditions, as observed during game sessions, it also brought difficulties for most of the team to establish effective cooperation strategies. There is a crucial need for research about group and team flow states in multiplayer condition with experimented players. The latter may control the game better and may also be able to build complete and consequently shared team mental models to serve their teamplay efficiency. It may then facilitate the emergence of collective and cooperative optimal experiences.

Conclusion

This study provided fruitful perspectives in the development of social forms of flow, namely 'group flow' and 'team flow' by addressing the question of the specific role of positive interdependence and its subtypes in their emergence. In line with previous research, it confirmed that social flow experiences are closely linked to the interdependence bonds between members of the team. Goal interdependence may guide individuals to share the same objective; however, they are still free to decide how they assume collective responsibility. Although task, and more specifically, action interdependence is a determinant of team flow state, as it forced players to act together cohesively in pursuing this common goal.

This research also brought important methodological results about new ways to detect optimal experience through players' behaviour observation. It notably shed light on the shared and concomitant social flow episodes that members of a team could experience at a very same moment during a game session. Moreover, the 'concentration-joy pattern' used to identify flow episodes seemed promising and needs to be enriched with new observation clues.

Finally, this study highlighted the importance of thoroughly analyzing game design to identify how gameplay mechanics could lead to the emergence of collective optimal states. We recommend that game designers and researchers identify precisely the subtypes of positive interdependence involved in the teamplay of a given game as it could allow them to grasp the very nature of structural and functional bonds which connect team members in this game.

References

Borderie, J. (2015). *La quête du team flow dans les jeux video coopératifs: Apports conceptuels et méthodologiques (The quest of team flow in cooperative video games: Conceptual and methodological contributions).* Unpublished doctoral thesis, Université Rennes 2, Rennes, France.

Borderie, J., & Michinov, N. (2014). Identifying social forms of flow in multi-user videogames. MULTI.PLAYER 2: Compete - cooperate – communicate. *International Conference on the Social Aspects of Digital Gaming.* Münster (Germany), August 14–15.

Borderie, J., & Michinov, N. (*In press*). Identifying flow in video games: Towards a new observation-based method. *International Journal of Gaming and Computer-Mediated Simulation.*

Brown, E., & Cairns, P. (2004). *A grounded investigation of game immersion.* Paper presented at the *Conference on Human Factors in Computing Systems.*

Cannon-Bowers, J. A., Salas, E., & Converse, S. (1993). Shared mental models in expert team decision making. In N.J. Castellan, Jr. (Ed.), *Current Issues in Individual and Group Decision Making* (pp. 221–246). Hillsdale, NJ: Erlbaum.

Chen, J. (2006). *Flow in games.* Unpublished master's thesis, University of Southern California, Los Angeles, CA.

Chou, T. J., & Ting, C. C. (2003). The role of Flow Experience in cyber-game addiction. *CyberPsychology & Behavior, 6*(6), 663–675.

Coan, J. A., & Gottman, J. M. (2007). The Specific Affect Coding System (SPAFF). In J. A. Coan & J. J. B. Allen (Eds.), *Handbook of emotion elicitation and assessment* (pp. 267–285): New York: Oxford University Press.

Cosma, J. (1999). *Flow in teams.* Unpublished master's thesis. Chicago School of Professional Psychology, Illinois.

Csíkszentmihalyi, M. (1990). *Flow: The psychology of optimal experience.* New York: Harper Perennial.

Csikszentmihalyi, M. (1992). A response to the Kimiecik & Stein and Jackson papers. *Journal of Applied Sport Psychology, 4*(2), 181–183.

Csikszentmihalyi, M. (1993). *The evolving self: A psychology for the third millennium.* New York: Harper Perennial.

Csikszentmihalyi, M., & Larson, R. (1987). Validity and reliability of experience sampling method. *Journal of Nervous and Mental Diseases, 175,* 526–536.

Ekman, P., Friesen, W. V., & Hager, J. C. (2002). *Facial action coding system: The manual.* Salt Lake City, UT: Research Nexus.

Entertainment Software Association (2013). Essential facts about the computer and video game industry. Retrieved from http://www.theesa.com/facts/pdfs/esa_ef_2013.pdf.

Ermi, L., & Mäyrä, F. (2005). *Fundamental components of the gameplay experience: Analysing immersion.* DiGRA conference. Changing Views: Worlds in Play, Vancouver, Canada.

Johnson, D. W., & Johnson, R. T. (1999). Making cooperative learning work. *Theory into Practice, 38*(2), 67–73.

Johnson, D. W., & Johnson, R. T. (2002). Cooperative learning and social interdependence theory. In *Theory and research on small groups* (pp. 9–35). Springer US.

Lazarovitz, S. M., (2003). *Team and Individual flow in female ice hockey players: The relationships between flow, group cohesion, and athletes performance.* Unpublished doctoral thesis. University of Calgary, Alberta.

Léger, P.-M., Sénécal, S., Aubé, C., Cameron, A.-F., Ortiz de Guinea, A., Brunelle, E., Courtemanche, F., Davis, F., & Cronan, P. (2013). The influence of group flow on group performance: A research program. *Proceedings Gmunden Retreat on NeuroIS 2013.* Gmunden, Austria, June 1–4.

Nacke, L., & Lindley, C. A. (2008). Flow and immersion in first-person shooters: Measuring the player's gameplay experience. In *Proceedings of the 2008 Conference on Future Play: Research, Play, Share* (pp. 81–88). New York: ACM.

Nacke, L. E., & Lindley, C. A. (2009). Affective ludology, flow and immersion in a first-person shooter: Measurement of player experience. *The Journal of the Canadian Game Studies Association. 3*(5). Retrieved from http://arxiv.org/ftp/arxiv/papers/1004/1004.0248.pdf.

Nakamura, J., & Csikszentmihalyi, M. (2002). The concept of flow. In C. R. Snyder & S. J. Lopez (Eds.), *Handbook of positive psychology* (pp. 89–105). Oxford: Oxford University Press.

Reese, D. D. (2010). Introducing flowometer: A CyGaMEs assessment suite tool. In R. V. Eck (Ed.), *Gaming & cognition: Theories and perspectives from the learning sciences* (pp. 227–254). Hershey, PA: IGI Global.

Reese, D. D. (2015). CyGaMEs Selene player log dataset: Gameplay assessment, flow dimensions and non-gameplay assessments. *British Journal of Educational Technology, 46*(5), 1005–1014.

Richter, S., & Lechner, U. (2009). Transactive memory systems and shared situation awareness: A World of Warcraft experiment. In *International Conference on Organizational Learning, Knowledge and Capabilities, The Netherlands.*

Salas, E., Dickinson, T. L., Converse, S. A., & Tannenbaum, S. I. (1992). Toward an understanding of team performance and training. In *Teams: Their training and performance.* Norwood, NJ: Ablex.

Sawyer, K. (2007). *Group genius: The creative power of collaboration.* Cambridge, MA: Basic Books.

Slater, M. (2002). Presence and the Sixth Sense. *Presence: Teleoperators and Virtual Environments, 11*(4), 435–439. doi: 10.1162/105474602760204327.

Sweetser, P., & Wyeth, P. (2005). GameFlow: A model for evaluating player enjoyment in games. *Computers in Entertainment (CIE), 3*(3), 3–3.

Walker, C. (2010). Experiencing flow: Is doing it together better than doing it alone? *The Journal of Positive Psychology, 5,* 3–11.

Wan, C. S., & Chiou, W. B. (2006). Psychological motives and online games addiction: A test of flow theory and humanistic needs theory for Taiwanese adolescents. *CyberPsychology & Behavior, 9*(3), 317–324.

4 Envisioning the Other

A Grounded Exploration of Social Roles in Digital Game Play

Jasmien Vervaeke, Frederik De Grove, and Jan Van Looy

In recent years, studies have shown that the presence of other people and broader social context when playing video games influences the playing experience (e.g., Gajadhar, de Kort, & IJsselsteijn, 2008; Kaye, 2016; Mandryk, Inkpen, & Calvert, 2006; Ravaja, Saari, Turpeinen, Laarni, Salminen, & Kivikangas, 2006). However, incorporation of the social influence in player experience models, for instance the SCI-model (Ermi & Mayra, 2005) or the GameFlow model (Sweetser & Whyeth, 2005), is still missing, as de Kort and IJsselsteijn (2008) rightfully address. Furthermore, researchers have been asking for models of player experience that incorporate the social context (e.g., de Kort & IJsselsteijn, 2008; Deterding, 2015; Kaye & Bryce, 2012). In the first section of this chapter, we will make a short chronological overview of the relevant literature regarding the influence of social settings on player experience, followed by an extraction of the common dimensions in this literature. Last, our biggest concern regarding previous research is shown: that too often social play is approached unidimensionally, alongside our proposal of how to tackle it, by means of a multidimensional and two-layered framework.

Relatively early in digital game research, it was shown that the social aspect of multiplayer games makes them compelling and interesting, in ways single-player games are not able to, because the social nature of humans (Bunten, 1996; Costikyan, 1994). The challenge that is being introduced by these types of games was particularly important as it differs from playing against a computer (e.g., Zagal, Nussbaum, & Rosas, 2000). Moreover, competition has taken on a different interpretation, by introducing human opponents (e.g., Vorderer, Hartmann, & Klimmt, 2003; Williams & Clippinger, 2002). What is more, such games are network-based and have different demands in terms of hardware and software than their single player counterparts. In 2002, Pantel and Wolf found that delay in real-time multiplayer games had an impact on performance and attractiveness, by letting two people sitting next to each other, compete in a racing game.

Since 2000, studies about the influence of the social context on the player experience started to appear. As both player experience and social context are broad, multifaceted concepts, there is a strong variability amongst these studies. For example, in an experimental study, players reported higher levels of aggressive feelings after playing *Monopoly* against a computer than after playing it against another human player in the same room (Williams & Clippinger, 2002). According to the authors, the context in which the game session takes place can contribute to aggressive feelings, as well as the aggression within the game. The pattern of their results was attributed to the presence of other people, as a form of social control. Competition has been regarded as a key enjoyment factor in social game play (Vorderer et al., 2003). Gamers rated *Tomb Raider* more enjoyable with a competitive element than without (Klimmt, 2001) and personal motivation to compete predicted best why gamers preferred a certain (competitive) game (Vorderer et al., 2003). Wanting to know how gameplay occurs in a natural setting, Carr, Schott, Burn, and Buckingham (2004) collected video footage of a gamer's living room when playing a single-player game whenever the player felt like it. Remarkably, they found that when friends were present and merely watching the game, they became actively involved in the game, by giving verbal advice and showing emotional reactions to the game.

Ravaja et al. (2006) measured the impact of the opponent (computer vs stranger vs friend) in a colocated competitive setting on an array of emotional outcomes, measured both subjectively and objectively. Results showed differences between a human and a computer opponent, but also between a friend and a stranger. They regarded the addition of observation by another human as a social-competitive situation in which task performance evaluation potential might be present, and this in turn increased arousal (Ravaja et al., 2006; Thorsteinsson & James, 1999). Mandryk et al. (2006) compared social contexts in which players competed against a computer or against a friend in the same room and saw significant differences in subjective self-reports and physiological data. Interestingly, when one player was competing against the computer, the other player had to leave the room. Indeed, an influence of an observer on the experience of the player would be expected (Kimble & Rezabek, 1992).

When studying players of *World of Warcraft*, Ducheneaut, Yee, Nickell, & Moore (2006) found that players preferred to play as classes that can be played on their own, without a necessity for other players. Although Massively Multiplayer Online Role-Playing Games like *World of Warcraft* are often regarded as social, and this social factor is often stated by players as their motivation to play, players of this genre are 'alone together', as they play *not with* others, but *surrounded by* others. Ducheneaut et al. (2006) stated that other people involved in gameplay have different roles than just direct support and camaraderie, as previously thought. They can also assume the role of an audience, to perceive how well the player performed, and provide social presence, as well as a spectacle.

De Kort and IJsselsteijn (2008) advocate that player experience and engagement is influenced by the social context of gameplay. This social surrounding is broader than just the presence or absence of others, but it includes a certain role for this other, which can be acting, observing, competing, cooperating or coacting. Dichotomies for persons surrounding gameplay should be avoided and continuums should be proposed instead. Turn-taking versus real-time competing games also influences the gamer's interaction, and hence also his or her experience, just as a broad range of game interface characteristics (e.g., size and orientation of the screen) (de Kort & IJsselsteijn, 2008). Player experience and aggression were compared in different competitive social settings with colocated and mediated friends, strangers and computers by Gajadhar et al. (2008) and an effect of familiarity (friend vs. stranger) and location (colocated vs mediated) was found, alongside the finding that it was more fun to play against humans than against computers. According to the authors, there are clear social roles in gameplay and these roles influence player experience (Gajadhar et al., 2008).

After a myriad of experimental research into social play, Kaye and Bruce (2012) claimed that real-life game experiences should be investigated qualitatively. Using focus groups with regular gamers, they found that social contexts can enhance the subjective experiences of gaming, with particularly differences between competitive versus collaborative play. They followed up with a retrospective study, comparing solo with social gaming in online and offline settings, with collaborative and competitive game play. Again, player experience differed between solo and social play. However, the other variations in contexts did not yield different outcomes. The lack of a significant impact may be due to the fact that participants had to recall a past experience, instead of playing and experiencing a game (Kaye & Bruce, 2014). Hudson (2015) conducted a similar study as Gajadhar et al. (2008), but worked with a cooperative setting instead of a competitive one. Because the player experience measure, the Social Presence Gaming Questionnaire from de Kort, IJsselstein, and Poels (2007), was not suited for this cooperative design, we cannot compare these two studies directly. Nevertheless, Hudson (2015) also found that social presence was higher when playing with a human teammate, but there was no influence of the location of the teammate in this study. He also found that players assume that they paid more interest to their teammates' actions than vice versa. The importance of the social context in game play has also been demonstrated by the work of Eklund (2015). In a descriptive survey in Sweden asking about social play, Eklund (2015) found that the other parties involved (family, friends or strangers) influenced the player's engagement. The level of an observer's involvement in game play then was investigated by Maurer, Aslan, Wuchse, Neureiter, and Tscheligi (2015) and showed to have a significant influence on overall game experience.

Table 4.1 Four properties of social play settings

Property	Refers to	Related to	Possible example
Spatiality	Real life	Location of the players	In the same room
Longevity	Real life	Duration of the relation	Friends
Adversarity	Game	Role in the game	Opponents
Synchronicity	Real life	Time of play	At the same time

All this demonstrates that game experience consists of a broad range of factors, including but not limited to motivation, frustration, competition, enjoyment, and arousal. During this literature review, it became apparent that several properties of the interpersonal relations have been identified as potential moderators of the social playing experience, and that these properties are recurring, but not always under the same name. We aimed to extract returning aspects of different social contexts into four coined terms: spatiality, longevity, adversarity and synchronicity (Table 4.1).

The first of these properties is the location of the other individual, which we will describe as the *spatiality* of the social play. In game research, there are two common distinctions (colocated or mediated; e.g., de Kort & IJsselsteijn, 2008) but other possibilities have been proposed too, such as in the next room (Gajadhar et al., 2008), or at a distance (Williams & Clippinger, 2002). Spatiality for our aim also includes socio-fugal settings, which are seating and viewing arrangements (Sommer, 1967), as sitting oriented towards each other has more opportunities for eye contact and interpretable facial expressions, than next to each other (de Kort & IJsselsteijn, 2008).

The *longevity* of the relation with the other, has often been referred to as being a friend or a stranger (e.g., Ravaja et al., 2006), but this does not cover the whole range of possible relations. With this term, the duration of the relationship between the player and the other is described, more specifically whether or not the relationship continues when the game session ends.

Adversarity designates the side the other is on, and whether he or she is an opponent, teammate, or a neutral party (Kaye & Bruce, 2012). This will partly depend on the game, as some are cooperative (same side) or competitive (other side), but it can also depend on the relationship with the other, meaning that friends can introduce competitive elements into a cooperative game.

Synchronicity, finally, refers to the temporal aspect of the social play, whereby it is possible to differentiate between players acting concurrently, in turns or delayed, largely dependent on the specific game. Although no papers found that compared real-time versus turn-based game play (probably because there is no game that can be played in both temporal modes in exactly the same way), there is ample research about the influence on game experience of a temporal delay in real-time games, making it clear that time is an important factor when investigating game experience (Pantel & Wolf, 2002; Quax, Monsieurs, Lamotte, De Vleeschauwer, & Degrande, 2004). In the current chapter, all interactions with other people about a game session are included, exceeding the game played and thus also including the player's testimonials during or after the game. In the latter case, there is an interval between the game session and the socialisation, making this a delayed interaction.

The four dimensions (spatiality, longevity, adversarity, and synchronicity; see Table 4.1) are helpful when describing a game setting and investigating game experience, but should not be treated as stand-alone variables. Most of the social play studies make a distinction between computers and humans, but the distinction between humans is rarely made beyond 'friend or stranger' or 'versus- or coplayer'. Usually, the influence of only one dimension on game experience is measured at a time, while neglecting possible interactions with other values on other dimensions, as shown in the literature study discussed previously. As reality is more complex than simple dichotomies, this chapter aims to demonstrate that there are important differences within each category that cannot be investigated by a single variable approach. To this end, the social roles gamers attribute to other people involved in and/or surrounding digital game play are explored as well as how these roles relate to game experience, by investigating, within each role, the values of the four proposed social play dimensions.

Method and Procedure

In this study, the grounded theory framework (Glaser & Strauss, 1967) was used. In this framework, theory is generated from the data itself and validated by new data, which shapes the theory further. This adapted theory is verified again with additional data and so on, until further data collection is redundant. According to this method, iterative cycles of data collection and analysis are interwoven with each other. In the current study, two waves of interviews with gamers were conducted. For the first wave, 40 people (15 female, 25 male), with a mean age of 28.65 years (SD = 11.48 years, modus = 22 years) and with different gaming habits (17 daily, 11 weekly, 7 monthly, and 5 yearly or less) were interviewed with the aim of getting a broad view on their experiences with other people while gaming, how they perceive those other people, and what role they fulfill according to the player.

The goal of the second wave of interviews was twofold: first, validating the archetypes that emerged after analysis of the first wave by exploring their boundaries. The second goal was to link the discovered archetypes to dimensions of social play commonly used in the gaming literature. For these purposes, 10 regular gamers (eight daily and two weekly) were interviewed (6 male), with a mean age of 22.7 years old (SD = 10.02). To qualify for this study, people were asked to answer questions about their gaming behaviour on an online survey, posted on multiple Belgian gaming websites and fora. From the completed surveys, 10 gamers were carefully selected to include the full range of game genres, gaming frequencies, and gaming media. These interviews took place at the participants' homes and audio was recorded. All interviews were transcribed and coded in NVivo 10 (QSR International Pty Ltd, 2012). Names in this study were altered to ensure anonymity. When referring to a player in this text, we used the male pronoun for reasons of simplicity.

The first wave of interviews aimed to get an overview of the different roles attributed by the player to the other person involved in a game session. 'Game session' refers to one instance or unit of game play. That is, the event of one uninterrupted period, during which the player plays a game. As soon as the player quits the game, the game session is discontinued. Because of the broad range of games, additional demarcations are needed. In some games, especially shooters, there are short periods during which the player is not able to play (e.g., when he dies in-game and waits to be revived). In this case, the player is still involved in the game, as the game developers intended, even if he is not actually playing. Therefore, the gaming session is not ended. In other games, it is also possible to not be playing for a short time, when it is not meant by the rules of the game (e.g., passing the console). Here, the game session is ceased and a new one will begin only when the player receives the controller anew and plays again.

Results

First Interview Wave

Analyzing the first wave of interviews led to uncovering three properties that, through their combination, allow for categorising the other person: Involvement, Focus, and Meaning construction. *Involvement* refers to the extent to which the other is able to directly exert influence on the events happening in the game of the player. *Focus* designates whether the focus of the play situation is more on the game or more on the social interaction with the other. *Meaning construction* refers to how the actions of the player can be seen and interpreted by others and to what extent the player is aware of this possibility.

If the player believes his or her actions are seen by others, they become shared. These three properties form the constitutional foundation through which four archetypes, or roles, emerged in the interviews. Table 4.2 provides an overview of these roles and their determining properties.

Table 4.2 Overview of the four emerging roles and their properties

Role	Involvement	Focus	Meaning Construction
Witness	Passive	Game	Shared meanings
Co-Player	Active	Game	Shared meanings
Companion	Active/Passive	Sociability	Shared meanings
Tool	Active	Game	No shared meanings

A first archetype is *the witness*. The witness plays a passive role and is therefore unable to influence what is happening in the game of the player. Despite this passive involvement, the focus of the interaction is on the game and not on the social situation surrounding it. What is more, meanings and experiences are shared between the player and the witness. Indeed, even if one just watches somebody play, the events happening in the game are shared and their meanings are negotiated between the player and the other, as Mark (male, 25, weekly gamer) illustrates:

> I don't think a lot of people just watch another person play, but I think it's the best. [...] I just like to be able to share it with somebody. To say how beautiful it [the game world] is.

There were several reasons for the existence of a witness. It could be because the witness just enjoyed watching and did not have the urge to play himself. Yet, there were also situations where there were more wanting-to-play persons than controllers. Another possibility is where the player and the other were not in the same room, but the other was still able to observe the game or evidence that the game was played and this changes the game experience, as illustrated by Peter (male, 21, daily gamer):

> With the iPhone, there's also a social aspect to it [infinity blade]. You can add friends and they can see which achievements you've acquired, just like the PS3. I really like that feature [...] It adds a competitive aspect.

Indeed, achievements, scoreboards and even video streams, can serve as a medium for a witness, to observe the progress of a player. This indicates that the witness is not bound by temporal or spatial constraints.

A second archetype is *the coplayer*. In contrast to the witness, the coplayer is actively involved in the game of the player. Hence, he can influence the player and vice versa, and can play either as an opponent or as an accomplice. Similar to the witness, the focus is on the game and meanings and experiences are shared. Furthermore, through the active involvement of the other, not only actions become shared, but also the consequences of those actions, as Adrian (male, 20, daily gamer) illustrates with a racing game (*Gran Turismo*):

> *If you win [against a human player], there is more fun and if you lose then, uhm, against the computer, you don't know him. You can try to drive him off the track but that's not funny.*

In this passage, it becomes obvious that shared meaning construction, something that can only happen between humans, changes the game experience of Adrian. A consequence of combining shared meanings with a focus on the game is that social play can lead to the creation of additional game-related goals. One of our respondents regularly played a football game with his brother. They often played the game at its easiest setting but challenged themselves by trying to win against the computer with a score of at least 10 to 0. The difference between focus on the game or on the sociability of the situation is not always clear-cut, however. Another respondent, playing football games with his friends, often uses the games' rules to make playing more fun by making those who score a goal drink a shot of alcohol each time.

The focus on the sociability of the situation rather than on the game itself, leads to another archetype: that of *the companion*. Meanings are shared between the player and the companion and the other can assume an active or a passive role. Maintaining the social relationship with each other is the main reason of the game session, whilst the game that is played is often of secondary importance. As such, the game is used as a means to be together. Several respondents reported playing with one or more companions during local area network (LAN) parties or on occasions with party games. For instance, Ross (31, male, daily gamer) says that LAN parties are not just about gaming, and that the actions you do in a game do not matter. For him, it is more about being together and making the LAN party a social event. Kurt (22, male, daily gamer) mentions the following about an evening with party games:

> *In a party game, you are in a living room with a bunch of friends, having fun. And the game is of secondary importance. It is something social.*

The fourth and final archetype is *the tool*. The tool has a purely functional role, in that the player needs his presence to be able to play the game. The tool is thus actively involved, since he can alter the game of the player. The focus lies on the game and sociability surrounding the situation is completely absent. Although the tool can influence the events in the game of the player, the absence of any sociability prevents that meanings and experiences are shared. As such, the tool is merely used to gain an advantage. This can range from being able to play a certain game to getting special items. The player is aware of the other in the game, but interaction is limited to what is required according to the rules of the game. In the interviews, Peter (21, male, daily gamer) stated that playing *Call of Duty* or *Counterstrike*, it did not matter to him whether he played with real people or not, but when playing *World of Warcraft*, he has to play with real people, because the game requires it. This is similar to what Joshua (22, male, weekly gamer) says:

> *If I am online, there are always strangers online too. You can play with or against them. [...] I don't have a bond with them. To me, playing against a computer or against that stranger is the same.*

To comprehend all the findings about the four archetypes above correctly, three things are important to consider. First, as mentioned previously, the roles are attributed to the other by the player in-game. It is therefore not always the way the other would see himself, but only what is perceived through the eyes of the player. Second, the role of the other can change during a game session and these shifts happen frequently, but also over several game sessions. Rob (male, 18, daily gamer) shows how one role can gradually develop into another, at a LAN party:

> *In the beginning, everybody is like "I'm gonna beat you". In the end, it is like "Oh well, you beat me". [...] In the end, you don't care anymore, you've won and you've lost, it doesn't matter anymore, you just play for fun.*

In this scenario, the people surrounding Rob are coplayers at the start as there is fierce competition. This fades over time, however, and by the end of the event they become companions. Third, because these roles are seen through the eyes of the player, properties of the player, of the other, of the game, and of the situation affect the attributed role. Two similar situations can thus elicit a different role to the other, because of a different player. For instance, a player deprived of friends after moving away, plays with a companion to have some social contact and to maintain their friendship, while a different player can play the same game, with a friend as a coplayer.

Second Interview Wave

Exploring the Four Roles

The four identified roles are treated as archetypes, or ideal forms. In practice, categorising is not always as straightforward. The goals of the second wave of interviews were to confirm and challenge the four archetypes by searching for their boundaries, as instructed by the grounded theory framework. This was done in two ways. First, based on purposeful sampling, respondents were sought that were expected to have experience with one or more archetypes, based on their game preferences. In contrast to the first wave of interviews, questions were specifically aimed at deepening our understanding of the archetypes and their constituting dimensions. Secondly, questions were developed to link our archetypes to recurring variables in social play research, which are adversarity, longevity, spatiality, and synchronicity, to see how each one affects game experience within and over archetypes.

Knowing that archetypes do not exist in real life and that the roles are dynamic because they can change during a game session, caution is in order. Hence it is useful to explore the boundaries between the archetypes. For example, the tool and the companion behave like opposites. For the former, there is a total lack of sociability and an almost exclusive focus on the game. This is in stark contrast to the companion, with whom there is most focus of all the archetypes on the sociability, making the game of secondary importance here.

The tool and the witness also have a clear distinction, mainly in terms of involvement. The tool can change events in the game directly, whereas the witness cannot. The meaning construction differs too. Meanings are not shared with a tool, while they are when playing with a witness watching the game.

The difference between the witness and the coplayer is straightforward, and the differing dimension is again the involvement. If there is a direct influence of the other in the game session of the player, the other is a coplayer; if not, a witness, all other things being equal. The events in the game cannot ever be changed by the witness, but he or she can have an indirect influence, by cheering or giving advice. To illustrate this boundary, an example in which the role of the other shifts from witness to coplayer, is described by Jeff (male, 17, daily gamer):

> *When I'm stuck in a certain fight and he knows how to pass, because he already did it a few times, he can tell me which attack I should use, but I don't know how to use that attack. Then he takes my PSP and shows me.*

In the beginning of the fragment, the other is a witness and merely watching the game. By giving advice, the involvement explores the boundaries of what is still to be considered as passive, yet it can still be considered so as the influence on the actions in the game remains indirect. The moment the other takes the PSP, he becomes actively involved and therefore a coplayer.

A more blurred distinction exists between the coplayer and the tool. The focus and involvement are similar, but their role in constructing meaning to the player's actions differs. In most interviews, there is mention of how playing with a friend enriches the experience compared to playing with an artificial intelligence or a stranger. However, a friend does not automatically assume the role of coplayer nor does a stranger always equal a tool. It is important to note that the other can evolve from tool to coplayer over the course of multiple and/or extended gaming sessions, as illustrated by Kenny (male, 13, weekly gamer), when playing *Call of Duty* online:

> *Although I added a friend after talking to him, a guy from England, he had his microphone on and was making silly noises. I put mine on and start to make silly noises myself. [...] We started talking and he said "I'm in your closet", [...] and I said "Haha, he's in my closet". [...] We played together, by saying stuff like "Go upstairs", or "hide in a corner" or "he's over there". Then you can work together and this creates a bond. [...] Afterwards, I've sent him a friend request.*

At first, before they started to communicate, the other person is a tool. Kenny has no emotional connection with him and 'uses' him to play the game. By working together, this role slowly changes into that of a coplayer, with whom Kenny shares meanings, which in turn changes his game experience.

The last two distinctions that will be discussed are also not clear-cut and demarcate the companion versus the witness and the companion versus the coplayer. The defining property for the companion is the focus on the sociability of the situation. It is the only archetype that does not have its focus on the game and thus this is the defining criterion for the companion. Meanings are shared with a companion, as well as with a witness and a coplayer, but the consequences of the actions of the player are only shared with a coplayer. Even though in theory, active companions receive a consequence in the game, this is of secondary importance and they give less weight to it. Gamers playing with a companion care less than coplayers about the events going on in the game itself, including their consequences. In Jeff's (17, male, daily gamer) words: *"You can hardly call it a competition"* and *"We do not play to win, we play to game and to be together"*.

Both the passive companion and the witness do not have a direct influence on the events in the game of the player. In case of an active companion, the influence is direct, as is the influence of a coplayer. Therefore, focus should be brought into account as well. If the player primarily wants to play the game, he will engage with a coplayer, otherwise the other will be a companion. Social events with games are prone to having companions, for example an evening at somebody's place where a party game is played. In the case of Jennifer (female, 22, daily gamer), at New Year's Eve, she had some friends over, that brought their Wii.

Past midnight, they all played on it. The primary goal of the evening was celebrating the new year, something that is considered a social event. This gathering would have happened, regardless of the Wii. Playing with the companion typically gives less weight to winning or losing than playing with the coplayer, as Rob (male, 18, daily gamer) describes:

> *I experience competition a lot less while playing on the Wii [with others]. I have the feeling of 'this is for fun, for having pleasure, it doesn't matter if I win or not, I have some exercise' more, when playing on the Wii.*

Both the passively involved companion and the witness see the actions of the player and share their meanings, but are not actually involved in the game of the player, apart from indirect influence, as stated earlier. The other assumes the role of witness if the player believes the common interest is in the game itself. If the player thinks the other is present for their social interaction, the archetype of the companion is imposed. The border between a companion and a witness is explored by Kyle (male, 23, daily gamer):

> *If one of my friends are online, I ask him how or what he's doing. He's usually playing a different game than me, but through the chat, we can talk about both games.*

This fragment has indicators of both the companion and the witness. On the one hand, Kyle asks his friend about his well-being, but on the other hand, they talk about the game they are playing. Additional information would be needed in order to classify the role of Kyle's friend appropriately here.

Playing with another person assuming a different role can not only change the meaning construction of the player's actions, but also the whole game experience. Shared meanings can lead to a shared and thus different experience because of the social nature the game session now has, compared to a game session without shared meanings. The role of other people in a gaming session matters to the experience of that session for the player. As a consequence, the roles described above, are important to understand player experience. The commonly researched social play dimensions have their limitations if used in a freestanding manner. There were respondents who mentioned that for them, it does not matter if they play with or against a friend, but that it did matter if they are playing against a friend or a stranger. This shows that adversarity on its own is not enough. Combining these regularly used dimensions with the archetypes yields a broader and at the same time more thorough view into the experience of the player, and thus describes a more complete picture.

In the following section, the four archetypes will be discussed in terms of the four identified dimensions from the literature that are known to affect game experience. The aim is to observe if and how game experience is influenced by each of these four dimensions (spatiality, synchronicity, adversarity, longevity), within each archetype, and if there is a difference in game experience, over archetypes, when looking at one dimension at a time.

Variations in Game Research Dimensions

When describing the archetypes, it was mentioned that there is an abundance of situations in which a witness can exist. These multiple settings result in a large variability of the witness in terms of the social play dimensions: all values of each dimension are possible with the witness. The witness can be in the same room as the player, but he does not have to be. He can watch the player's game live, but it can also be delayed. A witness is usually neutral, because he is not involved in the game, but as stated earlier, cheering for or against the player can occur. The duration of the relationship varied in the interviews, but witnesses who do not know the player at all were rare. Nevertheless, it happens that somebody watches a gamer's live streaming channel, he can then be regarded as a witness if the gamer notices him, as opposed to a walkthrough video on YouTube, where is no viewer information available to the gamer.

The coplayer can find himself in the same room as the player, or at any different location. Our respondents talked about engaging with a coplayer in both colocated and online social play, with a slightly higher frequency for online play. The gaming session is often played together, thus concurrently. This was almost always the case in the interviews, but playing at the same time is not a necessity, as shown by Amy (female, 50, daily gamer), who plays *Wordfeud*, a word game similar to Scrabble, on her tablet:

> You play in turns. The person I'm playing against now hasn't played yet. It's possible that she sees it [my move] in half an hour and that she'll play. It is likely that I'll only check this evening and play my turn. It is possible that you can put 3 or 4 words after each other down on the board, if you and the other are both playing at the same time. It is also possible that a game lasts a week, or two, until it is finished.

The coplayer can be a teammate or an opponent; both occurred at roughly the same percentage. In most of our interviews, the coplayer was somebody our interviewees knew, usually a friend. However, there were also players that regarded strangers as coplayers, as Joey (male, 23, daily gamer) describes, talking about a game of *Warcraft* online. He and his whole alliance fight together against the other fraction. He says the following about the other people in his alliance:

> *Even though they are strangers, it [the fight] is something that binds. In Warcraft, you have to play together in some aspects anyway and then I sometimes get to know other people.*

It is apparent in the previous example that the bonding occurs before Joey gets to know the other player. When bonding, the meaning construction is shared. Therefore, there exist strangers that are seen as coplayers. However, in all of the interviews, testimonies regarding a stranger as a coplayer included some form of getting to know this stranger eventually. As a consequence, it is expected that they will be playing together again in the future, just like when a player would see his friend as a coplayer, but this need not always be the case. It is very likely that although Joey bonds with a couple of alliance members, he will not befriend them all. These people border on the archetype of the tool and that of the coplayer. This statement of Joey also showed that the attributed roles are subject to the player's personality traits. A fair number of interviewees regarded strangers on their team as tools, not as coplayers.

The companion is in most cases in the same location as the player, although in some instances they are spatially separated, as in the case of Kyle (male, 23, daily gamer):

> *If I'm playing a game at home and somebody else is playing a different game, you can talk [...] through the Xbox, even when you're at the homepage [of Xbox]. You can do other stuff sitting in your couch and still be able to communicate while the other plays a different game.*

In this example, Kyle and the companion are interacting concurrently, but turn-based games can be played with a companion—for instance, a poker game. The stance of Kyle's companion is likely to be neutral because they are not in the same game. It is possible that the companion encourages Kyle verbally or laughs when he hears Kyle fail, making this companion pro and contra Kyle, respectively. This was reported in other interviews, too. Active companions are said to be playing with the player as well as against the player, but this does not actually matter a lot because the game itself and its consequences are of secondary importance. Kyle knows the companion and it is expected that they will play together again in the future, as is the case for most companions. However, this is not a necessity, for example in a group of friends, where someone brought along a new friend.

The tool rarely has the same spatial location as the player, but it is not impossible. The player and the tool usually play at the same time (e.g., in a shooter game), but again, this is not necessary, as in the case of Sarah (female, 21, daily gamer). When she plays *Candy Crush Saga*, she asks for an extra life from her sister or mother, but that is the only interaction with others she has in the game, which makes the focus evident on the game, even though she has a real, lengthy relationship with her sister and mother. There is usually a period between this request and the answer, making it asynchronous. The side the tool is on can vary because, in both competitive and collaborative games, other players can be needed to be able to play the game. The relation between the player and the tool is in most cases no longer than the gaming session, but can be, as in the example of Sarah.

Discussion

The current study wanted to explore the attributed roles of other people involved in the game of the player by means of interviews. From these interviews, three distinguishing properties arose, that through their combination, allow for categorising these roles. Four archetypical roles were found: the witness, the coplayer, the companion and the tool. Within each archetype, practically all values of social play research dimensions (spatiality, synchronicity, adversarity, and longevity) are existent. This large variability within each archetype shows that there is not one 'true' setting per archetype. Each social play dimension has been proven to affect game experience in previous studies and their variability has implications for the game experience. It is not a wild guess to assume that within each archetype, changing a value on a certain dimension will influence the game experience. Furthermore, these dimensions on their own sometimes lack subtlety or context and each value encloses a wide array of shades. Comparing for instance co- and versus-play, does not take into account that the other player can be a coplayer, tool, or companion. This is important because each archetype can provide a different game experience. Indeed, the presence of other people does not only change intensity, it also changes the meaning of the game experience variables themselves. For example, competition is experienced *differently* with a coplayer than with a companion, as seen in several of the testimonies shown previously. Thus, game experience is not only influenced by the social play dimensions, but also by the broader role of the other person in the game of the player.

The current chapter hopes to offer a framework that allows for taking these nuances into account. More specifically, our framework consists of two layers. The first layer holds the four archetypes. Within each archetype, there is a second layer that contains the social play research dimensions. This framework enables more nuanced comparisons between similar gaming situations and makes it possible to discover subtle differences in game experience. Research on the social aspect of play should reckon with the role of other people involved in the player's game, by adopting this framework, to gain a broader insight in the game experience of the player.

Next to enabling future research for more insights into the study of social play, the current chapter also has its limitations. First of all, the interviews conducted did not handle variables of game experience directly. Therefore, this paper has no solid proof that the roles in themselves have a different influence on all or even on some variables of game experience. The aim here was only to explore whether or not the involvement of other people could be categorised. A future study could look into specific aspects of game experience; for example, how spatiality affects game enjoyment when playing with each of the four archetypes. That way, it would be known if all of the social play dimensions have the same influence on all aspects of game experience within each archetype. A second limitation of this study is that properties of the player and others are overlooked—for instance, personality, gender, and age. This was outside the scope, but is a nonnegligible part of the categorisation and player experience (Eklund, 2015; Vermeulen, Núñez Castellar, & Van Looy, 2014; Williams & Clippinger, 2002). A follow-up study could research this, including not just traits of the player and other people, but also of the game and of the situation.

In summary, different roles for people involved in social digital game play are found to matter for the game experience of the player, above and beyond variables found in the literature. Therefore, a two-layered framework is offered, that enables researchers to categorise the role of these other people and to look into these social play research variables to see how each one affects game experience within a certain role. Future research could look into the specific aspects of game experience and into personal traits of the player and other people involved in social play to see if and how they impact game experience.

References

Bunten, D. (1996). On-line multi-player games. Carr, D., Schott, G., Burn, A., & Buckingham, D. (2004). Doing game studies: A multi-method approach to the study of textuality, interactivity, and narrative space. *Media International Australia Incorporating Culture and Policy, 110,* 19–30.

Costikyan, G. (1994). I have no words & i must design. Interactive Fantasy 2. Retrieved from http://classes.dma.ucla.edu/Winter15/157/wp-content/ihavenowords.pdf.

de Kort, Y., & IJsselsteijn, W. (2008). People, place, and play: Player experience in a socio-spatial context. *Computers in Entertainment (CIE), 6*(2), 1–11. doi:10.1145/1371216.1371221.

de Kort, Y., IJsselsteijn, W., & Poels, K. (2007). Digital games as social presence technology: Development of the Social Presence in Gaming Questionnaire (SPGQ). *Proceedings of PRESENCE, 195203.*

Deterding, S. (2015). The joys of absence: Emotion, emotion display, and inter-action tension in video game play. In *Proceedings of Foundations of Digital Games* (FDG 2015), June 22–25, Pacific Grove, CA.

Ducheneaut, N., Yee, N., Nickell, E., & Moore, R.J. (2006). *"Alone together?" Exploring the social dynamics of massively multiplayer online games.* paper presented at the *human factors in computing systems (CHI)*, Montreal, Canada. doi: 10.1145/1124772.

Eklund, L. (2015). Playing video games together with others: Differences in gaming with family, friends and strangers. *Journal of Gaming & Virtual Worlds, 7*(3), 259–277. doi: 10.1386/jgvw.7.3.259_1.

Ermi, L., & Mayra, F. (2005). Fundamental components of the gameplay experience: Analysing immersion. *Worlds in Play: International Perspectives on Digital Games Research, 37*(2).

Gajadhar, B., de Kort, Y., & IJsselsteijn, W. (2008). *Influence of social setting on player experience of digital games.* Paper presented at the *Conference on Human Factors in Computing Systems*, Florence, Italy. doi: 10.1145/1358628.1358814.

Glaser, B. G., & Straus, A. L. (1967). *The discovery of grounded theory: Strategies for qualitative research.* Chicago: Aldine.

Hudson, M. (2015). *Social presence in team-based digital games* (Unpublished doctoral dissertation). University of York, York.

Kaye, L.K. (2016). Exploring flow experiences in cooperative digital gaming contexts. *Computers in Human Behavior, 55,* 286–291.

Kaye, L.K., & Bryce, J. (2012). Putting the "fun factor" into gaming: The influence of social contexts on experiences of playing videogames. *International Journal of Internet Science, 7*(1), 23–37.

Kaye, L.K., & Bruce, J. (2014). Go with the flow: The experience and affective outcomes of solo versus social gameplay. *Journal of Gaming and Virtual Worlds, 6*(1), 49–60. doi: 10.1386/jgvw.6.1.49_1.

Kimble, C.E., & Rezabek, J.S. (1992). Playing Games Before an audience: Social facilitation or choking. *Social Behavior and Personality: an international journal, 20* (2), 115–120.

Klimmt, C. (2001). Computer-spiel: Interaktive unterhaltungsangebote als synthese aus medium und spielzeug [Computer-games: Understanding interactive entertainment and combination of media and toys]. *Zeitschrift fuer Medienpsychologie [The Journal of Media Psychology], 13*(1), 22–32.

Mandryk, R.L., Inkpen, K.M., & Calvert, T.W. (2006). Using psycho-physiological techniques to measure user experience with entertainment technologies. *Behaviour & Information Technology, 25*(2), 141–158. doi: 10.1080/01449290500331156.

Maurer, B., Aslan, I., Wuchse, M., Neureiter, K., & Tscheligi, M. (2015). Gaze-based onlooker integration: Exploring the in-between of active player and passive spectator in co-located gaming. In *Proceedings of the 2015 Annual Symposium on Computer-Human Interaction in Play,* 163–173. New York: ACM.

Pantel, L., & Wolf, L.C. (2002). On the impact of delay on real-time multiplayer games. *Proceedings of the 12th International Workshop on Network and Operating Systems Support for Digital Audio and Video, USA* (pp. 23–29). doi: 10.1145/507670.507674.

QSR International Pty Ltd (2012). NVivo qualitative data analysis software, version 10.

Quax, P., Monsieurs, P., Lamotte, W., De Vleeschauwer, D., & Degrande, N. (2004). Objective and subjective evaluation of the influence of small amounts of delay and jitter on a recent first person shooter game. *Proceedings of 3rd ACM SIGCOMM Workshop on Network and System Support For Games, USA* (pp. 152–156). doi: 10.1145/1016540.1016557.

Ravaja, N., Saari, T., Turpeinen, M., Laarni, J., Salminen, M., & Kivikangas, M. (2006). Spatial presence and emotions during video game playing: Does it matter with whom you play? *PRESENCE: Teleoperators and Virtual Environments, 15*(4), 381–392. doi: 10.1162/pres.15.4.381.

Sommer, R. (1967). Small group ecology. *Psychological Bulletin, 67*(2), 145–152.

Sweetser, P., & Whyeth, P. (2005). GameFlow: A model for evaluating player enjoyment in games. *Computers in Entertainment, 3*(3), 3–3. doi: 10.1145/1077246.1077253.

Thorsteinsson, E.B., & James, J.E. (1999). A meta-analysis of the effects of experimental manipulations of social support during laboratory stress. *Psychology and Health, 14*, 869–886.

Vermeulen, L., Núñez Castellar, E., & Van Looy, J. (2014). Challenging the other: Exploring the role of opponent gender in digital game competition for female players. *Cyberpsychology, Behavior, and Social Networking, 17*(5), 303–309. doi: 10.1089/cyber.2013.0331.

Vorderer, P., Hartmann, T., & Klimmt, C. (2003). *Explaining the enjoyment of playing video games: The role of competition.* Retrieved from http://www-users.cs.umn.edu/~bstanton/pdf/p1-vorderer.pdf.

Williams, R.B., & Clippinger, C.A. (2002). Aggression, competition and computer games: Computer and human opponents. *Computers in Human Behaviour, 18*, 495–506.

Zagal, J.P., Nussbaum, M., & Rosas, R. (2000). A model to support the design of multiplayer games. *PRESENCE, 9*(5), 448–462.

Part II
Online Gaming

5 Multiplayer Games as the Ultimate Communication Lab and Incubator

A Multimedia Study

John L. Sherry, Andy Boyan, Kendra Knight, Cherylann Edwards, and Qi Hao

One of the features that most clearly differentiates Massively Multiplayer Online Games (MMOGs) from the rest of the gaming world is the communication that occurs among players. This communication both facilitates game play and creates potential problems in these game spaces (as discussed in chapters 8 and 9 within this volume; Tang & Fox, 2016). Many of the most frequently cited studies of multiplayer games tend to focus on this social nature of gaming. For example, Cole and Griffiths (2007) surveyed 912 MMOG players about the friendships and social interactions developed online. Yee (2006) conducted a massive survey of online gamers to determine their motivations for game play, which included a large social component consisting of socializing, relationship building, and teamwork. Others have looked at these game spaces as a place to relieve loneliness (Kowert & Oldmeadow, 2014; Martončik & Lokša, 2016) or for people with autism to manage social interactions (Wang, Laffey, Xing, Ma, & Stichter, 2016). Although most of these studies focus on the uses and effects of communication in MMOGs, few of them focus on the actual communication. How do communicative exchanges play out in these games? Is MMOG communication a unique type of communication or does it follow patterns that are similar to other types of communication? Does it matter how open and large the play group is? Or how constrained the communication is by the types of talk needed for rapid game play? This chapter takes a closer look at the communicative interactions that occur in MMOGs and compares those interactions to those found in other mediated communication contexts.

Social Interactions in MMOGs

One of the benefits of working with digital games is that game transcripts provide access to records of spontaneous, real-life communication that can be challenging or impossible to replicate in laboratory settings. These instances of online communication include chat used to communicate with other players for relational and teamwork tasks under sometimes rigid time constraints. Within the MMOG world, players are free to determine and modify common goals, experiment in the construction of self, play out fantasies, and create networked groups for cowork. These spontaneous, self-directed exchanges render digital games a prime space to investigate basic communication phenomena that have often been ignored by communication researchers. In particular, the multiplayer nature of digital games should be of interest to communication scholars. For game designers, multiplayer game communication features are often a cost-effective feature to implement in games (Fang, Sun, & Leu, 2015) to expand the gaming experience. As a result, communication is one of the core reasons people play games (Yee, 2006).

There have been few studies that take a close look at sequences of in-game communication. Peña and Hancock (2006) examined the interactions of a small group of players involved in role-play using the MMOG *Jedi Knight II: Jedi Outcast*. They scraped 5,826 server chat messages from a random sample of six hours of play from a two-week period. The chat messages were coded according to Bales' (1950) categories for utterances during small group communication. Bales had set out to create a comprehensive set of conversational categories to be used to study the "microscopic social systems" (p. 257) that small groups represented. These categories were divided into socioemotional reactions (positive and negative) and task-related questions and answers. From this, he could empirically derive conversational norms for different social contexts based on the relative occurrence of different categories of utterances. Based on a number of studies, Bales found that the most frequently used categories were giving an opinion as a task answer, providing information/clarification as a task answer, and showing a positive emotional reaction by agreement. Unlike the Bales results within face-to-face small group communication, Peña and Hancock found that the online gamers used significantly more socioemotional talk than task-related talk. However, similar to Bales, they found that their sample of online gamers was significantly more likely to use positive emotional messages than negative emotional messages. They concluded that the type of messages found in their sample were a function of the recreational nature of this instance of game play and that they would find more task-related messages in a more instrumental communication context.

The conclusions drawn by Peña and Hancock (2006) represent a simple linear conception of the communication process. That is, utterances are a linear function of the communication task such that recreational tasks are more likely to evidence emotional messages and instrumental tasks are more likely to evidence task-related talk. This is a common sense conclusion that is consistent with their data; however, deep understanding of communication has historically defied simple linear explanation (Schegloff, 1998). Effect sizes in interpersonal and small group communication studies are typically quite small, suggesting that the vast majority of variance in the communication process remains unexplained.

Another way to think about human communication is as a dynamic, emergent process (Sherry, 2015). Sometimes called the "transactional nature of communication" (Miller, 2004) or simply 'interaction', communication is a process that unfolds over time in a set of moves and countermoves between those involved in the conversation. In the past few decades, scientists have moved to a third paradigm of science (Weaver, 1948) that facilitates looking at these types of systems. Research on complex adaptive systems has discovered that phenomena that appear to be highly complex are often the result of a process with simple rules unfolding over time (Holland, 2014; Miller & Page, 2009). Such processes often generate richly patterned phenomena that display self-similarity, such as the beautiful fractal patterns that can be seen in natural phenomena such as trees and vegetables (broccoli and sunflowers are particularly good examples) to manmade objects such as motion pictures, fabric design, steel cable, or cell phone antennae. Certainly, human communication has many of the markers of a pattern of generative self-similarity (Sherry, 2015). If communication is a complex adaptive system, similarity resulting from such patterns should be evident across communication modalities and situations.

Thinking about communication in this way moves us away from the static, linear conception of communication and forces us to take a closer look at the sequence of utterances that make up the interaction (Donohue, Sherry, & Idzik, 2015). If MMOG communication differs from other types of communication, we are most likely to see those differences in the sequence of utterances that typify each communication situation. We might ask ourselves:

- Will we see the same types of utterances in MMOG communication that we see in other communication contexts?
- Will MMOG communication be more or less predictable than other types of communication?
- Will there be similarities in the sequencing of certain types of utterances found in MMOGs versus other contexts?

One of the most fruitful areas of communication research examining patterns of human speech in conversation is speech act theory and conversation analysis (Searle, 1969; Nofsinger, 1991). Conversation analysis focuses on illocutionary acts (also known as speech acts) as the central unit of analysis. According to Searle, illocutionary acts can "state, assert, describe, warn, remark, comment, command, order, request, criticise, apologise, censure, approve, welcome, promise, express approval, and express regret ... and a thousand such (other) expressions in English" (pp. 1). Searle (1969) defined illocutionary speech acts as a propositional statement (typically a verbal signal) animated by force (the speaker's intention) and modeled as $F(P)$, in which propositional content (P) is animated by illocutionary force (F) (Searle, 1969; Searle & Vanderveken, 1985). Illocutionary force is the speaker's intention for how the propositional content is interpreted and acted upon by the receiver. Searle (1979) categorised speech acts into five types of force for analysis: assertives, directives, commissives, expressives, and declaratives. Assertive force commits the sender to something being the case. Basic statements of fact or opinion fall into this category, as well as boasts, complaints, and conclusions. Directives are attempts by the sender to get the receiver to do something. Examples of directive force include invitations, questions, advice, and insistences. Commissive force commits the sender to some course of future action, including promises, vows, plans, and bets. Expressives express the psychological state of the sender. These include apologies, thanks, and condolences. Declarative force establishes that some particular cases come into existence in the world. For example, when someone is officially nominated for a position the statement 'I nominate ... .' is declarative in that now the person is a nominee.

The focus on illocutionary acts requires putting communication into social and cultural context to understand their intent (Goodwin & Heritage, 1990), for the intent of conversation analysis is to understand the transfer of meaning and the moves executed by the participants to accomplish that transfer. One major assumption of this perspective is that communication is a rule-based activity and patterns of behaviour can emerge from different specific sign systems (Searle, 1969). If this is the case, we expect to see differences across conversational media, contexts, and goals. However, if communication generates patterns from a small set of rules, there should be evident similarities in speech acts across different media, contexts, and goals.

Conversation analysis is typically used to analyse face-to-face conversations among dyads; however, patterns of communication should exist regardless of group size and communication context. Theories of computer-mediated communication (CMC) predict that participants will interact via computer similarly to how they act in face-to-face contexts because social information remains the basic component of interactions offline and online (Walther, 1996). To examine patterns of human interactions in different contexts, data will be presented that show four different interactions varying in terms of rule systems and number of participants: a dyadic CMC conversation, a CMC *World of Warcraft* (*WoW*) raid group, a CMC casual multiplayer online game session, and the dialog from the popular science fiction/fantasy film *Return of the Jedi*. These interaction types are representative of various types of communication research, and all exemplify the complexity of a process-based phenomenon.

Method

Searle's (1979) categorization scheme has proven to comprehensively categorise most speech acts by providing a sense of the function of each act. These coding systems have been used in a large body of work on conversation.

We applied Searle's (1979) classification system to create categories of units typically found in communication. Patterns among those categories formed the elements that may reveal patterns in the process of communication. Over lengthy interactions, do patterns of speech acts emerge? Are dynamics of speech acts predictable in communication contexts?

Corpora

The study corpus was chosen to represent different types of communication tasks under two sets of constraints: group size and lexical flexibility (see Table 5.1). The corpus contained:

Jedi Knight II: Jedi Outcast – Transcripts were provided by Jorge Pena from his study on MMOG interaction (Peña & Hancock, 2006). The transcripts consisted of 5,826 text messages from 65 players on a "Jedi Knight II: Jedi Outcast", server in March 2002. "We recorded six 1-hour segments randomly sampled from the same server (i.e. same IP address) at random times of the day across a 2-week period. The server was selected on the basis of the highest number of connected users. The participants were not aware of the recording process and agreed to take part in the study only after contacted" (p. 98–99). We coded 197 lines of an interaction among 8–10 players who were engaged in attempting to recreate an action scene from the film *Star Wars: Return of the Jedi*.

WoW: Mists of Pandaria – Within a month of the new release of the *Mists of Pandaria* expansion set for *WoW* in 2012, a member of the research team took part in four pickup raids. Pickup raids are group-based gaming missions during which between 10 and 25 players are randomly assigned to the group by the game matchmaking system. To be successful in the raid, members of the pickup group must be experienced enough with the general mechanics of raiding that they can work together without knowing each other's individual abilities and tendencies. The raids resulted in four sets of transcripts with a total of 501 highly jargon-laden utterances.

CMC interactions – A set of dyadic interaction transcripts from another study were randomly chosen for inclusion in this analysis, resulting in 563 utterances. The study asks zero-history partners to communicate a simple idea using chat software. The partners do not know with whom they are interacting and cannot see or hear each other during the communication task.

Return of the Jedi motion picture script – Dialogue lines from an online transcript of *Star Wars: Return of the Jedi* were chosen, resulting in 488 utterances. The film was chosen because it contained the same set of characters and actions as the *Jedi Knight* game, but was from a different medium.

Table 5.1 Study corpus by group size and discursive flexibility constraints

		Group Size	
		Small and Exclusive	*Large and Inclusive*
Discursive Flexibility	Narrow and Limited	*Return of the Jedi* script $n = 488$ $k = 9$	WOW raid $n = 501$ $k = 4$
	Large and Free	CMC interactions $n = 563$ $k = 9$	*Jedi Knight II: Jedi Outcast* $n = 197$ $k = 3$

Note: n = the total number of utterances for that media category; k = the number of inter-action episodes for that media category.

The corpus was chosen to compare different types of multiplayer game play with a broad set of communication situations that maintained threads of common content or experience. *Jedi Knight* and *WoW* are similar in that they are both multiplayer games, though the type of play differed between games. The MMOGs use the same communication mechanism as the CMC interactions (keyboard-based synchronous chat). The film script was a written rendition of the same characters and settings as one of the MMOGs. Thus, all utterances come from communication that was conducted via a written modality (either typed script or computer chat) and with participants who were not colocated and were likely unknown to each other in the physical world. This controlled for differences between the allowances and constraints of spoken language versus written languages. Further, the multiplayer games either recreate directly or indirectly the type of action-via-cooperative-aggression that is found in the *Return of the Jedi* film.

The communication situations were also conceptualised as varying along two dimensions: discursive flexibility and group size (see Table 5.1). Discursive flexibility refers to the relative amount of freedom that communicants have in choosing language. For example, the *WoW* raids are conducted with a limited range of coded language used by game insiders that facilitates rapid communication needed due to the urgency of the game situation. *WoW* raiders use a limited, highly code dependent set of utterances (e.g. damage per second, tanking, aggro). Actors executing the movie script for *Return of the Jedi,* are limited to a set of prescripted utterances. These utterances are carefully planned to serve the plot and the semiotic needs of Hollywood science fiction films. On the other hand, participants in the CMC interactions and in the *Jedi Knight II: Jedi Outcast* game are free to select any language they feel fits the conversational system.

Two different sizes of interactive groups were used. In the CMC transcripts and the *Return of the Jedi* movie script, conversations primarily take place between two (CMC) to five (*Jedi* movie) individuals. The members of the system are set from the beginning and no new members are can gain entry. Conversely, both the *Jedi Knight II: Jedi Outcast* game room and the *WoW* raids have a large number of individuals in the group who are free to speak at any time. Additionally, these spaces are open systems that can (and do) admit additional members at any time.

Coding

Each utterance from the transcripts of the four groups was coded for Searle's (1979) speech act categories. An utterance was defined as one line on the transcript; so in the case of the online games and the CMC conversations, an utterance would end when a participant pressed the *Enter* key. In the script transcript, an utterance was considered an uninterrupted sequence of dialog by a single character.

The Searle (1976) classification system for illocutionary acts was used to generate definitions that guided the coding procedure. The five categories of illocutionary acts were defined as: (1) Assertive—utterance commits the sender to something being the case; statement of a fact, (2) Directive—attempts by the sender to get the receiver to do something, (3) Commissive—commit the sender to some course of future action, (4) Expressive—express the psychological state of the sender, and (5) Declarative—utterances that create some particular case to come into existence in the world (see Table 5.2 for examples).

After training in the Searle (1979) scheme for coding conversations, coders were provided with identical subsets of the transcripts and asked to code individually. Scores from the first coding session were compared and discrepancies identified. Discrepancies between coders were discussed; typically, they were due to coder error or message ambiguity. Discussion was used to improve the reliability of the coding rules and the procedure was iterated with different subsets of subject shapes until acceptable reliability was attained (Krippendorf α = .97). More than 98% of the utterances fell into one of the five Searle categories.

Table 5.2 Examples of illocutionary acts from the study corpus

Illocutionary Act	Example
Assertive	"this aint gonna work if the dps is not adds......too many staying on boss" – *WoW* Raid
Directive	"If they don't go for this, we're gonna have to get outta here pretty quick Chewie." – *Return of the Jedi*
Commissive	"Now I'm gonna die." – *Jedi Knight*
Expressive	"Awesome! :)" – CMC Interactions
Declarative	"KICK" – *WoW* Raid

Interaction Strings

When coding of all utterances was completed, interaction strings were created by retrieving all contiguous codes from a single episode (e.g. a single WoW raid). Therefore, an interaction string is an ordered one-dimensional array of Searle coded utterances representing a complete conversational episode. Episodes were delineated as follows: *Return of the Jedi* script were scenes; WoW raids were a complete raid (there were four complete raid transcripts); CMC was a single experiment interaction; and the *Jedi Knight* transcripts were broken up by natural breaks/shifts in the conversation.

Results

First, we look at the distribution of Searle's speech acts among the four groups (see Figure 5.1). The groups that have less lexical flexibility have the most similar distribution of speech acts. Testing the null hypothesis that percentages of categories from different groups are different, we found the movie script and the WoW raids are statistically equivalent for the percent of directive statements (35% and 36%; $Z = -0.29$, p = ns) and the percent of assertive statements (45% and 46%; $Z = -0.26$, p = ns), but the other two categories are statistically different (commissive; $Z = 3.79$, $p < .01$; expressive: $Z = 1.37$, $p < .01$). The large discursive flexibility groups both have 29% directive speech acts and an equivalent percentage of commissive statements (CMC = 2%, Jedi game = 4%, $Z = 1.63$, p = ns). However, they differ widely in that the CMC interactants depend primarily on assertive speech acts (63%), whereas the *Jedi* gamers mix in a generous amount of expressive statements (36%) with their assertives (31%).

Uncertainty

Another way to think about comparing the groups is in terms of the amount of uncertainty among the types of utterances used in each setting. Uncertainty in this case is the ability to predict the next type of speech act in the sequence; therefore a more predictable pattern should have less uncertainty. Uncertainty in communication can be indexed using Shannon's (1948) measure of entropy from his theory of communication. In that article, Shannon defines entropy (H) as:

$$H = -\Sigma p(x)log_b p(x)$$

where $p(x)$ is the probability of x in the distribution and the base of the log (b) is the number of bits. In computer science, this is of base 2 log because computers use two bits, 1 and 0. However, the Searle codes have five possible codes, so we used base 5 log (see Table 5.3). Entropy scores can be placed on a scale from 0 to 1, with 0 = highly predictable to 1 = completely random.

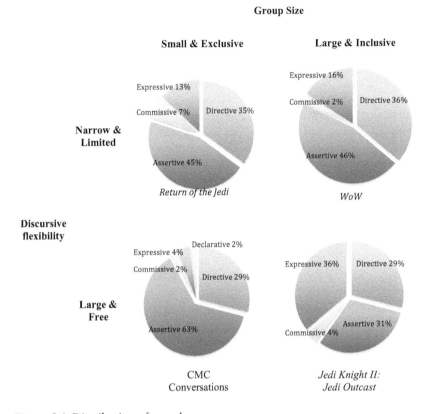

Figure 5.1 Distribution of speech acts across groups.

Table 5.3 Shannon entropy Searle codes

| | | Group Size | |
		Small and Exclusive	Large and Inclusive
Discursive flexibility	Narrow and Limited	H = 0.74 n = 488	H = 0.68 n = 501
	Large and Free	H = 0.53 n = 563	H = 0.76 n = 197

* *Note*: Shannon entropy ranges from 0 = highly predictable to 1 = completely random.

In the corpora, all four types of interaction showed evidence of being nonrandom, with the two-person CMC interactions the least random. Of the Searle codes, there is no clear pattern of more entropy by group size or by lexical diversity. In fact, the greatest similarities are found in diagonal pairings.

Sequence Alignment

In bioinformatics, DNA, RNA, or protein sequences can be compared with one another to determine the degree to which two or more sequences share a common structure/ordering using a technique called protein sequence alignment. In protein sequence alignment, an algorithm is used to locate identical sequences of protein coded on two or more arrays of DNA and to determine the amount of shared sequences. We used the same algorithm to examine interaction arrays from each medium to determine the degree to which interaction arrays within and between media were similar. Similarity is reported as an identity score (I), which represents the percent of shared sequence (see Table 5.3). The percent of shared sequence can be compared with the percent that would be shared among five arrays that are generated randomly. We ran 100 simulations on randomly generated arrays and found that the identity scores among random arrays would be $MI = 42.25\%$, $SD = 3.90$. Therefore, identity scores of $I > 50.05\%$ are significantly different from random at 95% probability. As can be seen in Table 5.4, all four groups have greater similarity within group than would be expected by chance.

Table 5.4 Sequence analysis: Identity between interactions within group for Searle codes

		Group Size	
		Small and Exclusive	*Large and Inclusive*
Discursive flexibility	Narrow and Limited	I = 62.33% $k = 9$	I = 61.43% $k = 4$
	Large and Free	I = 61.21% $k = 9$	I = 52.5% $k = 3$

Note: A simulation was conducted using random values to determine what would be expected if there were no common sequence. The results of 100 simulations was $M = 42.25$, $SD = 3.90$.

Table 5.5 Sequence analysis: Identity between interactions between group for Searle codes

	CMC	*Jedi Game*	*WoW*
Jedi Game	I = 39.95%		
World of Warcraft	I = 49.44%	I = 57.08%*	
Return of the Jedi Script	I = 56.44%*	I = 61.19%*	I = 64.64%*

Note. * = $p < 0.05$

Next, we looked at the extent to which the different media in our sample shared common interaction sequences. This was done by comparing every communication sequence in one group with every communication sequence in the comparison group (see Table 5.5). The highest percentage of commonality is among the two online games ($I = 57.08\%$) and between the *Return of the Jedi* film script and the other three groups. Only the CMC conditions with the two games failed to be significantly more similar than would be expected by random.

Discussion

We began this project with the assumption that MMOGs will provide fertile ground for studying both (1) the game affordance of player communication and (2) human communication in general because MMOGs are played primarily though communication. That is, MMOG players are dependent upon communication to achieve substantial success. We wondered about the nature of that communication and whether it is genre-specific, game-specific, or maybe simply an extension of natural communication? In particular, we were interested to see if we could discover patterns of common structure in multiplayer communication during MMOG play and then compare those patterns to the patterns of structure found in other communication. This proved to be a more difficult task than we had originally envisioned and so the goals were scaled back to comparing the constituent parts of different communication, verifying whether MMOG communication is patterned, and assessing the degree of structural commonality among different types of communication. Three somewhat unconventional methods were used to assess the research questions in this study: (1) descriptive comparison of constituent parts; (2) entropy analysis to determine the presence of deep patterning; and (3) sequence analysis to assess the degree of common structural patterning. Each of these methods provided insight into the general questions of the study.

At the most basic level, descriptive comparisons of the speech acts used in the four corpora were conducted, netting patterns of similarity and difference. MMOG discourse during *WoW* raids turned out to be remarkably similar to the *Return of the Jedi* film script. Discourse during the *Jedi* MMOG displayed much greater amount of expressive speech acts, but the other categories were proportionally similar to *WoW* and the film script distributions after controlling for the greater percentage of expressives. The CMC interactions were the only group that didn't share some level of similarity of distribution of speech act categories.

The differences between the two MMOGs (greater expressives in the *Jedi* game) can be understood as a function of the role of game play in the specific contexts of the MMOGs, as was the case in the Peña & Hancock (2006) study. The *Jedi* game does not have a predetermined scenario like that found in the WoW raid. Instead, discourse is situated within free play, as the players recreate their own rendition of scenes within the *Star Wars* universe. Without a clear and constrained task, free play leads to greater negotiation over procedure, outcome, and leadership. Although much play in WoW is constituted by free play, the raid context givens players a highly scripted and codified set of behaviours that they are supposed to engage in. Thus, expressing one's self to co-players is far more prevalent in the *Jedi* game than is found in play sessions that are more directed by game-originated outcome goals. Further, WoW pickup raids often function as strangers meeting to achieve a common goal, and persisting social relationships may not be expected to continue afterwards (similar to a game of pickup basketball). The social aspect of the WoW raids is about working together to overcome a challenge, not necessarily to build and maintain relationships—to clarify, these findings would not likely bear out for all of play in WoW, but we argue are found specifically due to the nature of the highly codified language and expectations within raids. Had we examined other situations within WoW it is likely that expressives would be similar in both games. In the *Jedi* game transcripts, it was clear that the players were participating in an ongoing group relationship. On the other end of the spectrum, the CMC discourse was the most constrained, having only two interlocutors and a single, very narrow information transfer task. This shifted almost all the speech acts to task-related categories of either assertion of facts (63%) or directing behaviour (29%).

The lack of clear patterns in the transcripts led us to ask a more fundamental question: is it possible that the sequences of utterances found in the transcripts are unordered? If communication is a complex, self-organizing system, sequences of speech acts should be non-random. We used Shannon's (1948) measure of entropy to test this question and found that all of the corpora were nonrandom, but not equally so. CMC conversations were clearly the most predictable form of communication in the corpora. Perhaps this is not surprising given the low number of participants ($n = 2$) and the highly restrained task. Interestingly, the communication forms with the greatest uncertainty were the film script and the *Jedi* MMOG (74% and 76%, respectively). Of course, these two groups are less task-oriented than the other two and have approximately the same number of people/characters per group.

The final analysis was unique in our field. We wanted to see the degree to which there are common sequences of speech acts among the various groups. An utterance sequencing algorithm modified from protein-sequencing analysis was applied to the conversations, and we found that sequences aligned at greater than random percentages both with other sequences in their own contexts and with utterances between most of the contexts. Again, the greatest degree of similarity is found between the *Return of the Jedi* script and the *WoW* raids ($I = 64.64\%$). Although this further supports our observation that narrowing the discursive flexibility makes interactions more similar, there is a bigger issue to contemplate here. Not only do these two very different types of communication share the same relative percentages of speech acts, those speech acts appear to be sequenced in very similar ways as well. Although it is logical that similar restraints would lead to similar distributions of speech acts (as discussed above), there is no reason why those speech acts should be delivered in the same order unless there is a deeper organizational structure to the discourse.

Conclusions

This study provides a compelling argument for further research into the deep structure of communication in MMOGs and other media. Results show that similar tasks and discursive constraints lead to similar distributions of speech acts, that these patterns are non-random, and that the similarities are present in the deep structure of the communication. One way that we might advance this kind of study is by paying closer attention to discursive flexibility and to communication contexts and tasks within games. If game communication was selected that compared two-player games (that require player–player communication) to games with four to seven players communicating, and games that contained larger groups communicating, we might be able to assess the impacts of group size relative to the utterance sequencing algorithm. We might also extend our understanding of communication in MMOGs by analyzing utterance sequences using different conceptual conversation analytic schemes from the Searle (1969) categories. For example, Bales' (1950) categories used by Peña and Hancock (2006) have 12 categories of speech acts, splitting some of Searle's categories into more detailed subcategories. Possibly a more detailed framework would erase similarities from the utterance sequencing? A different coding scheme could also focus on different aspects of the communication itself, with even more attention paid to the interactive nature of the communication process. For example, Searle (1969) categories have no indicator of whether a given utterance is in response to another utterance. This linking of related utterances seems crucial for understanding how communication sequences are structured; however, capturing this characteristic of the process is not readily apparent in many preestablished coding schemes.

These results are exciting, as they suggest that there is an underlying pattern to communication that can be assessed using a complex systems framework. We think that there is promise in methods that capture the nature of interaction over time in the communication process, which will help to understand communication in MMOGs, among various player groups as well as outside gaming contexts.

References

Bales, R. F. (1950). A set of categories for the analysis of small group interaction. *American Sociological Review, 15,* 257–263.

Cole, H., & Griffiths, M. D. (2007). Social interactions in massively multiplayer online role-playing gamers. *CyberPsychology & Behavior, 10,* 575–583.

Donohue, W. A., Sherry, J. L., & Idzik, P. (2015). Interaction dynamics predict successful negotiation in divorce mediation. *Journal of Language and Social Psychology, 35*(4). 0261927X15603090.

Fang, F., Sun, Y., & Leu, J. (2015). Profit analysis for video game releasing strategies: Single-player vs. multiplayer games. *Journal of Supply Chain and Operations Management, 13,* 58–77.

Goodwin, C., & Heritage, J. (1990). Conversation analysis. *Annual Review of Anthropology, 19,* 283–307.

Holland, J. H. (2014). *Complexity: A very short introduction.* Oxford: Oxford University Press.

Kowert, R., & Oldmeadow, J. A. (2014). Playing for social comfort: Online video game play as a social accommodator for the insecurely attached. *Computers in Human Behavior, 53,* 556–566. doi:10.1016/j.chb.2014.05.004.

Martončik, M., & Lokša, J. (2016). Do *World of Warcraft* (MMORPG) players experience less loneliness and social anxiety in online world (virtual environment) than in real world (offline)? *Computers in Human Behavior, 56,* 127–134. doi:10.1016/j.chb.2015.11.035.

Miller, J. H., & Page, S. E. (2009). *Complex adaptive systems: An introduction to computational models of social life.* Princeton, NJ: Princeton University Press.

Miller, K. (2004). *Communication theories: Perspectives, processes, and contexts.* McGraw-Hill.

Nofsinger, R. E. (1991). *Everyday conversation.* Newbury Park, CA: Sage.

Peña, J., & Hancock, J. T. (2006). An analysis of socioemotional and task communication in online multiplayer video games. *Communication Research, 33,* 92–109.

Schegloff, E. A. (1993). Reflections on quantification in the study of conversation. *Research on Language and Social Interaction, 26,* 99–128. doi:10.1207/s15327973rlsi2601_5.

Searle, J. R. (1969). *Speech acts: An essay in the philosophy of language.* London, UK: Cambridge University Press.

Searle, J. R. (1979). *Expression and meaning: Studies in the theory of speech acts.* London, UK: Cambridge University Press.

Searle, J. R., & Vanderveken, D. (1985). *Foundations of illocutionary logic.* CUP Archive.

Shannon, C. E. (1948). A mathematical theory of communication. *Bell System Technical Journal, 27,* 379–423. doi:10.1002/j.1538-7305.1948.tb01338.x.

Sherry, J. L. (2015). The complexity paradigm for studying human communication: A summary and integration of two fields. *Review of Communication Research, 3.* doi: 10.12840/issn.2255-4165.2015.03.01.007.

Tang, W. Y., & Fox, J. (2016). Men's harassment behavior in online video games: Personality traits and game factors. *Aggressive Behavior.*doi: 10.1002/ab.21646.

Walther, J. B. (1996). Computer-mediated communication impersonal, interpersonal, and hyperpersonal interaction. *Communication Research, 23*, 3–43.

Wang, X., Laffey, J., Xing, W., Ma, Y., & Stichter, J. (2016). Exploring embodied social presence of youth with autism in 3D collaborative virtual learning environment: A case study. *Computers in Human Behavior, 55*, 310–321. doi:10.1016/j.chb.2015.09.006.

Weaver, W. (1948). Science and complexity. *American Scientist, 36*(4), 536–544. Retrieved from http://www.ncbi.nlm.nih.gov/pubmed/18882675.

Yee, N. (2006) Motivations for play in online games. *CyberPsychology & Behavior, 9*, 772–775.

6 The MMORPG Designer's Journey

Casualization and its Consequences for Social Interactions

Daniel Pietschmann, Benny Liebold, and Georg Valtin

Massive Multiplayer Online Roleplaying Games (MMORPGs or MMOs) are often considered highly social gaming spaces (Cole & Griffith, 2007). Thousands of players share the same persistent game environment and control a single character, often in a fantasy or science-fiction scenario. As roleplaying games, they usually follow the hero's journey narrative (Campbell, 2008) with the development of the players' characters as the main goal of MMOs. They start out as nobodies and become stronger as they advance through the narrative. During their travels, players typically face challenges that force them to cooperate and create social ties. Most games also force players to choose a specific role during character generation to either deal damage to opponents (damage), support other players by healing them (healer), or draw enemies away from them (tank). These archetypes are often referred to as "holy trinity". They first appeared in pen-and-paper RPGs like *Dungeons and Dragons* and still shape MMORPG game design today. To achieve the game's goals, players with different roles typically have to cooperate. Depending on the game, players form groups of four up to 40 people with their given variations of the basic roles and tackle game objectives together. This style of game play strongly supports social ties and contributed to the image of MMORPGs as highly social games with their own subcultures including slang, social rules, and taboos.

The phenomenon of the newly established virtual cultures attracted researchers of the social sciences trying to understand the complex fabric of MMORPGs and its relevant aspects like community building (Ducheneaut & Moore, 2004), cultural practices (Hsu, Wen, & Wu, 2009; Taylor, 2006), communication (Steinkuehler, 2004; Williams, Caplan, & Xiong, 2007), player motivations (Choi & Kim, 2004; Griffiths, Davis, & Chappell, 2003), player identification (Filiciak, 2003; van Looy, Courtois, & De Vocht, 2010), demographics (Squire & Steinkuehler, 2006; Yee, 2006), economics (Castronova, 2008), and social interactions (Cole & Griffiths, 2007; Schroeder, 2002). The involved disciplines and methodologies vary heavily, but the unique scenario offered by MMORPGs in terms of social interaction provided a common ground for multidisciplinary research. Yet, changes in MMO design rationales over the last years suggest that as a result the social ecosystem of MMOs also underwent a considerable change.

In a study of MMORPG players ($N = 912$), Cole and Griffiths (2007) examined the demographics of play and analysed with whom players spent their time in the game. They found that most of the users (26.3%) played together with real-life friends and family. Several years later, a survey of $N = 1.414$ long-time *World of Warcraft* (WoW; Blizzard Entertainment, 2004) players found that players now seem to spent a significant part of their playtime playing alone (19%; Valtin, 2014). They still enjoy the company of other players, but something has changed. Current MMORPGs seem to be different social worlds compared with a decade ago. In essence, they evolved into a shared single-player environment, where players can choose between content to either play together or alone. Ducheneaut, Yee, Nickell, and Moore had referred to the role of other players as "audience" already in 2006, with some players preferring to interact with this audience only infrequently. According to this new trend, many players did not partake in joint activities until in the late stages of the game, where cooperation was still necessary. Another 10 years later, modern games do not force the players into cooperation as early games did, rendering true multiplayer content and therefore social interactions optional. We will present several examples of design changes through which catalysts of social interaction in MMOs were removed over the years. The evolution trough these changes can be seen as a gradual process of casualization.

Casualisation is a phenomenon referring to design changes of various aspects of computer games such as game mechanics, difficulty, and effort required to successfully master the game. The changes were most likely carried out to expand the reach of MMOs beyond the traditional video game audience. This notion directly refers to the differentiation between casual games and core games (Juul, 2009). Traditional MMORPGs required the players to invest a considerable amount of playtime to progress within the game. The resulting need to exchange information, coordinate group play, and receive help fostered player interaction and eventually led to the establishment of new online gaming cultures and corresponding social interactions. Over the years, however, MMORPGs step-by-step shifted their focus towards solo play by altering the game balance and introducing tools for automated group creation. As a result of the lower demands of the game, cooperation became mostly obsolete and social interaction in standard game play situations was no longer necessary. Research shows that emotional communication predominated task-oriented conversations even before casualization (Peña & Hancock, 2006). Lomanowska and Guitton (2012) found that players even tend to adjust their in-game spatial location in relation to other players to sustain close proximity and to promote social interactions. However, with the shift to more solo play, the colocation of game characters not only becomes optional for players, but sometimes impossible: For example, *WoW* introduced "phasing" and instancing of the game world to make each player feel more narratively immersed in the world – the game world changed according to the player's actions, but other players in different world phases were not visible unless they were in the same stage of the story.

The disappearance of most of the former MMORPG player culture presents several implications, which we will explore in this chapter: (1) social aspects might no longer be the main motivation for players; (2) social interaction during standard game play situations might no longer be a common phenomenon; (3) existing theories and findings about socially motivated player behaviour may not hold true anymore; and (4) research paradigms on social interaction might be limited to fewer social meaningful settings.

In this chapter, we discuss key design changes causing casualization and its corresponding effects on social interactions within MMORPGs as well as issues of ecological validity social researchers face when studying modern MMORPGs.

The Call to Adventure: Need for Cooperation

The first commercial MMORPGs were released with the advent of affordable Internet connections during the 1990s. Games such as *Meridian 59* (Archetype Interactive, 1996), *Ultima Online* (Origin Systems, 1997), and *EverQuest* (Verant Interactive, 1999) were able to attract a small but dedicated community of players who paid a monthly subscription fee to be a part of a virtual world. However, during their first decade, MMORPGs primarily catered to niche markets, reaching around 5 million players across all available games worldwide in 2004 (Van Geel, 2013). This first generation of MMORPGs was characterised by painfully slow progress, severe penalties for mistakes, clumsy combat systems, significant balancing issues, and overly complicated user interfaces. The resulting game experience was far from today's standards for mainstream MMORPG game play. The game worlds were mostly open, but the games did not tell players what to do or where to go, so they had to explore for themselves. This, however, had an interesting side effect: Even though MMORPGs were conceptualised to be played together in the first place, social interactions arose in large parts as the result of the difficult living conditions in the virtual world. Typically, new players were supported by veterans who chaperoned their first steps, explained the basic game play and often provided them with some equipment and in-game money (Kasavin, 1997). On their way to the maximum character level, the game mechanics forced the players to cooperate to achieve anything within the virtual world (Kasavin, 1997, 1999; Park, 2000). As a result of the on-going social interactions, those early player communities quickly became the role model for modern MMORPGs, forming societies with their own rules, culture, communication, and even language. The link between the need to cooperate and the development of culture is also consistent with anthropologic theories suggesting that the evolutionary environment of early humanity forced them into cooperation thereby establishing human culture (Tooby & Cosmides, 1992). Player interaction in early virtual worlds can be considered as a recapitulation of this process.

Social interaction was identified as the main factor of player experience and also long-time motivation for playing MMORPGs in several studies of *Lineage: The Blood Pledge* (NCsoft, 2001), *EverQuest,* and *Dark Age of Camelot* (Mythic Entertainment, 2001) players (Choi & Kim, 2004; Whang & Chang, 2004; Yee, 2006). In a study from Griffiths, Davies, and Chappell (2004), *EverQuest* players stated that "being able to play in a group with others" and "being part of a guild membership" were their main play motivations. They regarded their online social interactions with other players as important as their real-life friendships (Cole & Griffiths, 2007). A quarter of the players in the study made good friends with other players, 55.4% of female and 37.6% of male players even met their game contacts in the real world, also resulting in romantic relationships.

MMORPGs were soon identified to serve as a form of "third place" for informal sociability, where players establish and maintain social ties beyond the workplace and home (Steinkuehler & Williams, 2006). Much of the early research focussed on motivations and demographics to understand the makeup of the virtual communities (Choi & Kim, 2004; Griffiths, Davies, & Chappell, 2003; Yee, 2006). Other studies investigated identity patterns and identity construction in the games (Filiciak, 2003; Schroeder, 2002).

The Belly of the Whale: WoW

With the launch of *WoW*, MMORPGs left the niche and entered the mainstream market. The game immediately attracted millions of new players from a combination of various reasons:

1 *WoW* was based on an established and popular video game fantasy universe, following three previous *Warcraft* strategy games.
2 Blizzard, the developer of the game, had a reputation in the gamer community for releasing games with the highest quality standards.
3 The game had reasonable hardware requirements, so players with old machines could still enjoy it.
4 Broadband Internet connections and permanent connections were common enough to make the game accessible for a broad audience.

5 The game had a very clear and user-friendly interface and a likable cartoon look.
6 It streamlined many of the game mechanics used in other games, considerably reducing complexity.

Compared with prior games, *WoW* was considered more user-friendly and more accessible for players new to online gaming. As the first of the so-called theme park MMOs (Penelopae, 2012), *WoW* carefully guided the players through the virtual world, always providing ideal game objectives based on their current progress and skills. This was additionally skillfully flavored with a balance of serious and humoristic narratives. Players always had several possible game objectives they could choose from, depending on their preferred play style, available play time, or number of people they were playing with at the moment. The game thereby opened the genre to a high number of players who were formerly struggling with the idea of investing a great amount of time and effort in virtual online worlds. Because *WoW* still required the players to cooperate to achieve standard game goals – especially the end game content – similar social interaction patterns evolved as within earlier MMORPGs.

Many other games followed a similar recipe later, but could never reach the same level of success as *WoW*. The genre was at its peak with 23 million paying subscribers worldwide in 2011 (Van Geel, 2013). Then, the traditional subscription based economical model of most MMORPGs was slowly replaced by a free-to-play model, where players spend money for premium content or services[1].

Meeting with the Goddess: WoW *as a Social Scientist's Paradise*

In the early lifespan of the game, a game effect could be exploited by players that allowed them to infect and kill other players with a virtual undead plague (Ward, 2005). The plague was not intended to spread to the main cities of the game, but it did. As infected players logged out of the game while still carrying the plague, they infected other players even after logging back into the game days later. This phenomenon quickly garnered public and academic attention. Scientists studied the parallels of the game's virus outbreak to real-world epidemiological patterns (e.g. Balicer, 2007) and found that virtual worlds could serve as the perfect field to study social group behaviours. *WoW* inspired anthropology books wholly devoted to the game (Bainbridge, 2012; Corneliussen & Rettberg, 2008; Cuddy, 2009; Nardi, 2010), scientific blogs (e.g. Yee, 2009), and hundreds of research papers in various disciplines[2].

We cannot even try to cover all the different research topics, but for the sake of our argument of casualization, we solely focus on social behaviour research. In a first attempt to form a shared theory of the human social experiences in virtual worlds, Williams (2010) developed a research framework to map social behaviours. The dimensions of this model include group sizes (e.g. individuals, dyads, communities), traditional controls and independent variables (e.g. motivations, communication methods), contextual factors (e.g. world size, presentation, local culture), and directionality (e.g. online to offline, offline to online). Williams argues that only a minority of virtual situations will map to the real world and effects should not be overstated. This is particularly true for prosocial or antisocial behaviours: There is no adequate equivalent of emergencies in the virtual environment (i.e. saving a stranger's life after an accident). Avatars can be harmed and even be killed, but in most cases these character deaths are to be expected and not permanent. The only basic resource players can lose is valuable play time.

Wang and Wang (2008) studied prosocial behaviour in *WoW* and conducted a survey among regular players ($N = 402$). They found like in the nonvirtual world, women showed more prosocial behaviours than men. Furthermore, women tended to show this behaviour towards both sexes equally, whereas men more often helped women. They also verified a trend of male players deliberately identifying themselves as female players to obtain in-game items and other forms of favored treatment.

Physically attractive individuals are perceived as more socially desirable than less attractive individuals (e.g. Benson, Karabenick & Lerner, 1976). Comparable to real-world settings, attractive avatars generally induce more prosocial behaviour then less attractive avatars, especially attractive female avatars (Ohler, Pietschmann, &Valtin, 2007; van der Heide, Schumaker, Peterson, & Jones, 2013; Waddell & Ivory, 2015). In a series of so-called in situ experiments (virtual field studies) conducted between 2006 and 2014, Valtin and colleagues (2014) investigated prosocial behaviour by manipulating avatar attractiveness, form of address, and social setting in *WoW*, *Age of Conan* (Funcom Oslo, 2008), and *Star Wars: The Old Republic* (*SWTOR*; Bioware Austin, 2011). They approached other players with the researcher's avatars in social hubs of the game and asked them for help with game tasks and to lend them some money to buy equipment or to train new character skills. Because of the highly social nature of the game as a result of the necessity to cooperate, they encountered high degrees of prosocial behaviour. They also confirmed the positive effect of avatar attractiveness/ female avatars on prosocial behaviour to be consistent in all games. Playtime was identified as the most valuable resource for players in MMORPGs, because it translates into all other game resources. To be successful in the game and achieve goals, players need game resources, which can be obtained considerably faster and more efficiently together with other players.

Although this is merely a brief sketch of experimental research conducted on MMOs, the social aspects of the game were the driving force of the biggest part of research on the topic. However, what actual constitutes these social aspects might have changed over the past few years of MMO design.

The Ultimate Boon: Casualization and Current Evolvements

During its product lifecycle, WoW introduced major design changes representing the idea of casualization. This should not necessarily be seen as a bad thing per se, as it made the game even more approachable and resulted in better usability and user experience. But these design changes affected the social interactions in the game on a massive scale. Overall, casualization results in a lower time investment required by the players.

Conventional MMORPGs usually had a relative slow pace, lots of trial and error on the player's side, and only allowed for a slow character progress. They therefore demanded an almost unbearably high investment of playtime to reach the highest game levels. As part of the casualization process, the time required for character progression was reduced drastically so that players were not deterred by the required time it would normally take to reach the endgame content. Usually, this effect occurs when new game content is released (e.g. big world expansions like *WoW: Cataclysm*; Blizzard Entertainment, 2010). A faster progression made it easier for players to return to the game and catch up, but also for new players to quickly reach the new content and play with their friends, who already have high level characters.

Character classes and the game world were also changed, allowing players to survive and master content on their own, thus enabling solo play in the first place. Traditionally, MMORPGs relied on a triad of characters' roles (healer, tank, damage dealer). Each player had to play a specific part in a group to achieve common goals. Casualisation loosened this system, allowing players to adapt certain roles at will to complete game content more quickly. At the same time however, it made cooperation less likely, because playing together was no longer of benefit to the players. By playing alone, more of the valuable playtime could be spent actually playing the game instead of having to look and wait for other players.

Game expansions and their additional game content led to a larger game world. With a shrinking overall population, players would not always find others to play with at lower levels, because most players already concentrated on the respective end game content. Tools such as group finders and raid finders were introduced to allow for easier group forming and automatic transport to the location of the group encounter. Although this is very convenient for players and further reduced time required for organizational tasks, it removed the elements of searching for group members and collectively travelling – time which was typically used for conversation, social bonding, and recruiting guild members.

Endgame content typically involved complete evenings of guild members filled with strategic planning and coordination of large number of players to beat the next encounter. In this process, players had manifold possibilities to interact and bond with their fellow guild members. Yet, as these several hour long sessions were not always successful due to a large amount of trial and error, the overall difficulty of these encounters has been reduced. At the same time, convenience features were implemented to further reduce the level of frustration with these encounters (e.g. by providing hints to the best strategies within the game). Consequently, even players with a tight time budget for the game were able to experience all the game's content.

At the same time, standard player group size in MMORPGs gradually shrank over the years. Smaller groups could be assembled quicker and were easier to manage. In *Everquest* (1999), six players could form a standard group to play together and raid groups (players attempting very difficult tasks within the game) could reach up to 72 players. *Dark Age of Camelot* (2001) surpassed that with groups of eight players for standard content and more than 150 players for raid content. *WoW* (2004) only allowed five players to form a group. Raid groups could still have 40 players. Newer games following the trend of casualization reduced the standard group size to four players (*SWTOR*, 2011; *The Elder Scrolls Online*, Zenimax Online Studios, 2014) with raid groups of 16 and 12 players, respectively.

The player economy was also subject to changes to minimise player's efforts. In games such as *Dark Age of Camelot*, players had to advertise and trade items by chatting and meeting virtually, especially because certain high-quality items were only obtainable from other players, who were expert craftsmen. *WoW* was released with virtual auction houses in each of the capital cities where players could sell and buy items without having to interact with each other. The ability to send items to other players via the in-game mail system further minimised players' need for social encounters and negotiations.

Last, status and achievement are often represented in the player's equipment. Over the lifecycle of a MMORPG, an upward spiral (Kennedy, 1989) emerges, leading to an inflation of game currency and the necessity of newer and better virtual goods to keep players attracted. In the beginning of *WoW*, the best obtainable items required cooperation of big player groups of 40 players and lots of time. Due to the release of new expansions with more powerful items, the changes of the game mechanics and the increase of solo play, high-end gear became easily obtainable for every player. Instead of investing weeks of efforts in raiding (and socialising) with a larger player group, players can now use in-game tools to find random player groups to clear a game objective in a matter of minutes to obtain equipment. Consequently, it is no longer necessary to invest social capital to reach this level of end game content.

A recent example for the current state of casualization is *SWTOR*. The game was first released in 2011 with a subscription-based model and quickly attracted a millions of players due to the high production value and the popular *Star Wars* license. The game focussed heavily on storytelling and featured voiced dialogues for every character in the game world. All players had computer-controlled companions at their side, and thus did not require the help of other players for most of the game's standard tasks. Interestingly, the first player reached the maximum character level after just two days (Sonofalichs, 2011). The game content was considered as too easy by critics, and even regular players burned through most the content quickly, being able to reach the highest character levels within a couple of weeks. Over the course of its first year, *SWTOR* lost many players and switched to a free-to-play/pay-to-play hybrid model in late 2012. Since then, it has received several extensive content updates. *SWTOR*'s recent expansion *Knights of the Fallen Empire* (Bioware Austin, 2015), released in late 2015, is very remarkable when investigating the trend of casualization, as it completely contradicts the MMORPG idea. The expansion introduced a new storyline of 10 to 15 hours to the game that is only playable without other players. The expansion was heavily marketed as a "continuous storyline" with "choices that matter" ("Knights of the Fallen Empire", n.d.) and was well-received by critics and players[3]. Like *WoW* expansions before, *Knights of the Fallen Empire* also significantly lowered the time required to reach the new maximum level in *SWTOR*. Players could alternatively create a high-level character and immediately start the new storyline, without ever having to see another player, thus effectively playing a single player game. At the end of the story, other players suddenly reemerge in the game world. To go one step further, even the endgame content can be played without other players, which was not possible in other MMORPGs before. The only mechanical benefit of playing in groups now is to obtain slightly better equipment than what can be achieved when playing solo.

> *I rate this expansion highly because it gives me what I wanted from the initial launch up until now. This game has a memorable single player experience with optional multiplayer added on.*
>
> (Rystir, 2015)

Although the expansion attracted many players previously not interested in a MMORPG, not all long time players were happy about the further casualization of the game:

> *They totally destroyed the gameplay of SWTOR with this expansion. What they sell as streamlining and making more convenient for players is in fact a dumbing down of the game that makes it lose*

any challenge outside of [Player-versus-Player]. Some [...] people
say they like that they never die now, no matter how bad they play.
That you don't need to think at all, besides moving forward and let
your companion kill everything. [...] Myself and many mature play-
ers I know can only shake our heads what Bioware was thinking by
simplifying the game in such a way.

(Frosty1979, 2015)

The example of *SWTOR – Knights of the Fallen Empire* shows the ex-
treme end of the casualization process where the game is not a highly
social MMORPG anymore, but rather a single-player game in an online
environment. The result is a transformation of social spaces, social interaction, and social behaviour of yet unknown scale.

Refusal of the Return: Implications for Research on Social Aspects of MMOs

The observed trend of casualization within MMORPGs presents several implications for research on social interaction and gaming culture
on two levels. First, referring to existing theories and studies reporting patterns of socially motivated player behaviour to explain current
player behaviour should be carried out with caution. Changes from the
casualization have to be considered, when reviewing earlier research
results, which can often not be directly compared with newer studies.
Most interestingly, the social aspects of playing MMORPGs were often
considered a major motivator compared to single player games – the
trend of casualization, however, should have affected this link to player
motivation as well, as social interactions have grown less important over
time. A qualitative study by Chen, Duh, and Renyi (2008) of *WoW* players already showed that the introduction of new game features like the
group finder significantly changed the areas of social interaction and
affect interpersonal relationships and community size.

Second, conducting new studies on social interactions between players
should take these changes in the gaming culture into account, because
social interaction during standard game play situations is on the decline
and less common than in earlier MMOs. Thus, conducting studies on
social interaction would require the researcher to use settings which are
still socially meaningful, such as interaction within guilds or during
world events that require the cooperation of many players. Yet, this severely limits the number of research paradigms, because it only accounts
for a rather small proportion of the gaming time and conceptually moves
social interaction away from the basic idea of common day interaction
that is comparable to respective real-world situations.

However, this mainly holds true for the mainstream MMORPGs described in this chapter. There still are smaller communities playing "old

school" games, but they have to be considered a niche. Also, casualisation may have transformed the social interaction of players, but through this change also introduced new behaviours not covered in this chapter. Furthermore, many areas of research in online games may not be affected as much through casualisation (e.g. avatar identification, social competence).

Master of Two Worlds: Where Do We Go From Here?

Eventually, we have to conclude that players of MMORPGs seem to represent no special population of players anymore, because playing online can by now be regarded as the normal playing mode – whether it actually involves multiplayer and social interaction game play or not. Although this sounds like a rather pessimistic approach to social interaction in current MMORPGs, the process of casualization might also inform new types of research questions or revivify old ones: We could, for example, revisit the motivations to play MMORPGS. Through the need for cooperation in the classic MMORPG, players were always required to consider social encounters as a relevant part of the game. With this necessity being pulled out of the way, new target groups have been acquired and existing players are able to choose more freely to what degree they want to engage in social encounters. Revisiting this line of research after the substantial changes to the game genre might provide fruitful insights into the structure of player motivations and the role of social play.

There are, however, also virtual worlds that differ significantly from today's mainstream MMORPGs, for example *DayZ* (Bohemia Interactive Studio, 2013). This MMO takes players into a very dangerous postapocalyptic world and forces a so called "permadeath" on players. This means that a player character is permanently removed from the virtual world as soon as it dies within the game, resulting in the loss of all progress, items, and achievements obtained until this point. In combination with the many possible interactions with other players (hostile as well as friendly), the types of social behaviour players show in this game are very interesting, since the lone wolf playstyle has not proven to be a very reliable option. Research here could focus on basic and also evolutionary relevant social aspects as group hierarchies, the sharing of resources and the question of how to interact with other groups of players. This example shows that casualization does not automatically result in the end of social life in MMOGs.

As we have shown, not only do the player characters follow a hero's journey by exploring the shared virtual environments – the genre itself followed a similar journey and transformed key characteristics up to a degree that directly contradicts the original idea of MMORPGs. Whether the genre will manage to find its way back to its massively *multiplayer* roots or follow the trend to evolve into massively *single-player* online roleplaying games remains to be seen.

Notes

1 For a comprehensive overview and effects of the free-to-play model, see Lin & Sun (2011) or Luban (2011).
2 A database search in Academic Search Premier, Communication & Mass Media Complete, and PsychArticles for publication dates between 2004 and 2016 alone provides 158 academic journal papers with "World of Warcraft" in the title.
3 MMORPG.com user score, 8.1/10; IGN.com user score, 6.5/10; IMdB.com user score, 8.7/10 Metacritic.com user score, 7.5/10.

References

Bainbridge, W.S. (2012). *The warcraft civilization: Social science in a virtual world*. Cambridge, MA: MIT Press.

Balicer, R. (2007). Modeling infectious diseases dissemination through online role-playing games: Virtual epidemiology. *Epidemiology, 18*(2), 260–261.

Benson, P. L., Karabenick, S. A., & Lerner, R. M. (1976). Pretty pleases: The effects of physical attractiveness, race, and sex on receiving help. *Journal of Experimental Social Psychology, 12*(5), 409–415. doi:10.1016/0022-1031(76)90073-1.

Campbell, J. (2008). *The hero with a thousand faces* (3rd ed.). Novato, CA: New World Library.

Castronova, E. (2008). *Synthetic worlds: The business and culture of online games*: Chicago, IL: University of Chicago Press.

Chen, V. H.-h., Duh, H. B.-L., & Renyi, H. (2008). *The changing dynamic of social interaction in World of Warcraft: The impacts of game feature change*. Paper presented at the *Proceedings of the 2008 International Conference on Advances in Computer Entertainment Technology*, Yokohama, Japan.

Choi, D. & Kim, J. (2004). Why people continue to play online games: In search of critical design factors to increase customer loyalty to online contents. *CyberPsychology & Behavior 7*(1), 11–24.

Cole, H., & Griffiths, M. D. (2007). Social interactions in massively multiplayer online role-playing gamers. *Cyberpsychology and Behavior, 10*(4), 575–583. doi:10.1089/cpb.2007.9988.

Corneliussen, H.G. & Rettberg, J.W. (2008*). Digital culture, play, and identity: A World of Warcraft reader*. Cambridge, MA: MIT Press.

Cuddy, L. (2009). *World of Warcraft and philosophy: Wrath of the philosopher king*. Chicago, IL: Open Court.

Ducheneaut, N., & Moore, R. J. (2004*). The social side of gaming: A study of interaction patterns in a massively multiplayer online game*. Paper presented at the *Proceedings of the 2004 ACM Conference on Computer supported cooperative work*.

Ducheneaut, N., Yee, N., Nickell, E., & Moore, R. J. (2006). 'Alone together?' Exploring the social dynamics of massively multiplayer online games. *ACM Conference on Human Factors in Computing Systems (CHI 2006)* (pp. 407–416). 2006 April 22–27, Montreal, Canada. New York: ACM.

Filiciak, M. (2003). Hyperidentities: Postmodern identity patterns in massively multiplayer online role-playing games. In M. J. P. Wolf & B. Perron (Eds.), *Video game theory reader* (pp. 87–102). New York, NY: Routledge.

Frosty, 1979 (2015, October 28). User review posted to http://www.metacritic.com/game/pc/star-wars-the-old-republic---knights-of-the-fallen-empire.

Griffiths, M.D., Davies, M.N.O. & Chappell, D. (2003). Breaking the stereotype. The case of online gaming. *CyberPsychology & Behavior* 6(1), 81–91.

Hsu, S. H., Wen, M.-H., & Wu, M.-C. (2009). Exploring user experiences as predictors of MMORPG addiction. *Computers & Education, 53*(3), 990–999. doi: 10.1016/j.compedu.2009.05.016.

Juul, J. (2009). *A casual revolution: Reinventing video games and their players.* Cambridge, MA: MIT Press.

Kasavin, G. (1997, May 15). Meridian 59 review. *Gamespot.* Retrieved March 20, 2014. Retrieved from http://www.gamespot.com/reviews/meridian-59-review/1900-2542536/.

Kasavin, G. (1999, April 2). EverQuest review. *Gamespot.* Retrieved March 20, 2014. Retrieved from http://www.gamespot.com/reviews/everquest-review/1900-2535859/.

Kennedy, P. (1989). *The rise and fall of great powers.* London, UK: Fontana.

Knights of the Fallen Empire. The Old Republic (n.d.). Retrieved from http://www.swtor.com/fallen-empire/overview.

Lin, H., & Sun, C.-T. (2011). Cash trade in free-to-play online games. *Games and Culture: A Journal of Interactive Media, 6*(3), 270–287. doi:10.1177/1555412010364981.

Lomanowska, A., & Guitton, M. (2012). Spatial proximity toothers determines how humans inhabit virtual worlds. *Computers in Human Behavior, 28,* 318–323.

Luban, P. (2011, November 23) *The design of free-to-play games: Part 1.* Retrieved January 25, 2016, from http://www.gamasutra.com/view/feature/134920/the_design_of_freetoplay_games_.php.

Nardi, B. (2010). *My life as a night elf priest: An anthropological account of World of Warcraft.* Ann Arbor, MI: University of Michigan Press.

Ohler, P., Pietschmann, D., & Valtin, G. (2007). Social behavior in virtual Worlds [Soziales Verhalten in virtuellen Welten]. *GameStar/dev, 2,* 62–67.

Park, A. (2000, November 20). EverQuest. *Gamespot.* Retrieved March 20, 2014, from http://www.gamespot.com/articles/everquest/1100-2655176/.

Peña, J., & Hancock, J. T. (2006).An analysis of socioemotional and task communication in online multi-player video games. *Communication Research, 33*(1), 92–109.

Penelopae. (January 8, 2012). RPG defined - what is a themepark MMO? In *GiantBomb.* Retrieved March 18, 2014, from http://www.giantbomb.com/profile/penelopae/blog/rpg-defined-what-is-a-themepark-mmo/89885/.

Rystir (2015, October 29). User review posted to http://www.metacritic.com/game/pc/star-wars-the-old-republic---knights-of-the-fallen-empire.

Schroeder, R. (Ed.) (2002). *The social life of avatars: Presence and interaction in shared virtual environments.* London, UK: Springer.

Sonofalichs (2011, December 16). First level 50 world/EU? [Msg 1]. Message posted to http://www.swtor.com/community/showthread.php?t=35561.

Squire, K. D., & Steinkuehler, C. A. (2006). Generating cyberculture/s: The case of Star Wars galaxies. *Cyberlines, 2,* 177–198.

Steinkuehler, C. A. (2004). A discourse analysis of MMOG talk. *Proceedings from the Other Players conference* (pp. 2010–2022). Copenhagen, Denmark. July 31, 2004.

Steinkuehler, C. A., & Williams, D. (2006). Where everybody knows your (screen) name: Online games as "third places". *Journal of Computer-Mediated Communication, 11*(4), 885–909. doi:10.1111/j.1083-6101.2006.00300.x.

Taylor, T. L. (2006). *Play between worlds: Exploring online game culture.* Cambridge, MA: The MIT Press.

Tooby, J. & Cosmides, L. (1992). The psychological foundations of culture. In J. Barkow, L. Cosmides, & J. Tooby (Eds.), *The adapted mind: Evolutionary psychology and the generation of culture* (pp. 19–136). New York: Oxford University Press.

Valtin, G. (2014). *Prosocial behavior in virtual worlds based on the example of online roleplaying games. The Influence of situational and dispositional factors in comparison to real life helping behavior.* [Prosoziales Verhalten in virtuellen Welten am Beispiel von Online-Rollenspielen: Der Einfluss situativer und dispositionaler Faktoren im Vergleich zu realen Hilfesituationen]. Chemnitz, GER: Chemnitz University Press.

Valtin, G., Pietschmann, D., Liebold, B., & Ohler, P. (2014). Methodology of measuring social immersion in online role-playing games: Exemplary experimental research on social interactions in virtual worlds. In T. Quandt & S. Kröger (Eds.), *Multiplayer - Social aspects of digital gaming.* London, UK: Routledge.

van der Heide, B., Schumaker, E. M., Peterson, A. M., & Jones, E. B. (2013). The Proteus effect in dyadic communication: Examining the effect of avatar appearance in computer-mediated dyadic interaction. *Communication Research, 40*, 838–860. doi:10.1177/00936.50212438097.

Van Geel, I. (2013, December 29). *Total active subscriptions. MMOData blog.* Retrieved January 25, 2016, from http://mmodata.blogspot.de/.

Van Looy, J., Courtois, C., & De Vocht, M. (2010). *Playing a self: An exploration into the effect of avatar identification on gamer ratings of self, ideal self and avatar personality in MMORPGs.* Paper presented at the *Pre-conference to the ECREA 2010–3rd European Communication Conference, Avatars and Humans.* Representing Users in Digital Games.

Waddell, T. F., & Ivory, J. D. (2015). It's not easy trying to be one of the guys: The effect of avatar attractiveness, avatar sex, and user sex on the success of help-seeking requests in an online game. *Journal of Broadcasting & Electronic Media, 59*(1), 112–129. doi:10.1080/08838151.2014.998221.

Wang, C.-C., & Wang, C.-C. (2008). Helping others in online games: Prosocial behavior in cyberspace. *Cyberpsychology and Behavior, 11*, 344–346. doi:10.1089/cpb.2007.0045.

Ward, M. (2005). *Deadly plague hits Warcraft world.* Retrieved January 25, 2016, from http://news.bbc.co.uk/2/hi/technology/4272418.stm.

Whang, L. S., & Chang, G. (2004). Lifestyles of virtual world residents: Living in the on-line game "lineage". *Cyberpsychology & Behavior, 7*(5), 592–600. doi:10.1089/cpb.2004.7.592.

Williams, D. (2010). The mapping principle, and a research framework for virtual worlds. *Communication Theory, 20*(4), 451–470. doi:10.1111/j.1468-2885.2010.01371.x.

Williams, D., Caplan, S., & Xiong, L. (2007). Can you hear me now? The impact of voice in an online gaming community. *Human Communication Research, 33*(4), 427–449.

Yee, N. (2006). Motivations for play in online games. *CyberPsychology & Behavior, 9*(6), 772–774.

Yee, N. (2009). *The Daedalus Project*. Retrieved January 25, 2016, from http://www.nickyee.com/daedalus.

Referenced Games

Archetype Interactive (1996). *Meridian 59* [PC game]. Redwood City, CA: The 3DO Company.

Bioware Austin (2011). *Star Wars: The Old Republic* [PC game]. Electronic Arts.

Bioware Austin (2015). *Star Wars: The Old Republic – Knights of the Fallen Empire* [PC game]. Electronic Arts.

Blizzard Entertainment (2010). *World of Warcraft: Cataclysm* [PC game]. Irvine, CA: Blizzard Entertainment.

Bohemia Interactive Studio (2013). *DayZ* [PC game]. Bohemia Interactive Studio.

Funcom Oslo (2008). *Age of Conan: Hyborian Adventures* [PC game]. Eidos.

Mythic Entertainment (2001). *Dark Age of Camelot* [PC game]. Los Angeles: Vivendi Games.

NCsoft Corporation (2001). *Lineage. The Blood Pledge* [PC game]. NCsoft – North America.

Origin Systems (1997). *Ultima Online* [PC game]. Redwood City, CA: Electronic Arts.

Verant Interactive (1999). *EverQuest* [PC game]. San Diego: Sony Online Entertainment.

ZeniMax Online Studios (2014). *The Elder Scrolls Online* [PC game]. Bethesda Softworks.

7 Multiplayer Features and Game Success

André Marchand

Console video games attract some of the highest global consumer spending among media types and are continuing to be one of the most important game types (e.g. compared to PC, browser, social network, handheld, or mobile games) with impressive growth rates between 9% and 15% (ESA, 2016; Marchand & Hennig-Thurau, 2013). According to the Entertainment Software Association (ESA), more than 150 million U.S. consumers play video games regularly (ESA, 2016); however, not all console video games[1] are economically successful, even though hits such as *Grand Theft Auto V* (global revenues of more than $3.0 billion; Brightman, 2015) tend to attract the most attention. Video games demand large production budgets and thus high first-copy costs (e.g. $265 million for *Grand Theft Auto V*; Villapaz, 2013) but incur huge risks (e.g. the worst-selling game in the Sonic franchise, *Sonic Boom: Rise of Lyric*, sold only 620,000 copies; Sega Sammy Holdings, 2015). Moreover, the product lifecycles of video games are relatively short, and sales diffusion after the release of a video game tends to follow an exponential decay pattern (Hennig-Thurau, Houston, & Heitjans, 2009). These sales diffusions and the ongoing uncertainty about the revenue potential put video game developers and distributors under pressure and suggest a need to understand what makes video games economically successful.

This chapter will outline empirical research addressing the question of whether the multiplayer features of video games are positively related to short- and long-term game success[2]. Specifically, this research assesses the impact of local and online multiplayer features. Local multiplayer features refer to the option to play a game with others in front of the same screen (this has also been referred to as "colocated" play), whereas online multiplayer refers to the option to play a game with others who are not in front of the same screen but use another console in a different location. To evaluate the contribution of these features to a video games' success, longitudinal field data about video games was collected (for the Xbox 360 and PlayStation 3 consoles) over a period of seven years. After looking at short-term sales (i.e. the first week sales) and total sales of a video game, and controlling for other relevant success factors such as game genres, advertising spendings, and evaluations by ordinary consumers and experts, it was found that online multiplayer features are positively and directly associated with short-term sales and positively but only indirectly with total sales. The indirect effect with total sales is moderated by the age of the console generation, suggesting that online multiplayer features are economically beneficial at higher ages of a console generation with a higher installed base. This is discussed in more detail later.

Local and Online Multiplayer Features

Local Multiplayer

Other than single-player games where players compete with opponents steered by artificial intelligence and solve preprogrammed challenges, multiplayer features enable consumers to play games competitively or cooperatively with other humans. Local multiplayer features allow for colocated play. That is, it allows for more than one player to engage in the same video game content in front of the same screen. Pioneer games such as *Tennis for Two*, released in 1958, relied completely on the local multiplayer feature. As might be expected, games with local multiplayer features are often family-centered (Chambers, 2012) and allow a very limited number of players to play jointly. For example, the popular new game *FIFA16* allows only four players in front of the same television set. Theoretically, games with local multiplayer format are thought to be more valuable to its consumers as social consumption can satisfy a fundamental need for relatedness through interpersonal interactions (Deci & Ryan, 2000; Downie, Mageau & Koestner, 2008). As such, it was predicted that:

H1:   *The presence of a game's local multiplayer feature correlates positively with its (a) short-term and (b) total sales.*

ONLINE MULTIPLAYER

Games with online multiplayer features can be played by consumers from different sites who are connected through an online network like *PlayStationNetwork* or *Xbox Live*. Because many (sometimes more than 1 million) consumers play simultaneously, a widespread label refers to massively multiplayer online game, which can be specified to game genres (e.g. MMORPG for massively multiplayer online role-playing game, MMOFPS for massively multiplayer online first-person shooter game, MMORTS for massively multiplayer online real-time strategy game). Such complex and intensive game types can even integrate features of professional events (e.g. DreamHack), including world rankings (e.g. Call of Duty World League), tournaments with live broadcasts and local spectators, sponsorships, prize money, and even professional coaches. Online multiplayer features have been technically enabled since the sixth console systems generation (e.g. PlayStation 2).

By enabling direct communication among players (e.g. personal or group chats with text messages and voice; Williams, Caplan, & Xiong 2007), games with online multiplayer features also allow for social interactions during play and cooperation among factions. This allows consumers to develop existing relationships as well as make new friends, which can be particularly important for individuals who have difficulties developing and maintaining friendships in offline contexts (Kowert, Domahidi, & Quandt, 2014). Interactions within the game space include communication that enhances interpersonal relationships and goes beyond the fun of gaming itself (Ledbetter & Kuznekoff, 2011). It has been found that, when compared with real-life contexts, players can express themselves in other ways in virtual spaces because it enables them to hide their social class, appearance, and other personal attributes (Cole & Griffiths, 2007). Moreover, consumers do not just play a game but also create new virtual worlds which constitute cocreated narratives (Buchanan-Oliver & Seo, 2012) and let other players become a basic part of the social-servicescape experience (Tombs & McColl-Kennedy, 2003). Thus, it can be argued relying on the self-determination theory (Deci & Ryan, 2000) again that this influences enjoyment of playing a game, which leads to the second research hypothesis:

H2: *The presence of a game's online multiplayer feature correlates positively with its (a) short-term and (b) total sales.*

Interaction of Online Multiplayer Features with the Installed Base

In contrast to local multiplayer, online multiplayer features can make use of direct network effects, such that the value of these games increases with a larger installed base (Katz & Shapiro, 1994). Because games and consoles have a complementary relationship, a large installed base of video game consoles (player base) should also increase the utility of a video game with online multiplayer features (Shankar & Bayus, 2003). This means that the more consoles are in use, the more consumers can find other game partners online. It is thus easier for them to find suitable playing partners with equivalent playing experience and skills to experience flow.

When players consider both the system's generation age (which correlates strongly with the installed base of consoles) and multiplayer features, they likely confront a trade-off decision. Should they buy a game in late console's lifecycles when games appear similar to the existing ones in terms of technical innovations? In addition to this possible negative effect, there can be also a positive one. At late console's lifecycle stages, consumers have greater access to fellow players. It is possible, however, that the positive effect can surpass the negative effect because the added social value of multiplayer features should be higher than the weak ludic value of a less innovative or differentiated game experiences. This might explain why some older multiplayer games are still played despite their outdated graphics and other technical features. This leads to the third hypothesis:

H3:   *The impact of a game's online multiplayer feature on total sales is moderated by the system generation age, such that online multiplayer features are more effective when the system generation age is high.*

Empirical Study

Data

This empirical study consider a longitudinal field data set of 838 Xbox 360 (X360) and 664 PlayStation 3 (PS3) video games (sum of cases = 1,502) released in the United States between 16 November 2005 and 31 December 2011. It includes all console titles available on http://www. amazon.com. Among these games, 250 were released exclusively on the X360, and 114 appeared only for the PS3. To account for the rapid sales decay (often to a few percent of the first week sales after 10 weeks), the dependent variable for the total sales has been measured up to May 2012. Other consoles such as the Nintendo Wii and handhelds such as the Sony PlayStation Portable have been excluded, because they are not high-end console devices and feature only a few games with multiplayer online features. Table 7.1 provides descriptive statistics.

The research questions have been tested with ordinary least squares regressions and a residual centering approach (Lance, 1988) to form the interaction term (*multiplayer_online* × *console_age*). This has been done by regressing the product term of the interaction variables on both variables, then using the resulting residuals. Residual centering allows consideration of only that part of the interaction that is not explained by the particular interacting variables. This approach excludes potential multicollinearity issues and obtains an unbiased estimate.

To avoid multicollinearity concerns related to sales and the age of the consoles, they have been empirically separated with an auxiliary regression approach, in which console sales has been regressed on the console age. The residuals of the auxiliary regression are significant at $p < .001$, $R^2_{X360} = .177$; $R^2_{PS3} = .102$, and represent that portion of console sales that does not overlap with console age (*console_sales_release_res*). Furthermore, any heavily skewed variables (i.e. *game_sales, advertising*

Table 7.1 Descriptive statistics

Variable	X360					PS3				
Metric Variables	Mean	Median	SD	Min	Max	Mean	Median	SD	Min	Max
ln_game_sales_week1	9.88	9.89	1.79	4.16	15.27	9.73	9.70	1.59	2.64	14.65
ln_game_sales_total	12.08	11.97	1.25	6.12	16.09	12.00	11.94	1.15	8.29	15.43
age_rating	2.58	3.00	1.11	1.00	4.00	2.60	3.00	1.11	1.00	4.00
brand_awareness	3.38	1.00	4.91	.00	33.00	3.63	2.00	5.00	.00	33.00
ln_advertising	4.80	6.01	3.45	.00	10.33	4.97	6.16	3.46	.00	10.33
ln_competition_advertising	10.22	10.30	1.08	4.99	11.57	10.24	10.25	1.02	4.77	11.57
consumers_evaluation	7.16	7.50	1.36	2.00	9.40	7.43	7.70	1.22	2.50	9.50
experts_evaluation	68.53	70.50	15.06	20.00	96.19	70.52	72.46	14.23	16.00	97.01
console_generation_age	42.86	44.00	20.30	1.00	74.00	47.80	49.00	17.55	13.00	74.00
Binary Variables		Sum		%			Sum		%	
genre_action		168		20.05%			143		21.54%	
genre_adventure		39		4.65%			39		5.87%	
genre_fighter		48		5.73%			41		6.17%	
genre_platform		20		2.39%			23		3.46%	
genre_puzzle		7		.84%			2		.30%	
genre_racer		76		9.07%			61		9.19%	
genre_rpg		50		5.97%			44		6.63%	
genre_shooter		135		16.11%			101		15.21%	
genre_simulation		24		2.86%			15		2.26%	
genre_sports		161		19.21%			124		18.67%	
genre_strategy		20		2.39%			6		0.90%	
genre_other		90		10.74%			65		9.79%	
major_publisher		490		58.47%			410		61.75%	
christmas_release		353		42.12%			271		40.81%	
multiplayer_local		514		61.34%			391		58.89%	
multiplayer_online		488		58.23%			381		57.38%	
n		838					664			

and *competition_advertising*) have been log-transformed to approximate a normal distribution, consistent with related research (e.g. see Hennig-Thurau et al., 2009, for movie revenues).

Model

Two dependent variables were included in the empirical model: game sales for the first week (*ln_game_sales_week1*) and total (*ln_game_sales_total*) in the United States gathered from vgchartz.com. The multiplayer feature refers to whether consumers can play a game jointly with others in front of the same television set (*multiplayer_local*) or over the Internet (*multiplayer_online*). The information for these two binary variables was collected from http://www.gamespot.com. The age of the console generation was also considered (*console_generation_age*; see Gretz & Basuroy, 2013), by assessing the consoles' lifecycle stage using its age in months, which correlates strongly with the overall installed base and with the diffusion of rapid Internet access in U.S. households ($r > .9$, $p < .001$). This measure is less prone to external biases, such as the Microsoft Kinect introduction for Xbox 360 in 2010, which induced an abnormal increase of hardware sales. Finally, using console sales at the release week (*console_sales_release_res*) gathered from vgchartz. com, this study controls for changes in the installed base at any particular time. Because games sometimes sell as a bundle with a console, this variable might affect the short-term sales of video games.

Similar to movie search traits, this study treats two relevant control variables for this category: game genre (e.g. *genre_action*; see Hixson, 2006) gathered from http://www.vgchartz.com and Entertainment Software Rating Board (ESRB) rating of the game (*age_rating*; similar to Motion Picture Association of America ratings; Leenders & Eliashberg, 2011) gathered from gamespot.com. The ESRB age rating implies restrictiveness, because a higher rating limits the number of consumers who legally may buy the game. This tainted fruit effect (Bushman & Stack, 1996) could be strong for video games, in that at least 32% of all video game consumers are not adults (http://www.theesa.com), so a higher age rating could reduce demand for a video game. Alternatively, it could induce a forbidden fruit effect, in line with reactance theory (Brehm, 1966). That is, some young consumers may feel motivated to consume a restricted video game (e.g. without parental permission), which could increase total demand. The age rating signals mature content (Leenders & Eliashberg, 2011), so a higher rating also could induce a higher product demand among adults. This behaviour might be motivated by a willingness to consume negative content (Andrade & Cohen, 2007) or to breach taboos, such as when players engage in violence virtually.

Brands and their publishers' power could also be two important influencers for the game sales. For the first one, this study considers brand awareness, which can be enlarged through brand extensions (*brand_awareness*; see Dhar, Sun, & Weinberg, 2012; Hennig-Thurau et al., 2009). This variable has been measured as the number of all prequels of a game. A distinction was made between minor and major publishers based on survey of about 900 industry professionals that have named 10 major publishers each year based on their reputations and company size (see http://www.gamasutra.com for details about these regular surveys). It can be assumed that major publishers have more negotiating power for prominent product listings and distribution resources in general (*major_publisher*; see Elberse & Eliashberg, 2003; Hsu, 2006). This was operationalised as a binary variable with 1 if the publisher of the game was one of the top 10 biggest publishers in the release year of the game (according to http://www.gamasutra.com) and 0 otherwise.

Advertising budget is usually a strong success predictor. Nevertheless, many studies ignore this important variable because it is not easy to obtain. The weekly advertising expenses for each game has been acquired from http://www.kantarmedia.com and operationalise it in thousands of U.S. dollars and then log-transformed this variable (*ln_advertising*; see Zufryden, 1996). In this context, games usually release simultaneously with other game titles. That is why advertising expenditures were considered for all competing games released in the identical month. With this procedure, the competitive intensity for each game is able to be captured (*ln_competition_advertising*; see Krider & Weinberg, 1998).

To address general variations in demand over the year, this study includes release timing (*christmas_release*) to account for seasonal effects. Unlike the U.S. motion picture industry, which has more than one demand peak in each year (Einav, 2007), it can be anticipated that demand for video games should be significantly higher in the three months before Christmas than in the rest of the year. Video games are popular presents, and during the winter time, they likely become a more relevant leisure activity.

To get an idea about the experience traits, consumers rely on word of mouth. Today, a substantial amount of this happens online. Thus the valence of consumer evaluations (*consumers_evaluation*; see Holbrook & Addis, 2007; Moon, Bergey, & Iacobucci, 2010) from http://www.gamespot.com and experts' judgements (*experts_evaluation*; see Hennig-Thurau et al., 2012) on http://www.gamerankings.com were used. In other contexts, studies have investigated the positive effects of such ratings on product demand, because high ratings signal a better product quality. For the first-week performance model, the ordinary evaluations were excluded because they are not available until after at the release day, contrary to the evaluations of the professional reviewers who receive a game usually some time in advance.

Equations 1 and 2 display the final models used to test the research hypotheses, in which βs are the parameters to be estimated and $\varepsilon 1i$ and

$\varepsilon 2i$ are the respective error terms. With two dependent variables (*ln_game_sales_week1i* and *ln_game_sales_totali*) and *genre_vectori* as a vector of binary variables to indicate the genre of video game *i*, a first-week (1) and a total performance (2) model can be formulated.

1 $ln\_game\_sales\_week1_i = \beta_{1,0} + \beta_{1,1}$ *genre_vector*$_i$ + $\beta_{1,2}$ *age_rating*$_i$ + $\beta_{1,3}$ *brand_awareness*$_i$ + $\beta_{1,4}$ *major_publisher*$_i$ + $\beta_{1,5}$ *ln_advertising*$_i$ + $\beta_{1,6}$ *ln_competition_advertising*$_i$ + $\beta_{1,7}$ *christmas_release*$_i$ + $\beta_{1,8}$ *experts_evaluation*$_i$ + $\beta_{1,9}$ *console_generation_age*$_i$ + $\beta_{1,10}$ *console_sales_release_res*$_i$ + $\beta_{1,11}$ *multiplayer_local*$_i$ + $\beta_{1,12}$ *multiplayer_online*$_i$ + $\beta_{1,13}$ *multiplayer_online*$_i$ × *console_generation_age*$_i$ + ε_{1i}

2 $ln\_game\_sales\_total_i = \beta_{2,0} + \beta_{2,1}$ *genre_vector*$_i$ + $\beta_{2,2}$ *age_rating*$_i$ + $\beta_{2,3}$ *brand_awareness*$_i$ + $\beta_{2,4}$ *major_publisher*$_i$ + $\beta_{2,5}$ *ln_advertising*$_i$ + $\beta_{2,6}$ *ln_competition_advertising*$_i$ + $\beta_{2,7}$ *christmas_release*$_i$ + $\beta_{2,8}$ *consumers_evaluation*$_i$ + $\beta_{2,9}$ *experts_evaluation*$_i$ + $\beta_{2,10}$ *console_generation_age*$_i$ + $\beta_{2,11}$ *console_sales_release_res*$_i$ + $\beta_{2,12}$ *multiplayer_local*$_i$ + $\beta_{2,13}$ *multiplayer_online*$_i$ + $\beta_{2,14}$ *multiplayer_online*$_i$ × *console_generation_age*$_i$ + ε_{2i}

Each model will be tested for the X360 and the PS3 separately, which technically leads to four total equations.

Results

In the first-week performance model, the variance inflation factors were all less than 3.1 and less than 3.7 in the total performance model, so the results are not biased by multicollinearity (Hair, Black, Babin, & Anderson, 2009). The R^2 and F-statistics indicated that short-term and total success were well explained by the model variables, and the Durbin-Watson statistic of approximately 2 for all models eliminated the possibility of serial correlation in the residuals. The model parameters for the regressions, which have been executed separately for the X360 and PS3 and for short-term and total success, appear in Table 7.2.

The local multiplayer feature cannot be associated with higher sales in this model, so H_1 must be rejected. The online multiplayer feature exerted a positive effect on sales in the release week for both the X360 and the PS3 in support of H_{2a}. In the long run, although this effect remained positive, it lost significance, so it cannot be confirmed for H_{2b}. The nonmoderated influence of console generation age differed. It influenced short-term sales positively, but it lowered total sales, which can be explained with a saturation effect for a maturing console generation. For total game sales, a significant moderator effect of *multiplayer_online* × *console_age* has been found. The positive coefficient of this interaction indicated that when online multiplayer features were available in a game

Table 7.2 Software regression results

Group	Variable	First-Week Performance Model						Total Performance Model					
		X360			PS3			X360			PS3		
		B	Beta	t	B	Beta	t	B	Beta	t	B	Beta	t
Intercept	constant	4.393*		8.358	4.633*		8.166	8.497*		21.710	9.014*		21.996
Product characteristics	genre_action	.375*	.084*	2.266	.695*	.180*	4.068	-.170	-.054	-1.412	.157	.056	1.300
	genre_adventure	.301	.035	1.303	.618*	.091*	2.769	-.061	-.010	-.367	.102	.021	.657
	genre_fighter	.189	.024	.871	.901*	.136*	4.186	-.287	-.053	-1.821	.184	.039	1.222
	genre_platform	-.632*	-.054*	-2.164	.391	.045	1.503	-.211	-.026	-.995	.221	.035	1.220
	genre_puzzle	-.686	-.035	-1.493	.514	.018	.685	-.561	-.041	-1.682	.021	.001	.041
	genre_racer	.147	.024	.764	.218	.039	1.091	-.183	-.042	-1.304	-.015	-.004	-.110
	genre_rpg	.855*	.113*	3.850	1.104*	.173*	4.981	.033	.006	.206	.262	.057	1.673
	genre_shooter	.756*	.155*	4.192	.773*	.173*	3.988	.086	.025	.659	.120	.037	.890
	genre_simulation	-.202	-.019	-.752	-.596*	-.056*	-1.988	-.293	-.039	-1.498	-.363	-.047	-1.729
	genre_sports	.127	.028	.759	.318	.078	1.765	-.215	-.068	-1.762	.032	-.011	.259
	genre_strategy	.230	.020	.765	.237	.014	.523	-.143	-.017	-.656	.119	.010	.377
	age_rating	.336*	.207*	6.233	.249*	.173*	4.427	.136*	.120*	3.441	.100*	.096*	2.542
Brand/publisher power	brand_awareness	.040*	.110*	4.537	.040*	.125*	4.481	.024*	.096*	3.751	.028*	.120*	4.452
	major_publisher	.395*	.108*	4.615	.246*	.075*	2.794	.318*	.125*	5.117	.298*	.126*	4.861
Promotion	ln_advertising	.147*	.282*	11.480	.115*	.249*	8.723	.122*	.336*	13.161	.087*	.261*	9.424
	ln_competition_advertising	-.059	-.036	-1.342	-.088	-.056	-1.909	-.027	-.023	-.836	-.069*	-.061	-2.150
Distribution	christmas_release	-.207	-.057	-1.789	-.072	-.022	-.618	.243*	.096*	2.890	.239*	.102*	2.957
Product evaluations	consumers_evaluation	n.i.	n.i.	n.i.	n.i.	n.i.	n.i.	.140*	.152*	3.553	.181*	.191*	4.152
	experts_evaluation	.051*	.429*	17.074	.049*	.437*	15.508	.025*	.301*	7.040	.026*	.316*	6.758

(Continued)

Group	Variable	First-Week Performance Model						Total Performance Model					
		X360			PS3			X360			PS3		
		B	Beta	t	B	Beta	t	B	Beta	t	B	Beta	t
Indirect network effects	console_generation_age	.005*	.051*	2.061	.008*	.090*	3.190	-.004*	-.059*	-2.247	-.013*	-.201*	-7.391
	console_sales_release_res	.001*	.061*	2.144	.001	.050	1.574	-.001	-.030	-1.028	-.001	-.006	-.198
Direct network effects	multiplayer_local	.043	.012	.418	-.167	-.051	-1.586	.104	.040	1.398	-.084	-.036	-1.151
	multiplayer_online	.393*	.108*	3.875	.397*	.123*	3.637	.086	.034	1.173	.079	.034	1.043
Interaction effect	multiplayer_online × console_generation_age	-.001	-.005	-.193	.012*	.073*	2.544	.006*	.051*	2.015	.015*	.120*	4.327
Statistics	R^2	.607			.600			.576			.628		
	Adjusted R^2	.596			.585			.563			.614		
	F-statistic	54.60*			41.57*			45.92*			44.86*		
	n	838			664			838			664		

* Significant at $p < .05$; n.i. = variable was not included in the respective equation for reasons provided in the text. The dependent variable of the first-week performance model is $ln\_game\_sales\_week1$ and of the total performance model it is $ln\_game\_sales\_total$.

and the age of the console increased, total game sales also increased, in accordance with the arguments related to H_3.

To deeper investigate the interactions, a simple slopes analysis was calculated (Aiken & West, 1991). For the binary variable *multiplayer_online*, slopes for nominal values of 1 and 0 were calculated. The mean level of the moderator variable was shifted up and down by 1 standard deviation. Then the significance for each individual slope was assessed. The results, similar and consistent for both consoles, supported the theoretical arguments. As Figure 7.1 shows, games with the online multiplayer feature were more successful for older console generations. A spotlight analysis (Aiken & West, 1991) confirmed a significant increase in total game sales for both the X360 and the PS3.

A few control variables deserve particular mention. In terms of *age_rating*, studies about movies usually indicate a negative association between a higher age rating and economic success. For the Xbox 360 and PlayStation 3, the findings differ to the movie industry, such that a higher age rating leads to more demand, likely in line with the forbidden fruit theory of consumer behaviour. Similar to studies in the movie industry, brand awareness (measured by the number of prequels), a major publisher, and advertising correlated positively with sales. The seasonal effect (measured as a release between October and December) was not significant in the short term but grew significant and positive in the long term. It can be argued that the insignificant short-term effect might be due to the greater competition in the months before Christmas and the increase in releases during these months, even though shoppers might buy them later, closer to the gift-giving occasion (most video games are released between October and November but not in December). Evaluations by ordinary consumers and experts both related positively to sales, though the standardised parameters for the experts were stronger than those for consumers in the total performance model.

A post-hoc analysis reveals positive correlations of *multiplayer_online* with *consumers_evaluation* (r_{X360} = .256, r_{PS3} = .150, with both $p < .05$) and *experts_evaluation* (r_{X360} = .290, r_{PS3} = .228, with both $p < .05$), suggesting that online multiplayer features could also have a positive effect on consumer perceptions and quality judgements of a game.

Implications for Managers and Research Outlook

The findings imply that managers should release software titles before the overall demand for a console generation declines. This is particularly relevant for single-player software titles. When a console generation becomes older, an online multiplayer feature is capable of exerting the overall decline of demand. Therefore, video game developers should be advised to focus on video games with online multiplayer features in

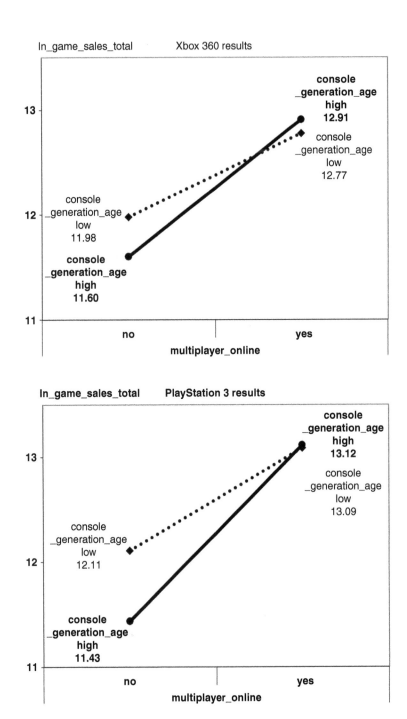

Figure 7.1 Slopes for moderating effects (total performance model).

later stages of a console lifecycle. With this strategy, they can counter the saturation effect in these stages.

Video games for consoles are a mass media phenomenon, accompanied by a growing number of exciting questions and possible strategies for managers. For example, multiplayer games can disrupt social structures (similar to some sports), allowing everyone to play one another, independent of social class. Other consumers also become part of the consumption experience, which might have negative value, such as when a consumer encounters rude language or abuse that damages the game experience. An automated recommendation system might help match similar consumers, to prevent this effect. With more games sold, more gamers are available to provide assistance, which lowers service costs for content providers. This opens many interesting opportunities for future research.

Notes

1 This article refers to them as *video games* throughout because several console video games such as Grand Theft Auto V are also available on personal computers.
2 Related aspects and some parts of this study have been published in Marchand (2016).However, this study employs a different empirical design and uses a different data set with a focus on the Xbox 360 and PlayStation 3 console games.

References

Aiken, L. S., & West, S. G. (1991). *Multiple regression: Testing and interpreting interactions.* Newbury Park, CA: Sage Publications.

Andrade, E. B., & Cohen, J. B. (2007). On the consumption of negative feelings. *Journal of Consumer Research, 34*(3), 283–300.

Brehm, J. W. (1966). *A theory of psychological reactance. Organization change: A comprehensive reader.* New York: Academic Press.

Brightman, J. (2015). GTA V ships 52m as Take-Two's annual revenue dips to $1.1 billion. gamesindustry.biz (assuming an average price of $60 per game). Retrieved from http://www.gamesindustry.biz/articles/2015-05-18-gta-v-ships-52m-as-take-twos-annual-revenue-dips-to-usd1-1-billion.

Buchanan-Oliver, M., & Seo, Y. (2012). Play as co-created narrative in computer game consumption: The hero's journey in Warcraft III. *Journal of Consumer Behaviour, 11*(6), 423–431.

Bushman, B. J., & Stack, A. D. (1996). Forbidden fruit versus tainted fruit: Effects of warning labels on attraction to television violence. *Journal of Experimental Psychology: Applied, 2*(3), 207–226.

Chambers, D. (2012). "Wii play as a family": The rise in family-centred video gaming. *Leisure Studies, 31*(1), 69–82.

Cole, H., & Griffiths, M. D. (2007). Social interactions in massively multiplayer online role-playing gamers. *Cyberpsychology & Behavior, 10*(4), 575–583.

Deci, E. L., & Ryan, R. M. (2000). The "what" and "why" of goal pursuits: Human needs and the self-determination of behavior. *Psychological Inquiry*, 11(4), 227–268.

Dhar, T., Sun, G., & Weinberg, C. B. (2012). The long-term box office performance of sequel movies. *Marketing Letters*, 23(1), 13–29.

Downie, M., Mageau, G. A., & Koestner, R. (2008). What makes for a pleasant social interaction? Motivational dynamics of interpersonal relations. *The Journal of Social Psychology*, 148(5), 523–534.

Einav, L. (2007). Seasonality in the U.S. motion picture industry. *The RAND Journal of Economics*, 38(1), 127–145.

Elberse, A., & Eliashberg, J. (2003). Demand and supply dynamics for sequentially released products in international markets: The case of motion pictures. *Marketing Science*, 22(3), 329–354.

ESA (2016). Industry facts. Entertainment Software Association. Retrieved from http://www.theesa.com/about-esa/industry-facts/.

Gretz, R. T., & Basuroy, S. (2013). Why quality may not always win: The impact of product generation life-cycles on quality and network effects in high-tech markets. *Journal of Retailing*, 89(3), 281–300.

Hair, J. F. J., Black, W. C., Babin, B. J., & Anderson, R. E. (2009). *Multivariate data analysis* (7th ed.). Upper Saddle River, NJ: Prentice Hal.

Hennig-Thurau, T., Houston, M. B., & Heitjans, T. (2009). Conceptualizing and measuring the monetary value of brand extensions: The case of motion pictures. *Journal of Marketing*, 73(6), 167–183.

Hennig-Thurau, T., Marchand, A., & Hiller, B. (2012). The relationship between reviewer judgments and motion picture success: Re-analysis and extension. *Journal of Cultural Economics*, 36(3), 249–283.

Hixson, T. K. (2006). Mission possible: Targeting trailers to movie audiences. *Journal of Targeting, Measurement and Analysis for Marketing*, 14(3), 210–224.

Holbrook, M. B., & Addis, M. (2007). Taste versus the market: An extension of research on the consumption of popular culture. *Journal of Consumer Research*, 34(3), 415–425.

Hsu, G. (2006). Jacks of all trades and masters of none: Audiences' reactions to spanning genres in feature film production. *Administrative Science Quarterly*, 51(3), 420–450.

Katz, M. L., & Shapiro, C. (1994). Systems competition and network effects. *Journal of Economic Perspectives*, 8(2), 93–115.

Kowert, R., Domahidi, E., & Quandt, T. (2014). The relationship between online video game involvement and gaming-related friendships among emotionally sensitive individuals. *Cyberpsychology, Behavior, & Social Networking*, 17(7), 447–453.

Krider, R. E., & Weinberg, C. B. (1998). Competitive dynamics and the introduction of new products: The motion picture timing game. *Journal of Marketing Research*, 35(2), 1–15.

Lance, C. E. (1988). Residual centering, exploratory and confirmatory moderator analysis, and decomposition of effects in path models containing interactions. *Applied Psychological Measurement*, 12(2), 163–175.

Ledbetter, A. M., & Kuznekoff, J. H. (2011). More than a game: Friendship relational maintenance and attitudes toward Xbox LIVE communication. *Communication Research*, 39(2), 269–290.

Leenders, M. A. A. M., & Eliashberg, J. (2011). The antecedents and conse-quences of restrictive age-based ratings in the global motion picture industry. *International Journal of Research in Marketing*, 28(4), 367–377.

Marchand, A. (2016). The power of an installed base to combat lifecycle dec-line: The case of video games. *International Journal of Research in Market-ing*, 33(1), 140–154.

Marchand, A., & Hennig-Thurau, T. (2013). Value creation in the video game industry: Industry economics, consumer benefits, and research opportunities. *Journal of Interactive Marketing*, 27(3), 141–157.

Moon, S., Bergey, P. K., & Iacobucci, D. (2010). Dynamic effects among movie ratings, movie revenues, and viewer satisfaction. *Journal of Marketing*, 74(1), 108–121.

Sega Sammy Holdings (2015). Appendix of consolidated financial statements year ended March 31, 2015. Consumer Business. Retrieved from https://www.segasammy.co.jp/english/pdf/release/201503_4q_tanshinhosoku_e_final_.pdf.

Shankar, V., & Bayus, B. L. (2003). Network effects and competition: An em-pirical analysis of the home video game industry. *Strategic Management Jour-nal*, 24(4), 375–384.

Tombs, A., & McColl-Kennedy, J. R. (2003). Social-servicescape conceptual model. *Marketing Theory*, 3(4), 447–475.

Villapaz, L. (2013). 'GTA 5' costs $265 million to develop and market, making it the most expensive video game ever produced: Report. *International Busi-ness Times*. Retrieved from http://www.ibtimes.com/gta-5-costs-265-million-develop-market-making-it-most-expensive-video-game-ever-produced-report.

Williams, D., Caplan, S., & Xiong, L. (2007). Can you hear me now? The im-pact of voice in an online gaming community. *Human Communication Re-search*, 33(4), 427–449.

Zufryden, F. S. (1996). Linking advertising to box office performance of new film releases. *Journal of Advertising Research*, 36(4), 29–41.

Part III

Gender Issues in Gaming Communities

8 Sexism in Video Games and the Gaming Community

Jesse Fox and Wai Yen Tang

Despite their growing popularity as a medium, video games are subject to many myths. One such myth is that video games are an almost exclusively male domain, with very few women playing. The statistics, however, indicate otherwise. According to the Electronic Software Association, 44% of those who play video games are women (ESA, 2015). Another survey found that women comprise 51% of PC-based game players (Chalk, 2014). Pew Research Center (2015) reported that across the United States, approximately 50% of men and 48% of women play video games. Women are clearly playing video games, so why does this myth persist?

One argument is that women and men engage with video games in distinct ways. Although men and women are relatively similar in terms of whether or not they play games, research has revealed some differences, such as gaming platforms (ESA, 2015), motivations for play (Chou & Tsai, 2007; Lucas & Sherry, 2004; Yee, 2008), and the types of games they play (Lucas & Sherry, 2004; Quandt, Chen, Mäyrä, & Van Looy, 2014; although see important critiques by Carr, 2005; Cassell & Jenkins, 1998; Jenson & de Castell, 2010). Importantly, men and women also differ in the degree to which they consider gaming an aspect of their identity (Shaw, 2012, 2015), with men twice as likely as women to self-identify as a gamer (Pew Research Center, 2015). Recently, scholars have suggested that some disparities in gameplay may also be attributable to women's experiences with sexism and harassment in gaming (Fox & Tang, *in press*).

Another issue in the gaming realm is a longstanding gender disparity among those who create video games (Cassell & Jenkins, 1998; Prescott & Bogg, 2013). A survey by the International Game Developers Association (IGDA; 2015) found that women composed only 22% of the video game industry workforce. Further, women's jobs were typically in areas such as human resources and marketing, which are uninvolved in the actual creation and development of games. Due to a variety of barriers, few women occupy key positions in game studios such as programmers, animators, and audio engineers (Ganguin & Hoblitz, 2014; IGDA, 2015; Prescott & Bogg, 2013). Some scholars have argued that this hegemony at the production level explains why women and women's experiences are often ignored, misrepresented, stereotyped, or objectified in games and gaming spaces (Chess, 2014; Fisher & Harvey, 2013; Fron, Fullerton, Morie, & Pearce, 2007; for more on this topic, see Chapter 9 in this volume).

These disparities in the nature of play and participation may explain why sexism and sexual harassment continue to be problematic in the gaming realm, across in-game player interactions, forums, conventions, and the industry. As T. L. Taylor (2006) argues, in many perspectives on games, "women are seen as 'intruders' rather than inhabitants of gamer culture" (p. 100). In this chapter, we will define sexism and sexual harassment and explain how the affordances of online games can aggravate these problems. We will describe factors at the individual, game, and industry level that perpetuate sexism in gaming and elaborate its consequences. Finally, we will consider the implications for gaming as a whole.

Sexism and Sexual Harassment in Online Environments

Sexism and Sexual Harassment

Sexism is defined as favorable or unfavorable beliefs and attitudes that reinforce gender disparity and inequality (Glick & Rudman, 2013). *Sexual harassment*, also known as *gender-based harassment*, includes unwelcome sexual advances or other conduct that targets someone based on their sex, gender, or gender identity. These behaviours may range from making discriminatory comments or sexist jokes to coercing someone to perform sex acts (Pina, Gannon, & Saunders, 2009; Tangri & Hayes, 1996). Because it is tied to a relatively immutable aspect of one's identity, sexual or gender-based harassment is distinguished from other forms of harassment and has particularly pernicious effects (Pina et al., 2009). Pryor and Whalen (1996) make an important distinction, noting that although sexual harassment can be driven by sexual motives, it can also be intended as "an expression of hostility toward a recipient perceived as an outgroup member" (p. 130). Most often, sexual harassment is perpetrated by men and targeting women (Pina et al., 2009; Pryor, 1987).

Although sexism and sexual harassment are often downplayed, the consequences of sexual harassment can be severe. Targets often attempt to extract themselves from the environment by avoiding or spending as little time as possible there; being precluded from participation or forced to avoid or circumvent harassers is in itself stressful (Fitzgerald, Drasgow, Hulin, Gelfand, & Magley, 1997). Victims report a range of psychological and physical effects, including emotional distress, decreased self-esteem, increased anxiety, sleeplessness, nausea, and depression (Larsen & Fitzgerald, 2011; Willness, Steel, & Lee, 2007). Larsen and Fitzgerald (2011) found that the outcomes can be so severe that victims meet the criteria for suffering from posttraumatic stress disorder.

Theories of sexual harassment outline two essential contextual factors (Fitzgerald et al., 1997), both of which apply to gaming contexts. First, these theories suggest that job gender context plays a role; sexual harassment is more frequent when men outnumber women and when the job tasks are perceived as masculine (Fitzgerald et al., 1997). Online video games meet these criteria as women are a minority in many popular genres of online games (Quandt et al., 2014). Further, playing video games is often seen as a masculine domain, and within games many tasks are stereotypically masculine (Gray, 2012b; Jenson & de Castell, 2010; Taylor, 2006; Yee, 2014). Second, these theories note that sexual harassment is more prevalent when there seem to be few consequences for harassment (Fitzgerald et al., 1997). Users perceive few consequences to sexual harassment online (Barak, 2005; Ritter, 2014). Further, video game companies, competitive gaming organizations, and the gaming industry as a whole have been publicly criticised for not addressing the widespread harassment of women (Fletcher, 2012). Thus, gaming meets the criteria for an environment in which sexual harassment is likely. Several features of games may also facilitate hostile behaviour toward women.

Affordances of Games and Online Interaction

Communication channels vary in their *affordances*, or properties that enable action (Sutcliffe, Gonzalez, Binder, & Nevarez, 2011). Although many benefits such as coordination of play (Sutcliffe et al., 2011) and the development of friendships (Cole & Griffiths, 2007) have been attributed to the affordances of online gaming environments, there is also a dark side to these attributes. Several theoretical perspectives, such as the *online disinhibition effect* (Suler, 2004) and the *social identity model of deindividuation effects* (SIDE; Lea & Spears, 1991), suggest that the distinctive affordances of online environments can facilitate disinhibited, and often socially undesirable, behaviour.

One such affordance is *anonymity*, or the ability to conceal one's identity. Very few gaming environments require individuals to disclose their actual offline identities. Rather, participants can choose screennames, player identifications, avatars, or other self-representations that do not disclose identifying details in games, meta-game platforms, forums, viewing channels, and other online gaming media. Such anonymity can promote the feeling that one's behaviour online cannot be tied to one's offline, "real" life (Suler, 2004).

This anonymity also reinforces a disassociation between the virtual, online world and the "real" offline world (Suler, 2004). Users feel they can engage in more deviant behaviour without consequence, leading to *toxic disinhibition* such as rude or hateful speech, threats, and other forms of harassment online (Suler, 2004). This disassociation is also applied to the targets of hostile behaviour; perpetrators of online hostility often minimise or excuse their hostile behaviour by suggesting that it is not a big deal and not hurtful towards victims because it happens online (Suler, 2004).

One explanation for this minimization is because many of the forms of computer-mediated communication that are prevalent in these environments, such as messaging and text chat, are *asynchronous* or *cue-filtered*, meaning they are limited in the number of nonverbal cues that are transmitted. The perpetrator often cannot observe the immediate nonverbal reactions of the target, such as a distressed facial expression. Lacking these responses, the perpetrator may feel that their hostile acts are not as impactful (Suler, 2004). SIDE also argues that because of the anonymity and lack of cues, users experience deindividuation, or a loss of a sense of self, in the social context. As a result, social identities become salient. Other anonymous users, particularly those in perceived outgroups, are depersonalised and stereotyped, and behavioural disinhibition occurs (Postmes, Spears, & Lea, 1998). SIDE has been applied to explain hostility towards women in games. Given the majority of avatars are male (Williams, Martins, Consalvo, & Ivory, 2009), and most tasks in networked games are competitive and aggressive, there are already cues in many environments that promote the salience of masculinity. As such, women are perceived as the outgroup, and players behave aggressively towards them.

Another feature of online interaction is the relative *visibility* or *privacy* of messages. Some online games allow both group chat, which is visible to all participants, and private chat limited to two players. Perpetrators may wish to capitalise on the visibility of public chat, harassing someone publicly in the hopes of impressing other players or eliciting their participation in ganging up on the target. Alternatively, perpetrators may not want a broader audience, choosing to harass the target privately so that other players are unaware. Private messaging systems also exist on some meta-game platforms, enabling perpetrators to extend their harassment outside of the game itself. Thus, the features of games and online communication may facilitate hostile interactions towards women. Another key predictor of this behaviour is personality traits.

Individual Predictors of Sexism and Sexual Harassment in Games

Hostile Sexism and Social Dominance Orientation

The theory of ambivalent sexism posits that individuals may hold both hostile and benevolent attitudes towards women, both of which have derogatory implications for women's nature and abilities (Glick & Fiske, 1996). Hostile sexism is defined by antipathy towards women and a sense of superiority over women. Hostile sexism characterises women as manipulative and trying to dominate men because of women's inherent inferiority. Benevolent sexism entails a paternalistic attitude towards women and rigid views of gender roles (Glick & Fiske, 1996). In this case, women are seen as weak, precious, and incapable of accomplishing the same things as men, and as such should be disempowered and protected by men.

Recent research has probed relationships between sexism and video games. Although one study found no relationship with general sexism (Breuer, Kowert, Festl, & Quandt, 2015), another study identified a positive relationship between hostile sexism and gameplay (Fox & Potocki, 2016). Hostile sexism has also been linked to players' sexist beliefs about women who play games (Fox & Tang, 2014) and men's harassment of other players within online multiplayer games (Tang & Fox, in press), whereas benevolent sexism was unrelated to either. One possible explanation for these links is that hostile sexist individuals are attracted to the inequitable elements evident in some video games, such as hypermasculine themes, sexist portrayals of women, or the perceived opportunity to demean or harass women during gameplay.

Another potential predictor that has been related to both hostile sexism and harassment is social dominance orientation (SDO; Russell & Trigg, 2004; Sibley, Wilson, & Duckitt, 2007). SDO reflects individuals' endorsement of inequality among social groups, resulting in prejudice and the belief in one group's superiority over other groups (Sidanius & Pratto, 1999). Although research is limited at this time, two studies have linked SDO with players' sexist beliefs about women's participation in games (Fox & Tang, 2014) and men's harassment behaviour in games (Tang & Fox, *in press*).

Masculinity

Because video games are seen as a space dominated by and oriented to men, masculine identity may be linked to sexism and sexual harassment in games. Jansz (2005) suggested that adolescent and young adult males often use game spaces to explore their masculinity and identity. Similarly, T. L. Taylor (2012) elaborates how the gaming community celebrates 'geek masculinity'. Additionally, interactions with other male players in networked video games provide opportunities to bond with other males (Frostling-Henningsson, 2009; Trepte, Reinecke, & Jeuchems, 2012). These bonding experiences may reinforce masculine norms in the video game setting, and this bolstering of the in-group (men) may also promote isolation or denigration of the outgroup (women).

In a related study, Hunt and Gonsalkorale (2014) found that masculinity drove in-group bonding among men and also predicted the likelihood of harassing women. Similarly, masculinity threats have been shown to increase the likelihood that men will sexually harass women (Maass, Cadinu, Guarnieri, & Grasselli, 2003). These findings may also explain why conformity to masculine norms has been linked to sexist beliefs among gamers (Fox & Tang, 2014). Thus, it is important to assess masculinity or the importance of masculine identity among gamers, as this may drive the exclusion, objectification, or harassment of women in the gaming environment.

Gamer Identity

Another important element of identity to consider may be the centrality of gaming to one's self-concept. Research specific to video games demonstrates that many players are highly involved and engaged with specific games as well as groups within the gaming community (De Grove, Courtois, & Van Looy, 2015; Grooten & Kowert, 2015; Shaw, 2015). High identification as a gamer has been associated with in-group preference and favoritism (Guegan, Moliner, & Buisine, 2015) as well as the denigration of outgroups and other in-group threats. For example, those who are highly involved with games have been shown to attack or discredit scientists reporting harmful effects of games (Nauroth, Gollwitzer, Bender, & Rothmund, 2014, 2015). Game involvement also predicts the likelihood of harassing other players (Tang & Fox, *in press*). Thus, investigating the role of gamer identity in the perpetration of harassment is an important direction for future research and may explain why a perceived outgroup like women are subject to harassment.

Those who identify as gamers also distinguish themselves from others who play video games. For example, those who play infrequently or play certain types of games are excluded from being identified as gamers. Individuals who play games on web browsers, social networking sites, or mobile devices are not considered true gamers, regardless of how involved they are or how frequently they play (Scharkow, Festl, Vogelgesang & Quandt, 2015; Shaw, 2012). Given that these gaming characteristics are common among women, this distinction is often gendered (Taylor, 2012; Vanderhoef, 2013) and used to deny women the designation of a 'real gamer'. Indeed, internalization of gendered norms or other myths about women's roles in gaming may explain why women are often reluctant to self-identify as gamers (Shaw, 2012) and why the default gamer identity is seen as male (Gray, 2012a; Shaw, 2012; Taylor, 2006).

Women's Participation and Representation in Game-Related Realms

Representation of Women in Video Game Content

Previous content analyses have determined that video games and video game-related media mirror traditional media in terms of how women are represented. Compared with men, women are drastically underrepresented (Beasley & Standley, 2002; Dietz, 1998; Downs & Smith, 2010; Smith, 2006; Williams et al., 2009). When women do appear in video games, it is often a highly sexualised or gender-stereotypical depiction (Beasley & Standley, 2002; Dill & Thill, 2007; Downs & Smith, 2010; Smith, 2006).

Representations in games are important to consider for many reasons. The symbolic annihilation of women in the virtual world may be seen as an allegory of gaming itself: if women do not belong as characters, perhaps they do not belong as players. Research has indicated that identification is a key motivator for players and specifically girls (Van Reijmersdal, Jansz, Peters, & Van Noort, 2013); when games lack female characters, girls in particular may be discouraged from playing or think that this is not a game for them. Sexualized and stereotypical portrayals are also a deterrent for women; an experiment found women rated fictional games with stereotyped female characters significantly lower than those with equitable portrayals (Hartmann & Klimmt, 2006).

Further, sexualised and stereotypical representations of women in virtual spaces have been shown to yield sexist attitudes among both men and women. Compared with nonsexualised portrayals, sexualised avatars have been shown to cause men and women to perceive women as less intelligent (Behm-Morawitz & Mastro, 2009), elicit hostile sexism in men and women (Fox & Bailenson, 2009), and promote rape myth acceptance in women (Fox, Bailenson, & Tricase, 2013; Fox, Ralston, Cooper, & Jones, 2015). Such depictions also make men more tolerant of sexual harassment (Dill, Brown, & Collins, 2008) and increase men's likelihood to sexually harass (Yao, Mahood, & Linz, 2010). Unsurprisingly, perhaps, users of sexualised female avatars reported the highest levels of harassment in a virtual world (Behm-Morawitz & Schipper, *in press*). These objectifying – and prevalent – portrayals of women may be perpetuating sexist attitudes and increasing the likelihood of sexual harassment in gaming spaces (see Chapter 9 for a more detailed discussion of this topic).

Representations of Women Across Gaming Media

The advertisements of video games and their characters are another source of sexist portrayals. Content analyses of advertisements in video game magazines and video game art found that women characters were underrepresented, and when they are depicted it is often in a subordinate or submissive role to the male protagonist (Burgess, Stermer, & Burgess, 2007; Near, 2013; Scharrer, 2004). Female characters are also far more likely than male characters to be sexualised (Burgess et al., 2007). The centrality of male characters in these media indicates that marketers presume men are their primary audience (Near, 2013). Such marketing strategies reinforce traditional gender roles and the perception that video games are a male-dominant medium (Dill & Thill, 2007).

Advertisements also often focus on the depictions of players. Chess (2011) evaluated gaming advertisements directed towards women and found that they reinforced existing gender role stereotypes, highlighting games in family interactions and beauty and weight maintenance. Advertisements that overlook women as players and portray gaming as an exclusively male activity may be detrimental to women's participation. Schott and Thomas (2008) reported that women who viewed ads from Nintendo's "For Men" advertising campaign felt excluded. Moreover, their initial positive impressions and intentions towards Nintendo's Game Boy Advance handheld diminished after seeing the ads.

Representations of women in video game magazines are also important to consider. These publications have an impact in the gaming community because they mediate communication between game developers and their consumers and influence the discourse of what is relevant to gamers. Similar to the gaming industry, the vast majority of video game journalists are male, which may explain the disparate treatment of male and female characters in games (Fisher, 2015; Ivory, 2006). Journalists mention physical appearance and discuss sexualization more often for female characters than for male characters (Fisher, 2015; Ivory, 2006). Journalists often review video games by playing the game from the male character's point of view, rarely noting that a game can be played as a female character. This absence further reinforces the invisibility of women within games and also overlooks the interests of women reading these magazines (Fisher, 2015). Other content analyses have shown how gaming magazines specifically targeted and catered to a male audience, such as players being portrayed as almost exclusively male (Cote, *in press-b*) and images of female characters being predominantly sexualised and consistently more so than men (Miller & Summers, 2007; Summers & Miller, 2014). The invisibility of the female player and the objectification of female characters in this space further reinforce gaming as a male space (Cote, *in press-b*).

Forums, social media, and other sites of interaction online also illustrate how sexism manifests. Indeed, blogs such as *Fat, Ugly, or Slutty* and Jenny Haniver's *Not in the Kitchen Anymore* are dedicated to recording and posting misogynistic interactions women experience when gaming. The online discourse on video games highlights how the majority of male gamers respond to gender issues by enforcing a masculine status quo. For example, a study of a *World of Warcraft* forum analysed the debate among players when the game removed a nonplayer character's sexist dialogue (Braithwaite, 2014). Many forum participants defended sexism in gaming content and blamed feminists for the changes (Braithwaite, 2014). In another occurrence, a male journalist accused a female gaming celebrity, Felicia Day, of being "nothing more than a glorified booth babe" on Twitter, attacking and downplaying her contributions (Tomkinson & Harper, 2015). Salter and Blodgett (2012) examined online discussion of the Penny Arcade "Dickwolves" incident, in which a controversy emerged regarding a comic that featured a rape joke. Across news sites, blogs, forums, and social media, the researchers noted "strong anti-feminine and anti-feminist undercurrents" in the debate around the original comic that evolved into "overtly hostile" discourse attacking the comic's critics (p. 409). Further, many women who spoke out against the comic received threats of sexual violence (Salter & Blodgett, 2012).

Women in the gaming community who have spoken out about inequality, such as developer Brianna Wu and critic Anita Sarkeesian, have also been targeted for longstanding campaigns of online harassment including rape and death threats (Chess & Shaw, 2015; Heron, Belford, & Goker, 2014). Perhaps the most salient example of online harassment in the gaming community is the GamerGate movement. The origins of GamerGate can be traced back to a scorned ex-boyfriend who summoned his online network to discredit and attack his ex-girlfriend, developer Zoe Quinn (Chess & Shaw, 2015; Heron et al., 2014). Perhaps unwittingly, the ex-boyfriend had tapped into a cesspool of sexism and loathing that was then galvanised to launch a series of public attacks and smear campaigns against other women in the gaming community, including Wu and Sarkeesian. Academics studying gender and games even came under fire, and the Digital Games Research Association was 'outed' as a feminist conspiracy against games (Chess & Shaw, 2015). These incidents suggest that there are zealous members of the gaming community that are resistant to highlighting and confronting sexism, and in some cases are openly against women's participation in gaming. Although it is very likely that this is a vociferous minority and not representative of gamers as a whole, the visibility and viciousness of this discourse perpetuates the idea that games are hostile spaces for women.

Participation and Representation of Women in Physical Gaming Spaces

The physical spaces of gaming are also an important factor to consider in examining gender (Bryce & Rutter, 2003; Lin, 2008). Early work noted differences in the presence of girls and women in gaming spaces such as public arcades (Kiesler, Sproull, & Eccles, 1985) and has been extended to explain how the physical environment of gaming studios assert and reinforce masculine norms (Johnson, 2014). Participation at gaming events also reflect gender disparities, because gatherings where individuals meet at a physical location to play video games together such as LAN parties are often male-dominated (Jansz & Martens, 2005).

At professional gaming events, the majority of competitors are male, and the few female competitors often receive unwanted attention from their male counterparts and audience members (Taylor, Jenson, &

de Castell, 2009). Furthermore, when women are present at video game venues, they often are in gendered roles, such as being cheerleaders to the male competitors or "booth babes" for video game products (Huntemann, 2013; Taylor et al., 2009). Several women journalists and regular attendees at conventions have reported being treated in a sexist manner or sexually harassed (Consalvo, 2012; Cote, *in press-a*).

Participation of Women in the Gaming Industry

Nearly half of industry workers feel that the gaming industry does not provide equal treatment and opportunity for women and other underrepresented groups (IGDA, 2015). It is unsurprising that few women enter and remain in the video game industry, because they face a number of barriers and an often hostile work culture (Consalvo, 2008; Prescott & Bogg, 2013). Given their minority status, it is very rare for women to occupy senior positions (Prescott & Bogg, 2013); as such, women are generally not in positions of power or able to effect change in the mainstream gaming industry. Other artifacts also demonstrate that gaming companies are not sufficiently equipped for managing gender disparity in the workplace. For example, only half of workers indicated their companies had policies regarding workplace harassment (IGDA, 2015).

Over time, women in the industry have become more vocal in regards to inequality, sexism, and sexual harassment in the workplace. For example, in response to a male game designer's Twitter query about the lack of "lady game creators", women developers launched the hashtag #1reasonwhy to publicise the struggles that women face in the gaming industry. Women shared stories of being overlooked for jobs, having their work dismissed by their peers, enduring coworkers' sexist comments and sexual harassment, and even being physically assaulted (Blodgett & Salter, 2013; Jenson & de Castell, 2013). Although there are many efforts to pursue and promote parity, particularly by women's collectives and independent studios, sexism continues to be an issue that women in the gaming industry must contend with (Jenson & de Castell, 2013; Prescott & Bogg, 2013; see Chapter 9 for more discussion of this topic).

Manifestations and Consequences of Sexism and Sexual Harassment in Games

Considerable research has shown that women are treated differently than men (Holz Ivory, Fox, Waddell, & Ivory, 2014; Taylor, 2006) and often disproportionately targets of sexism and harassment in gaming environments (Ballard & Welch, *in press*; Cote, *in press-a*; Fox & Tang, *in press*; Gray, 2012a, 2012b; Heron et al., 2014; Kuznekoff & Rose, 2013; Pew Research Center, 2014; Yee, 2014). Some studies have used quasiexperiments in natural settings and probed how sexism manifests in online environments. Holz Ivory and colleagues (2014) found that players in an online first-person shooter rewarded gender stereotypical behaviour: they accepted significantly more friend requests from a female confederate when she was nice than when she was hostile, although the reverse pattern held for male confederates. In another field experiment, Kuznekoff and Rose (2013) played an online game and interacted with other players using male or female prerecorded voices. The female voice received three times the amount of negative comments than the male voice had received. Kasumovic and Kuznekoff (2015) reanalysed this data set and also found that lower-skilled players were more hostile toward a female teammate than a male teammate.

Interviews and surveys with players have further illuminated women's experiences with harassment in games. Gray's research (2012a, 2012b) illustrates how players who allow sex-, gender-, race-, or ethnicity-related cues to leak in networked game play are subsequently targeted for harassment, a finding supported by Ballard and Welch (in press) for women and lesbian, gay, bisexual, transgender and queer (LGBT) players as well. Surveys have also found that men are more likely to be perpetrators of harassment in video games than women, and that women are more likely than men to be sexually harassed (Ballard & Welch, *in press*; Fox & Tang, 2013).

Experiences with sexism and sexual harassment have a number of consequences for women in games. Cote (*in press-a*) and Fox and Tang (*in press*) have explored how women respond to and cope with experiences of harassment. One strategy is to seek help from others, either inside or outside of the game (Fox & Tang, *in press*). This would include reporting harassment, asking others for advice, or soliciting support when being harassed, although some women report being uncomfortable asking other male players for assistance (Cote, *in press-a*). Women also avoided harassment by playing with people they knew rather than strangers (Cote, *in press-a*). Play style was also invoked strategically; women attempt to mitigate harassment by showing off their skills or expertise, hoping to get the perpetrator to refocus on the game itself (Cote, *in press-a*). Some women reported adopting an aggressive persona; when harassed or treated differently, women chose to do the same to the perpetrators (Cote, *in press-a*). Although these strategies vary in their level of success, importantly, women continue to maintain their presence and visibility in the game.

Other techniques, although successful in the short term, are problematic in the greater scheme. For example, some women deny that harassment is occurring or attempt to minimise it; others blame themselves for being victimised (Fox & Tang, *in press*). These strategies may trigger more negative experiences for the player. Another problematic method is gender-masking, in which women make efforts to hide their gender, such as choosing a gender-neutral screen name or avatar or not using voice chat to interact (Cote, *in press-a*; Fox & Tang, *in press*). Although it seems like an easy way to control harassment, by choosing to mask their sex or gender in play, women are inadvertently reinforcing the idea that they are in a small minority of players and that gaming is solely a masculine space. Similarly, one of the most common techniques was avoidance in which women self-selected out of these environments (Cote, *in press-a*; Fox & Tang, *in press*). Women would avoid interacting with other players, choose the single player option, or leave the game. Like masking, this strategy is problematic because it reduces women's participation and visibility in games, further reinforcing the appearance of a male-dominated environment. As Cote (*in press-a*) points out, however, "it is unfair to ask women to shoulder the entire burden of changing audience stereotypes and behaviors".

Research has shown that both general harassment (e.g., unwelcome hostile behaviour not tied to gender) and sexual harassment have been shown to predict women's withdrawal from games (Fox & Tang, *in press*). In the case of sexual harassment, however, the role of the gaming company is an important factor in determining whether women quit the game. *Organizational responsiveness* entails how the company handles reports of harassment and whether or not it punishes harassers. The responsiveness of gaming companies predicts whether or not women will leave a particular game after being sexually harassed (Fox & Tang, *in press*). As such, it is crucial for gaming companies to take action to retain women players.

Collectively, the differences in men's and women's experiences both within the game and within online and offline game-related venues is important for researchers to consider, particularly when speculating about gender differences. Gender itself may be a red herring, and the attributions and explanations for these differences may reinforce existing gender roles or stereotypes rather than identifying an important third variable. In reviewing some recent findings, it seems possible that some observed differences may be explained by women's expectations of or experiences with sexism or harassment. For example, Vermeulen and Van Looy (2014) found that men engaged in significantly more online communication in games than women. Both Cote (*in press-a*) and Fox and Tang (*in press*) found that women may limit or avoid communication with other players to preemptively thwart harassment, which may partially explain this difference. Additionally, many fast-paced cooperative games (such as collaborative first-person shooters) necessitate voice chat for quick decision-making and coordination. Women may be avoiding these games because the reliance on voice chat makes it difficult to mask their gender, explaining the male majority in these environments observed by Quandt and colleagues (2014). In general, women's distinct experiences in online games and the broader gaming community should be considered as a potential explanation for their gaming behaviour.

The Need for a Brighter Future

Although this chapter has focussed on sexism and sexual harassment, it is important to note that women are only one group targeted by toxic behaviour. Racism, homophobia, transphobia, and xenophobia are also common in these environments. Like women, other underrepresented groups such as LGBTQ individuals, ethnoracial minorities, and intersectional identities face symbolic annihilation or negative stereotyping in game content (Higgin, 2009; Kafai, Cook, & Fields, 2010; Shaw, 2015; Williams et al., 2009); harassment in social gaming contexts (Gray, 2012a, 2012b; Yee, 2014); and underrepresentation in the gaming industry (IGDA, 2015). As Leonard (2006), Shaw (2015), and many other gaming scholars argue, the erasure or nullification of marginalised identities from the discourse surrounding games has far-reaching implications.

Research with women players indicates that sexism and sexual harassment drives women away from games (Cote, *in press-a*; Fox & Tang, *in press*). This may discourage girls at a young age from participating in games or considering careers in video game or other computer-related industries. Women gamers may disproportionately miss out on the individual and social benefits associated with playing games, including enjoyment, relaxation, establishing friendships, and receiving social support (Cole & Griffiths, 2007; Taylor, 2006; Trepte et al., 2012). Gaming is perceived as a space in which women are treated inequitably (Pew Research Center, 2014); such perceptions, combined with news stories and other discourse about the toxicity of this environment, likely discourage participation by those who are not yet involved in gaming.

This reputation for toxicity is also problematic for the existing gaming community on a number of levels. Online hostility perpetuates and reifies existing stereotypes of gamers as immature and socially inept (Kowert, Festl, & Quandt, 2014). It may feed into nongamers' perceptions that games are useless and detrimental to individuals and society (Pew Research Center, 2015; Royse, Lee, Undrahbuyan, Hopson, & Consalvo, 2007). If gaming is to ascend the cultural hierarchy and be seen as a socially acceptable pastime or respected as an artistic medium by the general public, it must find ways to mitigate sexual harassment and promote equal representation and treatment of women and other underrepresented groups.

At the industry level, the lack of diversity contributes to the reification of certain viewpoints within games (Fron et al., 2007). The protagonists and story lines in many major titles are predictable and droll: gruff, White, muscular, heterosexual, cisgendered adult male with a traumatic event in his past seeks revenge or redemption by systematically killing his enemies. These homogeneous representations reflect the hegemony of both creators and the perceived audience. The growth of games as a medium and as an art form is stifled by a lack of diverse perspectives in the creative process as well as a continued focus to please the presumed target audience of young White male players. Recent efforts, however, have sought to make women and other underrepresented groups more visible as part of the gaming audience. For example, Tanya DePass originated the hashtag #INeedDiverseGames to ask developers to reflect their broad and multifaceted player base in the games they create.

In addition to more equitable hiring and representation, the gaming industry also needs to make consistent efforts to curtail sexism and sexual harassment across game content, game participation, and gaming events. Video game companies should be concerned with sexual harassment because many women avoid or quit games because of it (Fox & Tang, *in press*). Moreover, gaming companies need to visibly and publicly take a stand against harassment and have consequences for those who harass. If gaming companies are seeking motivation for taking action, they should be aware that their lack of responsiveness influences victims of sexual harassment to quit their games (Fox & Tang, *in press*) and likely hurts their bottom line. Some online games have made progress in curtailing harassment and reducing toxic interactions (Busch, Boudreau, & Consalvo, 2015). For example, Jeffrey Lin at Riot Games has led the successful implementation of a system designed to punish serial harassers in *League of Legends*. Lin's work is promising and presents a model for online games to follow.

Confronting sexism and sexual harassment in gaming would benefit players, the industry, and society as a whole. As researchers, we must acknowledge, assess, and consider the role that sexism and other forms of discrimination have on the participation and experiences of women and other marginalised identities in the realm of gaming. Our combined efforts may lay the groundwork for a brighter future in which women and other groups can participate more freely and are represented more fairly across games and the gaming community.

References

Ballard, M. E., & Welch, K. M. (*in press*). Virtual warfare: Cyberbullying and cyber-victimization in MMOG play. *Games & Culture*. doi: 10.1177/1555412015592473.

Barak, A. (2005). Sexual harassment on the internet. *Social Science Computer Review, 23*, 77–92. doi:10.1177/0894439304271540.

Beasley, B., & Standley, T. C. (2002). Shirts vs. skins: Clothing as an indicator of gender role stereotyping in video games. *Mass Communication & Society, 5*, 279–293. doi: 10.1207/S15327825MCS0503_3.

Behm-Morawitz, E., & Mastro, D. (2009). The effects of the sexualization of female video game characters on gender stereotyping and female self-concept. *Sex Roles, 61*, 808–823. doi: 10.1007/s11199-009-9683-8.

Behm-Morawitz, E., & Schipper, S. (*in press*). Sexing the avatar: Gender, sexualization, and cyber-harassment in a virtual world. *Journal of Media Psychology.* doi: 10.1027/1864-1105/a000152.

Blodgett, B. M., & Salter, A. (2013). Hearing "lady game creators" tweet: #1ReasonWhy, women, and online discourse in the game development community. Paper presented at the *Annual Conference of the Association for Internet Researchers* 14.0, Denver, CO.

Braithwaite, A. (2014). 'Seriously, get out': Feminists on the forums and the War (craft) on women. *New Media & Society, 16,* 703–718. doi: 10.1177/1461444813489503.

Breuer, J., Kowert, R., Festl, R., & Quandt, T. (2015). Sexist games = sexist gamers? A longitudinal study on the relationship between video game use and sexist attitudes. *Cyberpsychology, Behavior, & Social Networking, 18,* 197–202. doi: 10.1089/cyber.2014.0492.

Bryce, J. O., & Rutter, J. (2003). Gender dynamics and the social and spatial organization of computer gaming. *Leisure Studies, 22,* 1–15. doi: 10.1080/02614360306571.

Burgess, M. C. R., Stermer, S. P., & Burgess, S. R. (2007). Sex, lies, and video games: The portrayal of male and female characters on video game covers. *Sex Roles, 57,* 419–433. doi: 10.1007/s11199-007-9250-0.

Busch, T., Boudreau, K., & Consalvo, M. (2015). Toxic gamer culture, corporate regulation, and standards of behavior among players of online games. In S. Conway & J. DeWinter (Eds.), *Video game policy: Production, distribution, and consumption.* New York: Routledge.

Carr, D. (2005). Contexts, gaming pleasures, and gendered preferences. *Simulation & Gaming, 36,* 464–482.

Cassell, J., & Jenkins, H. (Eds.) (1998). *From Barbie to Mortal Kombat: Gender and computer games.* Cambridge: MIT Press.

Chalk, A. (2014, October 28). Researchers find that female PC gamers outnumber males. *PC Gamer.* Retrieved from http://www.pcgamer.com/researchers-find-that-female-pc-gamers-outnumber-males/.

Chess, S. (2011). A 36–24-36 cerebrum: Productivity, gender, and video game advertising. *Critical Studies in Media Communication, 28,* 230–252. doi: 10.1080/15295036.2010.515234.

Chess, S. (2014). Strange bedfellows: Subjectivity, romance, and hidden object video games. *Games & Culture, 9,* 417–428. doi: 10.1177/1555412014544904.

Chess, S., & Shaw, A. (2015). A conspiracy of fishes, or, how we learned to stop worrying about #GamerGate and embrace hegemonic masculinity. *Journal of Broadcasting & Electronic Media, 59,* 208–220. doi:10.1080/08838151.2014.999917.

Chou, C., & Tsai, M. J. (2007). Gender differences in Taiwan high school students' computer game playing. *Computers in Human Behavior, 23,* 812–824. doi: 10.1016/j.chb.2004.11.011.

Cole, H., & Griffiths, M. D. (2007). Social interactions in massively multiplayer online role-playing gamers. *CyberPsychology & Behavior, 10,* 575–583. doi: 10.1089/cpb.2007.9988.

Consalvo, M. (2008). Crunched by passion: Women game developers and workplace challenges. In Y. Kafai, C. Heeter, J. Denner, & J. Sun (Eds.),

Beyond Barbie and Mortal Kombat: New perspectives on gender and gaming (pp. 177–191). Cambridge: MIT Press.

Consalvo, M. (2012). Confronting toxic gamer culture: A challenge for feminist game studies scholars. *Ada: A Journal of Gender, New Media, and Technology, 1*. Retrieved from http://adanewmedia.org/2012/11/issue1-consalvo/.

Cote, A. C. (*in press-a*). "I can defend myself": Women's strategies for coping with harassment while gaming online. *Games & Culture*. doi: 10.1177/1555412015587603.

Cote, A. C. (*in press-b*). Writing "gamers": The gendered construction of gamer identity in *Nintendo Power* (1994–1999). *Games & Culture*. doi: 10.1177/1555412015624742.

De Grove, F., Courtois, C., & Van Looy, J. (2015). How to be a gamer! Exploring personal and social indicators of gamer identity. *Journal of Computer-Mediated Communication, 20,* 346–361. doi: 10.1111/jcc4.12114.

Dietz, T. L. (1998). An examination of violence and gender role portrayals in video games: Implications for gender socialization and aggressive behavior. *Sex Roles, 38,* 425–442. doi: 10.1023/A:1018709905920.

Dill, K. E., Brown, B. P., & Collins, M. A. (2008). Effects of exposure to sex-stereotyped video game characters on tolerance of sexual harassment. *Journal of Experimental Social Psychology, 44,* 1402–1408. doi: 10.1016/j.jesp.2008.06.002.

Dill, K. E., & Thill, K. P. (2007). Video game characters and the socialization of gender roles: Young people's perceptions mirror sexist media depictions. *Sex Roles, 57* (11), 851–864. doi: 10.1007/s11199-007-9278-1.

Downs, E., & Smith, S. L. (2010). Keeping abreast of hypersexuality: A video game character content analysis. *Sex Roles, 62,* 721–733. doi: 10.1007/s11199-009-9637-1.

ESA (Entertainment Software Association). (2015). *2015 sales, demographic and usage data: Essential facts about the computer and video game industry.* Washington, DC: Author.

Fisher, H. D. (2015). Sexy, dangerous-and ignored: An in-depth review of the representation of women in select video game magazines. *Games and Culture, 10,* 551–570. doi: 10.1177/1555412014566234.

Fisher, S. J., & Harvey, A. (2012). Intervention for inclusivity: Gender politics and indie game development. *Loading..., 7*(11). Retrieved from: http://journals.sfu.ca/loading/index.php/loading/article/viewArticle/118.

Fitzgerald, L. F., Drasgow, F., Hulin, C. L., Gelfand, M. J., & Magley, V. J. (1997). Antecedents and consequences of sexual harassment in organizations: A test of an integrated model. *Journal of Applied Psychology, 82,* 578–589. doi: 10.1037/0021-9010.82.4.578.

Fletcher, J. (2012, June 3). Sexual harassment in the world of video gaming. *BBC Online*. Retrieved from http://www.bbc.com/news/magazine-18280000.

Fox, J., & Bailenson, J. N. (2009). Virgins and vamps: The effects of exposure to female characters' sexualized appearance and gaze in an immersive virtual environment. *Sex Roles, 61,* 147–157. doi: 10.1007/s11199-009-9599-3.

Fox, J., Bailenson, J. N., & Tricase, L. (2013). The embodiment of sexualized virtual selves: The Proteus effect and experiences of self-objectification via avatars. *Computers in Human Behavior, 29,* 930–938. doi: 10.1016/j.chb.2012.12.027.

Fox, J., & Potocki, B. (2016). Lifetime video game consumption, interpersonal aggression, hostile sexism, and rape myth acceptance: A cultivation perspective. *Journal of Interpersonal Violence, 31,* 1912–1931.

Fox, J., Ralston, R. A., Cooper, C. K., & Jones, K. A. (2015). Sexualized avatars lead to women's self-objectification and acceptance of rape myths. *Psychology of Women Quarterly, 39,* 349–362. doi: 10.1177/0361684 314553578.

Fox, J., & Tang, W. Y. (2013, November). Harassment in online video games and predictors of video game sexism. Poster presented at the *99th Annual Conference of the National Communication Association,* Washington, DC.

Fox, J., & Tang, W. Y. (2014). Sexism in online video games: The role of conformity to masculine norms and social dominance orientation. *Computers in Human Behavior, 33,* 314–320. doi: 10.1016/j.chb.2013.07.014.

Fox, J., & Tang, W. Y. (*in press*). Women's experiences with harassment in online video games: Rumination, organizational responsiveness, withdrawal, and coping strategies. *New Media & Society.* doi: 10.1177/1461444 816635778.

Fron, J., Fullerton, T., Morie, J., & Pearce, C. (2007, September). The hegemony of play. In *Situated Play: Proceedings of Digital Games Research Association 2007 Conference.* (pp. 1–10). Tokyo, Japan: Author.

Frostling-Henningsson, M. (2009). First-person shooter games as a way of connecting to people: "Brothers in blood." *CyberPsychology & Behavior, 12,* 557–562. doi: 10.1089/cpb.2008.0345.

Ganguin, S., & Hoblitz, A. (2014). *High score & high heels: Berufsbiografien von Frauen in der Games-Industrie.* Berlin, Germany: Springer-Verlag.

Glick, P., & Fiske, S. T. (1996). The ambivalent sexism inventory: Differentiating hostile and benevolent sexism. *Journal of Personality & Social Psychology, 70,* 491–512. doi: 10.1037/0022-3514.70.3.491.

Glick, P., & Rudman, L. A. (2013). Sexism. In J. F. Dovidio, M. Hewstone, P. Glick, & V. M. Esses (Eds.), *The SAGE handbook of prejudice, stereotyping, and discrimination* (pp. 329–344). Washington, D.C.: Sage.

Gray, K. L. (2012a). Deviant bodies, stigmatized identities, and racist acts: Examining the experiences of African-American gamers in Xbox Live. *New Review of Hypermedia & Multimedia, 18,* 261–276. doi: 10.1080/ 13614568.2012.746740.

Gray, K. L. (2012b). Intersecting oppressions and online communities. *Information, Communication & Society, 15,* 411–428. doi: 10.1080/1369118X. 2011.642401.

Grooten, J., & Kowert, R. (2015). Going beyond the game: Development of gamer identities within societal discourse and virtual spaces. *Loading...,* 9(14). Retrieved March 16, 2016, from http://journals.sfu.ca/loading/index. php/loading/article/view/151.

Guegan, J., Moliner, P., & Buisine, S. (2015). Why are online games so self-involving: A social identity analysis of massively multiplayer online role-playing games. *European Journal of Social Psychology, 45,* 349–355. doi: 10.1002/ejsp.2103.

Hartmann, T., & Klimmt, C. (2006). Gender and computer games: Exploring females' dislikes. *Journal of Computer-Mediated Communication, 11,* 910–931. doi: 10.1111/j.1083-6101.2006.00301.x.

Higgin, T. (2009). Blackless fantasy: The disappearance of race in massively multiplayer online role-playing games. *Games & Culture, 4*, 3–26. doi: 10.1177/1555412008325477.

Holz Ivory, A., Fox, J., Waddell, T. F., & Ivory, J. D. (2014). Sex-role stereotyping is hard to kill: A field experiment measuring social responses to user characteristics and behavior in an online multiplayer first-person shooter game. *Computers in Human Behavior, 35*, 148–156. doi: 10.1016/j.chb.2014.02.026.

Hunt, C. J., & Gonsalkorale, K. (2014). Who cares what she thinks, what does he say? Links between masculinity, in-group bonding and gender harassment. *Sex Roles, 70*, 14–27. doi: 10.1007/s11199-013-0324-x.

Huntemann, N. B. (2013). Women in video games: The case of hardware production and promotion. In N. B. Huntemann & B. Aslinger (Eds.), *Gaming globally: Production, play, and place* (pp. 41–57). New York: Palgrave Macmillan.

International Game Developers Association. (2015). *Developer Satisfaction Survey 2015*. Author.

Ivory, J. D. (2006). Still a man's game: Gender representation in online reviews of video games. *Mass Communication & Society, 9*, 103–114. doi: 10.1207/s15327825mcs0901_6.

Jansz, J. (2005). The emotional appeal of violent video games for adolescent males. *Communication Theory, 15*, 219–241. doi: 10.1111/j.1468-2885.2005.tb00334.x.

Jansz, J., & Martens, L. (2005). Gaming at a LAN event: The social context of playing video games. *New Media & Society, 7*, 333–355. doi: 10.1177/1461444805052280.

Jenson, J., & De Castell, S. (2010). Gender, simulation, and gaming: Research review and redirections. *Simulation & Gaming, 41*, 51–71. doi: 10.1177/1046878109353473.

Jenson, J., & De Castell, S. (2013). Tipping points: Marginality, misogyny and videogames. *Journal of Curriculum Theorizing, 29*(2). Retrieved from: http://journal.jctonline.org/index.php/jct/article/view/474/pdf.

Johnson, R. (2014). Hiding in plain sight: Reproducing masculine culture at a video game studio. *Communication, Culture & Critique, 7*, 578–594. doi: 10.1111/cccr.12023.

Kafai, Y. B., Cook, M. S., & Fields, D. A. (2010). "Blacks deserve bodies too!": Design and discussion about diversity and race in a tween virtual world. *Games & Culture, 5*, 43–63. doi: 10.1177/1555412009351261.

Kasumovic, M. M., & Kuznekoff, J. H. (2015). Insights into sexism: Male status and performance moderates female-directed hostile and amicable behaviour. *PloS One, 10*(7). doi: 10.1371/journal.pone.0131613.

Kiesler, S., Sproull, L., & Eccles, J. S. (1985). Pool halls, chips, and war games: Women in the culture of computing. *Psychology of Women Quarterly, 9*, 451–462. doi: 10.1111/j.1471-6402.1985.tb00895.x.

Kowert, R., Festl, R., & Quandt, T. (2014). Unpopular, overweight, and socially inept: reconsidering the stereotype of online gamers. *Cyberpsychology, Behavior, & Social Networking, 17*, 141–146. doi: 10.1089/cyber.2013.0118.

Kuznekoff, J. H., & Rose, L. M. (2013). Communication in multiplayer gaming: Examining player responses to gender cues. *New Media & Society, 15*, 541–556. doi: 10.1177/1461444812458271.

Larsen, S. E., & Fitzgerald, L. F. (2011). PTSD symptoms and sexual harassment: The role of attributions and perceived control. *Journal of Interpersonal Violence, 26*, 2555–2567. doi: 10.1177/0886260510388284.

Lea, M., & Spears, R. (1991). Computer-mediated communication, deindividuation, and group decision-making. *International Journal of Man Machine Studies, 34*, 283–301. doi: 10.1016/0020-7373(91)90045-9.

Leonard, D. J. (2006). Not a hater, just keepin' it real: The importance of race- and gender-based game studies. *Games and Culture, 1*, 83–88. doi: 10.1177/1555412005281910.

Lin, H. (2008). Body, space and gendered gaming experiences: A cultural geography of homes, dormitories and cybercafes. In Y. Kafai, C. Heeter, J. Denner, & J. Sun (Eds.), *Beyond Barbie and Mortal Kombat: New perspectives on gender and gaming* (pp. 67–81). Cambridge, MA: MIT Press.

Lucas, K., & Sherry, J. L. (2004). Sex differences in video game play: A communication-based explanation. *Communication Research, 31*, 499–523. doi: 10.1177/0093650204267930.

Maass, A., Cadinu, M., Guarnieri, G., & Grasselli, A. (2003). Sexual harassment under social identity threat: The computer harassment paradigm. *Journal of Personality & Social Psychology, 85*, 853–870. doi: 10.1037/0022-3514.85.5.853.

Miller, M. K., & Summers, A. (2007). Gender differences in video game characters' roles, appearances, and attire as portrayed in video game magazines. *Sex Roles, 57*, 733–742. doi: 10.1007/s11199-007-9307-0.

Nauroth, P., Gollwitzer, M., Bender, J., & Rothmund, T. (2014). Gamers against science: The case of the violent video games debate. *European Journal of Social Psychology, 44*, 104–116. doi: 10.1002/ejsp.1998.

Nauroth, P., Gollwitzer, M., Bender, J., & Rothmund, T. (2015). Social identity threat motivates science-discrediting online comments. *PLOS ONE, 10*(2). doi: 10.1371/journal.pone.0117476.

Near, C. E. (2013). Selling gender: Associations of box art representation of female characters with sales for teen- and mature-rated video games. *Sex Roles, 68*, 252–269. doi: 10.1007/s11199-012-0231-6.

Pew Research Center. (2014). *Online harassment*. Washington, DC: Author. Retrieved from http://www.pewinternet.org/2014/10/22/online-harassment/.

Pew Research Center. (2015). *Gaming and gamers*. Washington, DC: Author. Retrieved from http://www.pewinternet.org/2015/12/15/gaming-and-gamers/.

Pina, A., Gannon, T.A., & Saunders, B. (2009). An overview of the literature on sexual harassment: Perpetrator, theory, and treatment issues. *Aggression & Violent Behavior, 14*, 126–138. doi: 10.1016/j.avb.2009.02.002.

Postmes, T., Spears, R., & Lea, M. (1998). Breaching or building social boundaries? SIDE effects of computer-mediated communication. *Communication Research, 25*, 689–715. doi: 10.1177/009365098025006006.

Prescott, J., & Bogg, J. (2013). *Gender divide and the computer game industry*. Hershey, PA: IGI Global.

Pryor, J. B. (1987). Sexual harassment proclivities in men. *Sex Roles, 17*, 269–290. doi: 10.1007/bf00288453.

Pryor, J. B., & Whalen, N. J. (1996). A typology of sexual harassment: Characteristics of harassers and the social circumstances under which sexual harassment occurs. In W. O'Donohue (Ed.), *Sexual harassment: Theory, research, and treatment* (pp. 129–151). Boston, MA: Allyn & Bacon.

Quandt, T., Chen, V., Mäyrä, F., & Van Looy, J. (2014). (Multiplayer) gaming around the globe? A comparison of gamer surveys in four countries. In T. Quandt & S. Kröger, *Multiplayer: The social aspects of digital gaming* (pp. 23–46). New York: Routledge.

Ritter, B. A. (2014). Deviant behavior in computer-mediated communication: Development and validation of a measure of cybersexual harassment. *Journal of Computer-Mediated Communication, 19*, 197–214. doi: 10.1111/jcc4.12039.

Royse, P., Lee, J., Undrahbuyan, B., Hopson, M., & Consalvo, M. (2007). Women and games: Technologies of the gendered self. *New Media & Society, 9*, 555–576. doi: 10.1177/1461444807080322.

Russell, B. L., & Trigg, K. Y. (2004). Tolerance of sexual harassment: An examination of gender differences, ambivalent sexism, social dominance, and gender roles. *Sex Roles, 50*, 565–573. doi: 10.1023/B:SERS.0000023075.32252.fd.

Salter, A., & Blodgett, B. (2012). Hypermasculinity & dickwolves: The contentious role of women in the new gaming public. *Journal of Broadcasting & Electronic Media, 56*, 401–416. doi: 10.1080/08838151.2012.705199.

Scharkow, M., Festl, R., Vogelgesang, J., & Quandt, T. (2015). Beyond the "core-gamer": Genre preferences and gratifications in computer games. *Computers in Human Behavior, 44*, 293–298. doi: 10.1016/j.chb.2014.11.020.

Scharrer, E. (2004). Virtual violence: Gender and aggression in video game advertisements. *Mass Communication & Society, 7*, 393–412. doi: 10.1207/s15327825mcs0704_2.

Schott, G., & Thomas, S. (2008). The impact of Nintendo's "For Men" advertising campaign on a potential female market. *Eludamos: Journal for Computer Game Culture, 2*, 41–52.

Shaw, A. (2012). Do you identify as a gamer? Gender, race, sexuality, and gamer identity. *New Media & Society, 14*, 28–44. doi: 10.1177/1461444811410394.

Shaw, A. (2015). *Gaming at the edge.* Minneapolis, MN: University of Minnesota Press.

Sibley, C. G., Wilson, M. S., & Duckitt, J. (2007). Antecedents of men's hostile and benevolent sexism: The dual roles of social dominance orientation and right-wing authoritarianism. *Personality & Social Psychology Bulletin, 33*, 160–172. doi:10.1177/0146167206294745.

Sidanius, J., & Pratto, F. (1999). *Social dominance: An intergroup theory of social hierarchy and oppression.* Cambridge: Cambridge University Press.

Smith, S. L. (2006). Perps, pimps, and provocative clothing: Examining negative content patterns in video games. In P. Vorderer & J. Bryant (Eds.), *Playing video games: Motives, responses, and consequences* (pp. 57–75). Mahwah, NJ: Erlbaum.

Suler, J. (2004). The online disinhibition effect. *Cyberpsychology & Behavior, 7*, 321–326. doi: 10.1089/1094931041291295.

Summers, A., & Miller, M. K. (2014). From damsels in distress to sexy superheroes: How the portrayal of sexism in video game magazines has changed in the last 20 years. *Feminist Media Studies, 14*, 1028–1040 doi: 10.1080/14680777.2014.882371.

Sutcliffe, A. G., Gonzalez, V., Binder, J., & Nevarez, G. (2011). Social mediating technologies: Social affordances and functionalities. *International*

Journal of Human-Computer Interaction, 27, 1037–1065. doi: 10.1080/10447318.2011.555318.

Tang, W. Y., & Fox, J. (*in press*). Male players' harassment behaviors in online video games: Personality traits and game factors. *Aggressive Behavior*.

Tangri, S. S., & Hayes, S. M. (1996). Theories of sexual harassment. In W. O'Donohue (Ed.), *Sexual harassment: Theory, research, and treatment* (pp. 112–128). Boston, MA: Allyn & Bacon.

Taylor, N., Jenson, J., & De Castell, S. (2009). Cheerleaders/booth babes/Halo hoes: pro-gaming, gender and jobs for the boys. *Digital Creativity*, 20, 239–252. doi: 10.1080/14626260903290323.

Taylor, T. L. (2006). *Play between worlds: Exploring online game culture*. Cambridge, MA: MIT Press.

Taylor, T. L. (2012). *Raising the stakes: E-sports and the professionalization of computer gaming*. Boston, MA: MIT Press.

Tomkinson, S., & Harper, T. (2015). The position of women in video game culture: Perez and Day's Twitter incident. *Continuum*, 29, 617–634.

Trepte, S., Reinecke, L., & Juechems, K. (2012). The social side of gaming: How playing online computer games creates online and offline social support. *Computers in Human Behavior*, 28, 832–839. doi:10.1016/j.chb.2011.12.003.

Vanderhoef, J. (2013). Casual threats: The feminization of casual video games. *Ada: A Journal of Gender, New Media, & Technology*, 2. Retrieved from: http://adanewmedia.org/2013/06/issue2-vanderhoef/.

Van Reijmersdal, E. A., Jansz, J., Peters, O., & Van Noort, G. (2013). Why girls go pink: Game character identification and game-players' motivations. *Computers in Human Behavior*, 29, 2640–2649. doi: 10.1016/j.chb.2013.06.046.

Vermeulen, L., & Van Looy, J. (2014). Happy together? A gender-comparative study into social practices in digital gaming. In T. Quandt & S. Kröger, *Multiplayer: The social aspects of digital gaming* (pp. 58–69). New York: Routledge.

Williams, D., Consalvo, M., Caplan, S., & Yee, N. (2009). Looking for gender: Gender roles and behaviors among online gamers. *Journal of Communication*, 59, 700–725. doi: 10.1080/00224490902954323.

Willness, C. R., Steel, P., & Lee, K. (2007). A meta-analysis of the antecedents and consequences of workplace sexual harassment. *Personnel Psychology*, 60, 127–162. doi: 10.1111/j.1744-6570.2007.00067.x.

Yao, M. Z., Mahood, C., & Linz, D. (2010). Sexual priming, gender stereotyping, and likelihood to sexually harass: Examining the cognitive effects of playing a sexually-explicit video game. *Sex Roles*, 62, 77–88. doi: 10.1007/s11199-009-9695-4.

Yee, N. (2008). Maps of digital desires: Exploring the topography of gender and play in online games. In Y. B. Kafai, C. Heeter, J. Denner, & J. Y. Sun, *Beyond Barbie and Mortal Kombat: New perspectives on gender and gaming* (pp. 83–96). Cambridge, MA: MIT Press.

Yee, N. (2014). *The Proteus paradox: How online games and virtual worlds change us--and how they don't*. New Haven, CT: Yale University Press.

9 Women Are From *FarmVille*, Men Are From *ViceCity*

The Cycle of Exclusion and Sexism in Video Game Content and Culture

*Rachel Kowert, Johannes Breuer,
and Thorsten Quandt*

From its early beginnings in the 1970s until today, video game play[1] has evolved from a niche activity to a mainstream activity enjoyed by millions of people worldwide. Representative data generated from the 2015 Pew Internet and American Life Project Survey reported that 49% of all American adults are active video game players (Duggan, 2015). The Entertainment Software Association (ESA) reports that 58% of American adults play video games (ESA, 2014), with 42% of Americans reporting regular game play of three hours per week or more (ESA, 2015). Similar rates of video game play among adults have also been found in other countries around the world, including Flanders (the Dutch-speaking part of Belgium; 41.2%) and Singapore (41.1%) (Quandt, Chen, Mayra, & Van Looy, 2014). University student samples and Internet-based samples typically report higher rates of video game play, with rates of around 90% (see Colwell & Kato, 2003; Kowert, Griffiths, & Oldmeadow, 2012; Salguero & Morán, 2002).

Although video game play has historically been a male-dominated leisure activity, with demographic reports consistently showing a disproportionate ratio of male to female players, recent reports indicate that female players now constitute between 44% (ESA, 2015) and 54.6% (Lucas & Sherry, 2004) of the American game playing community. An international comparison of video game player demographics by Quandt et al. (2014) also found that the gender gap in the diffusion rate of playing is not that large anymore. For Germany, the survey showed that 20.9% of females play video games (compared with 30.1% of males). In the other countries surveyed in this study, overall diffusion rates of playing were generally higher while the differences between males and females were less pronounced (Finland: 42.9% females, 57.6% among males; Flanders: 39.4% females, 43.0% males; Singapore: 48.0% females, 53.0% males).

Despite the diminishment in the gender divide among game players in recent years, there remains pronounced gender differences in relation to the frequency of, and motivations and preferences for video game play as well as the extent to which male and female players consider themselves a member of the 'gamer' community (for a review of the research in this area see Jenson & DeCastell, 2013; Richard, 2013). For example, several studies have noted that male players engage in video game play more often and for longer durations (Greenberg, Sherry, Lachlan, Lucas, & Holmstrom, 2010; Lucas & Sherry, 2004; Ogletree & Drake, 2007; Phan, Jardina, Hoyle, & Chaparro, 2012). Genre preferences also vary across gender lines (Carr, 2005; Greenberg et al., 2010; Hartmann, Möller, & Krause, 2014; Jansz & Tanis, 2007; Lucas & Sherry, 2004; Phan et al., 2012; Quandt et al., 2014; Van Looy et al., 2011; Vermeulen et al., 2011), with females reporting a strong preference for digital versions of traditional games (e.g. card/dice, board games, quiz/trivia) or other 'casual games' (i.e. games that do not require a special set of skills or a large time commitment to complete), whilst males prefer more 'core' genres (i.e. not casual), such as physical enactment (e.g. fighter, shooter, sports, racing/speed) and 'imagination' (e.g. fantasy/role playing, action/adventure, strategy, simulation) games. Female players also report a lower motivation to engage in video game play, for any reason (Greenberg et al., 2010; Lucas & Sherry, 2004; Phan et al., 2012; Van Looy et al., 2011; Van Reijmersdal, Jansz, Peters, & Van Noort, 2013) as well as are less likely than males to report video game play as their primary hobby (Phan et al., 2012). Male players are also twice as likely to call themselves gamers than are female players (15% vs 6%; Duggan, 2015).

These differences in engagement might seem puzzling, especially against the background of a diminishing gender divide in terms of the overall number of players. However, we believe that these differences can be attributed to an exclusion of females from the video game culture on three levels: (1) early media and gender socialization, (2) the video games industry, and (3) player communities. Together, these processes have created a cycle of exclusion and sexism for female players and, consequently, contributed to differences in levels of engagement in terms of participation within this medium as well as its associated industries and cultures. These levels of exclusion are discussed in more detail in the following sections.

The Exclusion of Females From Gaming Spaces: A Three-Tiered Process

Socialization: Gendered Media Spaces

The earliest and possibly also the most deeply rooted causes of exclusionary gaming culture are gender and media socialization processes in childhood and adolescence. From as early as kindergarten, video game play is typically seen as a more appropriate activity for boys than girls (Wilder, Mackie, & Cooper, 1985). This sex stereotyping has been found to extend into adulthood: adult males and females also report video game play to be more of a male-centric activity (Cruea & Park, 2012). These beliefs are further reinforced by the children's environment, as homes with a male child have been found to be more likely to own a video game console than homes with a female child (Woodard & Gridina, 2000). As an activity that is male-dominated and perceived as more appropriate for males from the point at which one can first hold a game controller or navigate a keyboard, the physical context in which games are played quickly becomes socially excluding for females. With video games being considered a "boy's toy" (Lucas & Sherry, 2004), females are more likely to be left out of group play and, if they do participate, are more likely to be rejected by their peers for engaging in behaviours that are stereotypically male (Greenberg et al., 2010; Kowert et al., 2012; Kowert & Oldmeadow, 2012; Lucas & Sherry, 2004; Van Looy et al., 2011; Walkerdine, 2004). As explained by Moller and colleagues (1992), "children who do not exhibit gender-appropriate behaviour are viewed as not fulfilling their gender role and are considered an anomaly. Such children may be actively rejected and alienated from their peers" (p. 333). Thus, young men are socially reinforced to engage in video game play whilst young women are discouraged from engaging in the same, cross-sex stereotyped activity. As such, video games provide opportunities for young boys to meet social needs for inclusion and affection but do not serve the same functions for young girls. The socialization of video game play as a "boy's toy" has led to video games being perceived as male-centric activities and the exclusion of females from participation at an early age.

This early process of gender socialization and sex stereotyping is also believed to influence the uses and gratifications male and female players become capable of obtaining from video game play itself (Lucas & Sherry, 2004). The early socialization of video games as a male activity can discourage females from engaging in video game play and contribute to their overall reduced motivation to participate. Consequently, female players are less likely to derive satisfaction from playing, such as feelings of social inclusion or acceptance (Hartmann & Klimmt, 2006a; Lucas & Sherry, 2004; Sherry, Greenberg, Lucas, & Lachlan, 2006). These differences are likely to also be the cause of females reporting less engagement with video games play than their male counterparts, in terms of play frequency, preferences, and the role that 'gaming' plays in their everyday lives. A recent experimental study by Kaye and Pennington (2016) has also found that confronting female players with the stereotype that male players typically outperform their female counterparts reduces female players' performance in a game. This process, known as stereotype threat, is another mechanism that likely contributes to the exclusion or marginalization of female gamers.

The Video Game Industry: Male Producers = Male Content?

Despite being one of the fastest growing industries of the 21st century (Krotoski, 2004), women are vastly underrepresented in all roles and levels within the video game industry (Prescott & Bogg, 2013). Although it is not clear why this is the case, it is possible that due to early socialization processes, males are given a head start in the acquisition of gaming literacy (Klimmt, 2009), contributing to advantage in both video game skills and knowledge. Consequently, the industry has become dominated by males and has been described as a "culture of masculinity" (Valenduc, et al., 2004).

Possibly in part due to the underrepresentation of women in game development, the video games industry has largely failed to provide game content that is relevant and relatable for female players or, at the very least, not offensive to the female members of the game-playing community (similar arguments have been made for the representation of females in film; Smith, Choueti, & Pieper, 2014). For example, many video game titles that have emerged from major game development studios contain competitive features and/or gratuitous use of violence, both of which are elements of video games that are particularly off-putting to female players (Hartmann & Klimmt, 2006a; Phan et al., 2012). Content analyses of video games have also consistently found women to be largely underrepresented within this medium (Beasley & Standley, 2002; Dietz, 1998; Downs & Smith, 2010; Ivory, 2006; Miller & Summers, 2007). A 2001 report by Children NOW found that only 16% of all video game characters are female, with 50% being portrayed as props or bystanders. In 2002, Beasley and Standley found similar results when they coded the characters in 47 video games that were randomly selected from the *Nintendo 64* and *PlayStation* consoles. Of the 597 game characters that were identified and coded, only 13.74% (82) were female. A study by Waddell et al. (2014) also found that female characters are also underrepresented in Massively Multiplayer Online Games.

Of the few female characters, and even fewer female protagonists (e.g. Lara Croft from the *Tomb Raider* Series) that do exist in video games, many are portrayed in ways that are vastly different to their male counterparts (Beasley & Standley, 2002; Children NOW, 2001; Dietz, 1998; Downs & Smith, 2010; Fox, Bailenson, & Tricase, 2013; Ivory, 2006; Jansz & Martis, 2007; Miller & Summers, 2007). For example, Beasley and Standley (2002) found that the large majority of female characters in video games expose more skin than male characters. Echoing the finding of the study by Beasley and Standley (2002), Dill and Thill (2007) found that female game characters were more likely to be scantily clad than male characters (39% vs 8%) as well as more likely to be sexualised than male characters (60% vs 1%). In a similar analysis, Downs and Smith (2010) found that female characters were 10 times more likely to be shown nude (partially or fully) than male characters. These differences in clothing are not trivial, as clothing can be viewed as a prime indicator of sex roles in society, even in video games (Duncan, 1990; Riffe, Place, & Mayo, 1993).

Video game content, in terms of game narratives, is also often male-centric, particularly within specific genres. For example, the popular *Grand Theft Auto* series includes a vast array of content that female players may find offensive or demeaning (Dickey, 2006), such as visiting a strip club, hiring a prostitute, or rescuing 'helpless' female characters. In fact, several tropes that commonly enlisted in video game narratives depict women in unflattering and chauvinist ways, such as "Damsel in Distress" (i.e. where a female must be rescued by a male hero) and the "Ms. Male Character" (where a female character is simply an established male character with stereotypical female identifiers, such as *Ms. Pac-Man*; Sarkeesian, 2013a, 2013b).

By primarily enlisting male-centric narratives, largely failing to provide female characters (particularly protagonists), and oversexualising the few female characters that are available, many video game developers contribute to the proliferation of the cliché that video games are primarily "boy's toys". These trends in video game designs, particularly among mainstream video game titles, creates an exclusionary atmosphere for female players by limiting their ability to identify with protagonists or relate to the in-game content, both of which are important factor for enjoyment of the medium (Trepte & Reinecke, 2010; Van Looy, Courtois, De Vocht, & De Marez, 2012).

The Players: Causes and Effects of Sexist Attitudes and Behaviour

Cultivation of Sexist Beliefs and Attitudes

Apart from being deterrents for female players, the under- and misrepresentation of female characters in video games might also have an impact on attitudes and beliefs of the players. As proposed by cultivation theory (Gerbner, Gross, Morgan, & Signorielli, 1994), long-term media consumption can influence a user's view of the world and contribute to changes in real-world beliefs, attitudes, and actions, towards one that is represented by the media content. Although cultivation theory was originally developed to explain the impact of television and film, it has also been applied to the influential power of video games on players' attitudes and beliefs (Behm-Morawitz & Ta, 2014; Breuer,

Kowert, Festl, Quandt, 2015; Festl, Scharkow, & Quandt, 2013; Van Mierlo & Van den Bulck, 2004; Williams, 2006). In fact, the ability for video games to cultivate beliefs, attitudes, and behaviours is believed to be particularly influential because of games' ability to 'teach' its users through active participation and interactivity within the medium (Downs & Smith, 2010). Therefore, from a theoretical standpoint, exposure to media where women are infrequently represented and portrayed in a highly stereotyped, and often sexualised, manner holds the potential to cultivate and/or reinforce biased gender roles or sexist beliefs. Empirically, however, there is mixed evidence regarding cultivation effects in general and on sexist beliefs and attitudes in particular. An experimental study by Dill, Brown, and Collins (2008) found that males exposed to stereotypical video game representations of women were more tolerant of sexual harassment. Similarly, Stermer and Burkley (2012) demonstrated that men who play video games that feature sexist content score higher on measures of benevolent sexism. However, this research has exclusively enlisted cross-sectional designs and/or has assessed only the short-term effects of video game exposure, making it difficult to conclude if video game play is cultivating sexist beliefs over time or if there may be a selection effect of sexism and game play (i.e. individuals with more sexist beliefs and attitudes are drawn to video games). In the only known longitudinal study of the cultivation of traditional sexist attitudes among video game players, no casual links were found (Breuer et al., 2015).

Although previous research has failed to demonstrate causal, cultivation links, the findings of the cross-sectional research in this area and the theoretical underpinnings of cultivation theory suggest that sexist game content may be a source of the gender divide in terms of video game engagement (e.g. play frequency, preference) as well as contributing to the exclusionary atmosphere of gaming communities through the cultivation of sexist beliefs.

Misogyny and Sexual Harassment in (Online) Player Communities

Various elements of "toxic gamer culture" (Consalvo, 2012), including the sexist and misogynistic climate of online gaming environments, have been well-documented by players themselves. Websites such as *Not in the Kitchen Anymore* (www.notinthekitchenanymore.com) and *Fat, Ugly, or Slutty* (www.fatuglyorslutty.com) have archived some of the offensive, sexist, and misogynistic comments that have been directed towards female video game players. Browsing these websites reveals that the majority of comments are sexual in nature, such as requests for sexual favors (*"1600 [in-game] gold for nude picture"*) or verbal sexual assaults (*"How did my genitals feel on your face?"*).

There are also numerous documentations of gender-based insults (*"[I hate losing] especially when it's a bitch"*, *"whore"*, *"slut"*) and comments expressing how female players are not capable of being real 'gamers' (*"... did you get those achievements or did your boy-friend?"*). There are also much more explicit comments that depict or threaten bodily harm (*"What do you tell a woman with two black eyes? You don't need to tell her anything because she's already been told... twice"*). Perhaps the most notable instance of misogynistic ha-rassment within the video game playing community has been the back-lash that was directed towards Anita Sarkeesian, who is the creator of *Feminist Frequency* (www.feministfrequency.com). When seeking funding for her *"Tropes vs Women"* video series, which aimed to high-light the ways in which women are commonly being portrayed in video games, Sarkeesian turned to the crowd-funding platform, *Kickstarter*. Almost immediately after posting her project, she became the vic-tim of a series of terrifying verbal attacks by members of the gam-ing community, which included threats of rape and murder (Dolan, 2013). The aggressors also constructed a rudimentary video game that showed Sarkeesian being physically injured, entitled *"Beat Up Anita Sarkeesian"* (Garcia, 2012).

Although from a scientific viewpoint, these examples provide only what is commonly referred to as anecdotal evidence – albeit in large quantities – researchers have also more systematically documented the presence of sexist, misogynistic, and offensive behaviour in online gaming communities. An informal survey study of online gamers con-ducted in 2012 found that 79.3% of the respondents believe that sexism is prominent in the gaming community, with women being four times more likely than male players to experience sex-based taunting or ha-rassment (Matthew, 2012). Similarly, in a survey of *World of Warcraft* players, Brehm (2013) found that 63.6% of the female respondents reported that they had experienced sexism or misogynistic behaviour from other players, whereas only 11.6% of male respondents reported such experiences. The perception of the extent to which this kind of behaviour was problematic also differed between genders, with 45.3% of female participants reporting that sexism is a problem in *World of Warcraft* but only 27.5% of the male players held the same opinion. An observational study by Kuznekoff and Rose (2012) further confirmed the presence of sex-based discrimination in online gaming spaces; they found that if an avatar is being controlled by a woman (as signified by hearing a woman's voice in the game), players will experience three times as many negative comments compared with hearing a male's voice or no voice, regardless of in-game performance. In an attempt to avoid gender-based discrimination within these spaces, females seem to have developed a range of strategies, such as obscuring or not dis-closing their sex and choosing to play male avatars and/or male or neutral user names (Fox & Tang, 2016; Gray, 2012; Matthew, 2012). Many female players have also reported that they have considered or actually did quit playing video games temporarily, or quit playing a certain game permanently, because of sexual harassment (Matthew, 2012). A recent survey study by Fox & Tang (2016) among female online gamers found that the relationship between sexual harassment experiences and the intention to withdraw from a game is moderated by the responsiveness of the video game company, suggesting that it is important if and how video game companies react to and handle reports of sexual harassment.

Recent editorial articles by Kowert (2014) and McIntosh (2014) also highlight the sex-based discriminations that game playing females often experience as well as discuss how these attitudes, beliefs, and behaviours are dangerously close to becoming an accepted part of gamer cultures. Although Kowert (2014) discusses the current "gamer identity crisis" more generally, with sexism and misogyny being one of the emerging features of these communities, McIntosh (2014) highlights the range of 'invisible benefits' that male game players enjoy and, consequently, the range of limitations that are involuntarily imposed upon female game players simply because of their gender. Such examples included never being asked to one's credibility as a gamer, not having to be harassed at gaming events or conventions, and never being told that video games or the surrounding culture is not intended for them, simply because of their gender.

With regard to the motivations for harassment targeted at female players in online games there has been much speculation. An experimental study by Kasumovic and Kuznekoff (2015) found that lower skill and poor performance in an online shooter game were associated with an increased hostility towards a female teammate. Based on their findings, the authors of this study conclude that lower-skilled players feel more threatened in their status by the entrance of a female player and, hence, react more negatively. Because this study was based on observational data from individual online matches, it may also be that – in the long run – the causality is reversed. That is, that harassing other players distracts from the actual performance and thus negatively impacts it. On a longitudinal scale, this could also be a reciprocal process: poor performance increases harassment, which (further) reduces performance. A survey among male online players by Tang and Fox (2016) sheds some further light on the potential reasons for harassment in online games. The authors found that social dominance orientation and hostile sexism predicted men's harassment behaviour in online games as did high game involvement. Taken together, these results suggest that some male players may view female players as a threat to their social identity and therefore attempt to demonstrate their superiority and defend what they to be consider 'their' domain by insulting and harassing female players.

An Integrated Model of Exclusion and Sexism in Video Game Content and Culture

Taken together, early socialization processes, the predominance of males in the video game industry, and cultivation processes may be contributing to a cyclical process of exclusion and sexism in video game content and culture that reinforces the gender divide in gaming communities that we see today (see Figure 9.1). The first two components (i.e. gender socialization processes and the lack of females in the video gaming

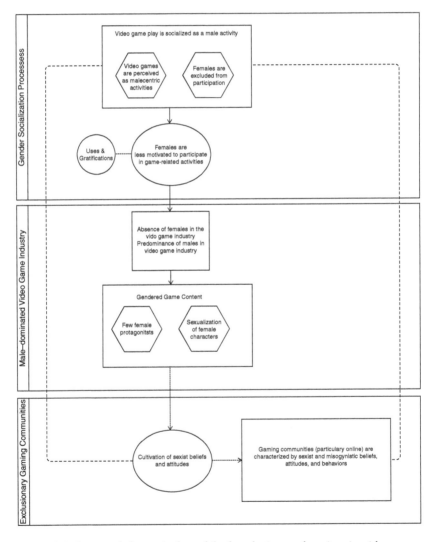

Figure 9.1 Proposed theoretical model of exclusion and sexism in video game content and culture.

industry) directly contribute to lower rates of active participation in, and motivation for, interacting within video game–playing communities and industries among females. Consequently, these processes of exclusion are also likely to contribute to the sexist and misogynistic cultures that have come to characterise many online gaming communities. This third component of the model (i.e. "exclusionary gaming communities") may be the crux for why gender differences in video game engagement within gaming communities and industries persist despite the popularization and growth of the medium.

Although previous research has noted cross-sectional relationships between video game use and sexist beliefs and attitudes (e.g. Dill et al., 2008; Stermer & Burkley, 2012), the theoretical underpinnings of these findings have often been linked to singular processes, such as gender socialization processes or the male-dominated video games industry. Our proposed model of exclusion and sexism in video game content and culture is the first to synthesise previous theoretical and empirical work in this area to create a more comprehensive model for understanding the perpetuation of sexism and exclusion of females within gaming content, culture, and industry. This model is built on the basic idea that gender socialization processes and the male-dominated video game industry and content contribute to the proliferation of sexist attitudes and behaviour among game players. Although cross-sectional work supports these suppositions, the exact causalities in these relationships warrant further investigation through longitudinal work.

Conclusion

It seems that a cycle of exclusion and sexism in gaming exists and persists despite changes in both the composition of the game-playing population and the video games market. As outlined by our model of sexism and exclusion in the video game culture (see Figure 9.1) there is no single cause or solution to this problem. To diminish gender differences in the access to video games, however, a combination of several measures might help. In addition to stronger penalties for sexual harassment and misogyny in games and gaming communities (enforced by the gaming companies, forum moderators, etc.), there is a need for an increased awareness for the subject as well as efforts to increase the number of women working in the video games industry. Measures like these could help to make reduce the social reinforcement of misogynist behaviour among game players, while at the same time help to dissipate the exclusionary climate of this activity for female players. Ultimately, it will take the combined efforts of the player community, the industry, and educators to break the cycle of sexism and exclusion that has been troubling video games for too long already.

Note

1 In this context, video game play refers to all digital games played via console, computer, or handheld device.

References

Beasley, B., & Standley, T. C. (2002). Shirts vs. skins: Clothing as an indicator of gender role stereotyping in video games. *Mass Communication & Society*, 5(3), 279–293.

Behm-Morawitz, E., & Ta, D. (2014). Cultivating virtual stereotypes? The impact of video game play on racial/ethnic stereotypes. *Howard Journal of Communication*, 25(1), 1–15. doi:10.1080/10646175.2013.835600.

Brehm, A. (2013). Navigating the feminine in massively multiplayer online games: Gender in World of Warcraft. *Frontiers in Psychology*, 4, 1–12.

Breuer, J., Kowert, R., Festl, R., & Quandt, T. (2015). Sexist games = sexist gamers? A longitudinal study on the relationship between video game use and sexist attitudes. *Cyberpsychology, Bheavior, and Social Networking*, 18(4), 197–202. doi: 10.1089/cyber.2014.0492.

Carr, D. (2005). Contexts, gaming pleasures, and gendered preferences. *Simulation & Gaming*, 36(4), 464–482.

Children NOW. (2001). *Fair play? Violence, gender, and race in video games*.

Colwell, J., & Kato, M. (2003). Investigation of the relationship between social isolation, self-esteem, aggression and computer game play in Japanese adolescents. *Asian Journal of Social Psychology*, 6, 149–158.

Consalvo, M. (2012). Confronting toxic gamer culture. *Journal of Gender, New Media and Technology*. doi:10.7264/N33X84KH.

Cruea, M., & Park, S.-Y. (2012). Gender disparity in video game usage: a third-person perception-based explanation. *Media Psychology*. doi:10.1080/15213269.2011.648861.

Dickey, M. D. (2006). Girl gamers: The controversy of girl games and the relevance of female oriented design for instructional design. *British Journal of Educational Technology*, 37(5), 785–793.

Dietz, T. L. (1998). An examination of violence and gender role portrayals in video games: Implications for gender socialization and aggressive behavior. *Sex Roles*, 38(516), 425–442.

Dill, K., Brown, B. P., & Collins, M. A. (2008). Effects of exposure to sex-stereotyped video game characters on tolerance of sexual harassment. *Sex Roles*, 44, 1402–1408.

Dill, K., & Thill, K. P. (2007). Video game characters and the socilization of gender roles: Young people's perceptions mirror sexist media depictions. *Sex Roles*, 57, 851–864.

Dolan, E. W. (2013). Anita Sarkeesian explains fight against "cyber mob" of misogynistic trolls. *The Raw Story*. Retrieved from http://www.rawstory.com/rs/2013/04/18/anita-sarkeesian-explains-fight-against-cyber-mob-of-misogynistic-trolls/.

Downs, E., & Smith, S. L. (2010). Keeping abreast of hypersexuality: A video game character content analysis. *Sex Roles*, 62, 721–733.

Duggan, M. (2015). *Gaming and gamers.* Pew Internet and American Life Project. Retrieved from http://www.pewinternet.org/2015/12/15/gaming-and-gamers/.

Duncan, M. C. (1990). Sports photographs and sexual differences: Images of women and men in the 1984 and 1988 Olympic Games. *Sociology of Sport Journal, 7*, 22–43.

Entertainment Software Association. (2014). GamePlayer Data. www.theesa. com. Retrieved from http://www.theesa.com/facts/index.asp.

Entertainment Software Association. (2015). Essential facts about the computer and video game industry. www.theesa.com. Retrieved from http://www.theesa. com/wp-content/uploads/2015/04/ESA-Essential-Facts-2015.pdf.

Festl, R., Scharkow, M., & Quandt, T. (2013). Militaristic attitudes and the use of digital games. *Games and Culture, 8*(6), 392–407.

Fox, J., Bailenson, J., & Tricase, L. (2013). The embodiment of sexualized virtual selves: The Proteus effect and experiences of self-objectification via avatars. *Computers in Human Behavior, 29*, 930–938.

Fox, J., & Tang, W. Y. (2016). Women's experiences with general and sexual harrassment in online video games: Rumination, organizational responsiveness, withdrawal, and coping strategies. *New Media & Society.* Advance online publication. doi: 10.1177/1461444816635778.

Garcia, A. (2012). Violent video game targets feminist blogger. *The raw story.* Retrieved from http://www.rawstory.com/rs/2012/07/08/violent-video-game-targets-feminist-blogger/.

Gerbner, G., Gross, L., Morgan, M., & Sign, orielli, N. (1994). Growing up with television: The cultivation perspective BT - Media effects: Advances in theory and research. In J. Bryant & D. Zillman (Eds.), *Media effects: Advances in theory and research* (pp. 17–41). Hillsdale, NJ: Lawrence Erlbaum Associates.

Gray, K. (2012). Intersecting oppressions and online communities. *Information, Communication & Society, 15*(3), 411–428.

Greenberg, B., Sherry, J., Lachlan, K., Lucas, K., & Holmstrom, A. (2010). Orientations to video games among gender and age groups. *Simulation & Gaming, 41*(2), 238–259.

Hartmann, T., & Klimmt, C. (2006). Gender and computer games: Exploring females' dislikes. *Journal of Computer-Mediated Communication, 11*(4).

Hartmann, T., Möller, I., & Krause, C. (2014). Factors underlying male and female use of violent video games. *New Media and Society, 17*(1), 1777–1794.

Ivory, J. (2006). Still a man's game: Gender representation in online reviews of video games. *Mass Communication & Society, 9*(1), 103–114.

Jansz, J., & Martis, R. G. (2007). The Lara phenomenon: Powerful female characters in video games. *Sex roles, 56*(3–4), 141–148.

Jansz, J., & Tanis, M. (2007). Appeal of playing online first person shooter games. *Cyberpsychology, Behavior, and Social Networking, 10*(1), 133–136.

Jenson, J., & DeCastell, S. (2013). Tipping points: Marginality, Misogyny, and videogames. *Journal of Curriculum Theorizing, 29*(2), 72–85.

Kasumovic, M. M., & Kuzenkoff, J. H. (2015). Insights into sexism: Male status and performance moderates female-directed hostile and amicable behaviour. *PLoS ONE, 10*(7), e0131613. doi: 10.1371/journal.pone.0131613.

Kaye, L. K., & Pennington, C. R. (2016). "Girls can't play": The effects of stereotype threat on females' gaming performance. *Computers in Human Behavior, 59*, 202–209. doi: 10.1016/ab.21646.

Klimmt, C. (2009). Key dimensions of contemporary video game literacy: Towards a normative model of the competent digital gamer. *Eludamos. Journal for Computer Game Culture, 3*(1), 23–31.

Kowert, R. (2014). The gamer identity crisis: Towards a reclamation. *First Person Scholar*. Retrieved March 05, 2014, from http://www.firstpersonscholar.com/the-gamer-identity-crisis/.

Kowert, R., Griffiths, M. D., & Oldmeadow, J. A. (2012). Geek or chic? Emerging stereotypes of online gamers. *Bulletin of Science, Technology & Society, 32*(6), 471–479. doi:10.1177/0270467612469078.

Kowert, R., & Oldmeadow, J. A. (2012). The stereotype of online gamers: New characterization or recycled prototype. In *Nordic DiGRA: Games in Culture and Society Conference Proceedings*. Tampere, Finland: DiGRA.

Krotoski, A. (2004). Chicks and joysticks: An exporation of women in gaming. Entertainment and Leisure Software Publishers Association (ELSPA).

Kuznekoff, J. H., & Rose, L. M. (2012). Communication in multiplayer gaming: Examining player responses to gender cues. *New Media & Society, 15*(4), 541–556.

Lucas, K., & Sherry, J. (2004). Sex differences in video game play: A communication-based explanation. *Communication Research, 31*(5), 499–523.

Matthew, E. (2012). Sexism in video games: There is sexism in gaming. Pricecharting.com. Retrieved from http://blog.pricecharting.com/2012/09/emilyami-sexism-in-video-games-study.html.

McIntosh, J. (2014). Playing with privilege: The invisible benefits of gaming while male. Polygon. Retrieved April 28, 2014, from http://www.polygon.com/2014/4/23/5640678/playing-with-privilege-the-invisible-benefits-of-gaming-while-male.

Miller, M. K., & Summers, A. (2007). Gender differences in video game characters' roles, appearances, and attire as portrayed in video game magazines. *Sex Roles, 57*, 733–742.

Moller, L. C., Hymel, S., & Rubin, K. H. (1992). Sex typing in play and popularity in middle childhood. *Sex Roles, 26*, 331–353.

Ogletree, S. M., & Drake, R. (2007). College students' video game participation and perceptions: Gender differences and implications. *Sex Roles*. doi:10.1007/s11199-007-9193-5.

Phan, M. H., Jardina, J. R., Hoyle, S., & Chaparro, B. S. (2012). Examining the role of gender in video game usage, preference, and behavior. *Proceedings of the Human Factors and Ergonomics Society Annual Meeting, 56*, 1496–1500.

Prescott, J., & Bogg, J. (2013). The gendered identity of women in the games industry. *Eludamos. Journal for Computer Game Culture, 7*(1), 55–67.

Quandt, T., Chen, V., Mayra, F., & Van Looy, J. (2014). (Multiplayer) gaming around the globe? A comparison of gamer surveys in four countries. In T. Quandt & S. Kroger (Eds.), *Multiplayer. Social aspects of digital gaming* (pp. 23–46). London: Routledge.

Richard, G. T. (2013). Gender and gameplay: Research and future directions. In B. Bigl & S. Stoppe (Eds.), *Playing with virtuality: Theories and methods of computer game studies* (pp. 269–284). Frankfurt: Peter Lang Academic.

Riffe, D., Place, P. C., & Mayo, C. M. (1993). Game time, soap time and prime time TV ads: Treatment of women in Sunday football and rest-of-week advertising. *Journalism Quarterly, 70*, 437–446.

Salguero, R., & Morán, R. (2002). Measuring problem video game playing in adolescents. *Addiction, 97*(12), 1601–1606.

Sarkeesian, A. (2013a). Damsel in distress: Part 1. (A. Sarkeesian, Ed.). Feminist frequency. Retrieved from http://www.youtube.com/watch?v=X6p5AZp7r_Q.

Sarkeesian, A. (2013b). Ms. male character. (A. Sarkeesian, Ed.). Feminist frequency. Retrieved from http://www.youtube.com/watch?v=eYqYLfm1rWA.

Sherry, J., Greenberg, B., Lucas, S., & Lachlan, K. (2006). Video game uses and gratifications as predictors of use and game preference BT - Playing computer games: Motives, responses and consequences. In P. Vorder & J. Bryant (Eds.), *Playing computer games: Motives, responses and consequences.* Mahwah, NJ: Erlbaum.

Smith, S. L., Choueti, M., & Pieper, K. (2014). Gender bias without borders: An investigation of female characters in popular films across 11 countries. USC Annenberg: Media, Diversity, & Social Changes Initiative.

Stermer, S. P., & Burkley, M. (2012). SeX-Box: Exposure to sexist video games predicts benevolent sexism. *Psychology of Popular Media Culture.*

Tang, W. Y., & Fox, J. (2016). Men's harassment behavior in online video games: Personality traits and game factors. *Aggressive Behavior.* doi: 10.1002/ab.21646.

Trepte, S., & Reinecke, L. (2010). Avatar creation and video game enjoyment. *Journal of Media Psychology: Theories, Methods, and Applications.* doi:10.1027/1864-1105/a000022.

Valenduc, G., Vendramin, P., Guffens, C., Ponzellini, A. M., Lebano, A., d'Ouville, L., ... & Webster, J. (2004). *Widening women's work in information and communication technology.* European Commission.

Van Looy, J., Courtois, C., De Vocht, M., & De Marez, L. (2012). Player identification in online games: Validation of a scale for measuring identification in MMOGs. *Media Psychology.* doi:10.1080/15213269.2012.674917.

Van Looy, J., Courtois, C., & Vermeulen, L. (2011). Why girls play digital games: An empirical study into the relations between gender, motivations, and genre. In *DiGRA 2011 Conference: Think Design Play.* Hilversum.

Van Mierlo, J., & Van den Bulck, J. (2004). Benchmarking the cultivation approach to video game effects: a comparison of the correlates of TV viewing and game play. *Journal of Adolescence, 27*, 97–111.

Van Reijmersdal, E. A., Jansz, J., Peters, O., & Van Noort, G. (2013). Why girls go pink: Game character identification and game-players' motivations. *Computers in Human Behavior, 29*, 2640–2649. doi:10.1016/j.chb.2013.06.046.

Vermeulen, L., Van Looy, J., De Grove, F., & Courtois, C. (2011). You are what you play? A quantitative study into game design preferences across gender and their interaction with gaming habits. In *DiGRA 2011 Conference: Think Design Play.* Hilversum.

Waddell, T. F., Ivory, J. D., Conde, R., Long, C., & McDonnell, R. (2014). White man's virtual world: A systematic content analysis of gender and race in massively multiplayer online games. *Journal of Virtual Worlds Research, 7*(2).

Walkerdine, V. (2004). Remeber not to die: Young girls and video games. *Papers: Explorations into Children's Literature, 14*(2).

Wilder, G., Mackie, D., & Cooper, J. (1985). Gender and computers: Two surveys of computer related attitudes. *Sex Roles, 13,* 215–228.

Williams, D. (2006). Virtual Cultivation: Online Worlds, Offline Perceptions. *Journal of Communication, 56,* 69–87.

Woodard, E. H., & Gridina, N. (2000). *Media in the home 2000: The fifth annual survey of parents and children.* Philadelphia: Annenberg Public Policy Center of the University of Pennsylvania.

Part IV
Games for Change

10 The Key Features of Persuasive Games

A Model and Case Analysis

Ruud S. Jacobs, Jeroen Jansz, and Teresa de la Hera Conde-Pumpido

Digital games are increasingly being recognized as more than entertainment media by policymakers, the industry, and idealistic developers. They are claimed to be able to alter players' worldviews and change the way they think (Connolly, Boyle, MacArthur, Hainey, & Boyle, 2012). This view has been advocated strongly by the Games for Change platform that aims to 'catalyze social impact through digital games' ("Games for Change," n.d.). Some researchers believe games influence players on an abstract level by, for example, making players feel empowered and teaching them the virtues of confidence and persistence (Granic, Lobel, & Engels, 2013; McGonigal, 2011; Neys, Jansz, & Tan, 2014). Others have theorized the ability for games to promote societal change by focusing on specific knowledge, skills, and attitudes in players; for instance, by foregrounding the game's rhetorical potential (Bogost, 2007). Such games are tailor-made to serve a particular purpose, such as teaching math, promoting healthy diets, or considering humanitarian crises in the Global South. These games are generally labelled as 'serious games', with subdivisions as educational games, advertising games, and health games, among others.

This chapter will discuss *persuasive games* as a subset of serious games. We have embedded our definition of persuasive games in current theorising about persuasion (O'Keefe, 2002), defining them as serious games made with the primary intention of changing or reinforcing specific attitudes (O'Keefe, 2002), where an attitude is defined as "a learned, global evaluation of an object (person, place or issue)" (Perloff, 2014, p. 71). Although many games have this intention, we looked at games that place this intention front and center by being free to play. The present chapter aims to deepen our insight into the nature and possible impact of persuasive games by analyzing several existing games that are united in their intentions to change or reinforce attitudes. This investigation was aimed at answering the following research question: How are persuasive games equipped to persuade their players and maximize their impact?

Because the research field focusing particularly on persuasive games is nascent, most previous research cited a handful of examples of games that were made to persuade, like *Darfur is Dying* (Cohen, 2014;

Peng, Lee, & Heeter, 2010), *Food Force* (Raessens, 2015), *PeaceMaker* (Alhabash & Wise, 2012; Neys & Jansz, 2010) and *September 12th* (Bogost, 2007). Given the dynamic sociopolitical context these games are published in, we find it necessary to provide the community of game researchers with a broader set of contemporary examples of how these games aim to persuade players. However, because of the variety in the themes, styles, and formats of persuasive games, it is impossible to represent all forms of this genre in one study; therefore, we discuss in detail a set of 11 games that are playable online at the time of writing to serve as exemplary cases. Each case shows in its own way how a game can convey certain messages and how the message is translated into the game's operations. The focus of the current study is on manifest game content. By playing these games, we analysed them to determine how the persuasive elements emerged. This means that we did not study the games' actual impacts on their players. In sum, this chapter investigates 11 exemplar cases of contemporary persuasive games to get a better understanding of the elements that game developers use to persuade players.

A Conceptual Model to Analyze Persuasive Properties

Previous work on persuasive elements in games focussed on games as a consumable product that delivers a rhetoric embedded in the game's systems and rules (Bogost, 2007). This proceduralist view posits that games offer a unique opportunity to engage with a message through their interactive nature, proposing that developers and researchers interested in game rhetoric focus on the systems underpinning this interactivity. Because our analysis is concerned with the dynamics of game design, we needed to go beyond procedural rhetoric to a more holistic view of persuasive elements. De la Hera's (2015) conceptual model (displayed in Figure 10.1) describes many different ways to persuade players of persuasive games, combining methods of persuasion unique to games with those that could also be used in different media. Moreover, games are experiences that not only allow for interaction, but also interact with players to create a context of play. The conceptual model of persuasive dimensions distinguishes possible persuasive properties or features across three levels: signs, systems, and contexts (Figure 10.1). Signs (the inner ring of the figure) refer to the visual, auditory, linguistic, and tactile stimuli, incorporating all the information that reaches the players across different sensory modalities. Next, in the figure's middle ring, the system-level persuasive strategies establish meaningful ties between the signs and are divided into narrative, procedural, and cinematic persuasion. These dimensions cover the way a game's interplay of signs and structure can create a persuasive argument. For example, successions of linguistic and visual elements constitute a narrative of events that offers a different message than the signs could have offered independently. The third level describes how games could effect change through the social, tactical, sensorial, and affective contexts of play (displayed on the figure's outer ring). These contexts focus on how the players experience the game. Though browser-based persuasive games are experienced through endless combinations of players and social environments that all influence the play session, this level of persuasive dimensions refers to what the game could possibly stir up in players under ideal circumstances (for example, when users are emotionally and attentively engaged and make optimal use of all of the games' affordances). Taken together, these 11 dimensions describe the different ways a game can attempt to persuade players. In practice, games of course use several methods simultaneously. The current study applies this model of persuasive dimensions (originally posited by De la Hera, 2015) to the exemplar cases of browser-based persuasive games to determine which dimensions are used to effect the persuasive message and to what degree the games' arguments rely on each of these dimensions.

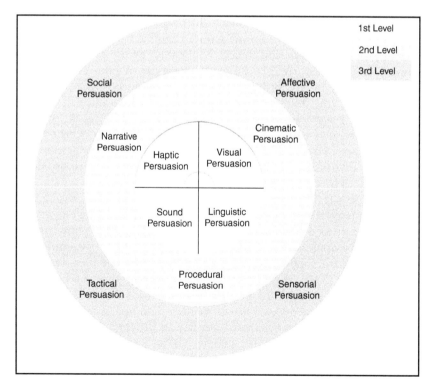

Figure 10.1 Model of persuasive dimensions employed in persuasive games.

Method

Selection

A set of criteria determined our selection of persuasive games: First of all, the games had to appear to primarily argue for a certain topic or stance in an effort to persuade players to change or reinforce their attitudes towards a particular subject. For example, the game *Darfur is Dying* was designed to convince players that the situation in Sudan was untenable to motivate them to act. Second, the games needed to be freely available online and in English. Games related to marketing efforts for commercial products or brands were excluded. Different methods were used in our online search. To identify the games, we used a wide range of search terms on Google, including persuasive games, political games, health games, news games, impact games, or games for change[1]. Forty-three persuasive games were found this way. This list was then compared to three online databases of serious games. These were the Health Games Research website (http://www.healthgamesresearch.org/db), the MIT Game Lab overview of purposeful games for social change (http://purposefulgames.info/), the Games for Change website (http://www.gamesforchange.org/), and the listing by the Center for Games and Impact (http://gamesandimpact.org/). After removing overlap, 66 unique games remained. Next, these games were played (to completion, where applicable) by the primary author. During these explorative play sessions, the styles of game play, themes, and topics were noted, and an inference was made as to the persuasive message the game intended to convey. From the 66 games that fit the definition, 11 were selected as exemplar cases for in-depth analysis. Our selection was based on two criteria. The first was concerned with the developers. Care was taken to select games from different game designers or institutions commissioning the game (organizations, single authors, activist groups) to represent the different ways in which such games are made. The second criterion was diversity. We chose games that were as different as possible while still sharing key elements. By focusing on shared elements, we tried to gain insight into how similar topics can be approached in different ways as well as how similar design choices can support games that proffer different messages. The application of these criteria resulted in a meaningful set of 11 games, which are listed in Table 10.1.

The games spanned three broad themes. The first was poverty and hardship. These games addressed poverty in different situations in an effort to promote empathy for people who are worse off, stir players towards action, or inform them about how to handle this kind of life. Games in this category included *Survive125*, *Poverty Is Not a Game*, *Ayiti: The Cost of Life*, and *My Cotton Picking Life*.

The second theme was about lived experiences and suffering from disorders. Though these are two different things, these games were grouped because they were all deeply personal experiences. These games wanted to let players experience life in a certain situation, either for its own sake or to promote action and included *Depression Quest*, *Power and Control*, *Dys4ia*, and *Auti-Sim*.

The third theme included games that dealt with the topic of violence and politics. Although these games usually included violent content, they strayed from entertainment games in that all of them carried messages about the consequences and futility of violent acts. This category included *September 12th*, *The Best Amendment*, and *Endgame: Syria*.

These three themes do not represent the breadth of topics that are currently being explored by developers of persuasive/serious/games for change. For example, there are games about animal abuse (e.g. PETA, n.d.), energy conservation (e.g. Bang, Torstensson, & Katzeff, 2006), and smoking cessation (e.g. Deleon, 2011), among many others. It is outside the scope of this chapter to provide a full overview of the entire catalogue of persuasive games. However, by including games that fit within these three themes, we aim to draw meaningful comparisons between the persuasive mechanisms in these games.

Analysis

After describing the games, they were analysed for their persuasive elements using the model by De la Hera (2015) and subsequently compared with the other game(s) in each of the three themes. The emphases games place on each of the 11 persuasive dimensions (De la Hera, 2015) were coded by one researcher, distinguishing different levels and kinds of emphasis for each dimension.

Results

The analyses are divided in three different themes. Table 10.1 contains an overview of how the games in this study attempted to persuade their players by noting to what degree each of the 11 persuasive dimensions of the model by De la Hera (2015) are used in each game.

The games' persuasive emphases were divided into strong, nominal, or no emphasis. In some instances, the message of the game as a whole seemed to be contradicted by an individual dimension, in which case the emphasis was marked as conflicted. Finally, some games used signs, systems, or contextual dimensions to support the other elements, rather than to bring across the game's message. In these cases, the emphasis was marked as supportive even if a dimension would not be persuasive by itself.

Table 10.1 Emphasis on persuasive elements of the games studied

Theme:		Poverty & Hardship				Personal Experience & Illness				Violence & Politics		
Level	Persuasive Dimension	Survive 125	PING	Ayiti	My Cotton Picking Life	Depression Quest	Power and Control	Dys4ia	Auti-Sim	September 12th	The Best Amendment	End-game: Syria
Signs	Linguistic	++	++	++	+	++	++	++	0	+	+	++
	Visual	0	+/-	+/-	+	+	&	+	++	+	+/-	&
	Aural	0	&	+/-	&	&	++	+	++	+	&	&
	Haptic	0	0	&	++	0	++	+	0	0	&	0
Systems	Procedural	+	+	++	++	+	+	+/-	+	++	++	+
	Narrative	++	++	+	0	++	+	++	0	0	0	++
	Cinematic	0	+	0	0	0	0	0	0	0	0	0
Contexts	Affective	+/-	&	+	0	++	+	+	+	+	0	0
	Sensorial	0	0	0	0	+	+	0	++	+	&	0
	Tactical	+	+/-	++	0	+/-	0	0	0	++	+/-	++
	Social	&	0	0	&	+	0	0	0	0	0	0

Legend: ++: Strong emphasis, +: Emphasis, +/-: Conflicting emphasis, 0: No direct emphasis, &: Supportive emphasis.

The following sections present the three themes we used to label the different games. Each game is first briefly described and next compared with the other games within the theme with respect to their persuasive intent. Overarching analyses are shared in the conclusion and discussion section.

Poverty and Hardship

Four persuasive games were found that dealt with the subject of poverty and hardship. These games are *Survive125* (Live58, 2014), *Poverty Is Not a Game* (iMinds, 2010), *Ayiti: The Cost of Life* (Global Kids, 2006), and *My Cotton Picking Life* (Rawlings, 2012b).

Survive125 is a short text-based narrative game where players have to survive as a working single mother in India for 30 days by making decisions about family and health matters. The presentation is minimalist because it only shows players how their actions affect their health and available money, though the actions do result in small snippets of text about their consequences.

Ayiti: The Cost of Life (*Ayiti*) describes a similar situation, but is about a family living in poverty in Haiti. In this strategy game, players control the actions of a family of five, determining the family members' access to education, work, health care, and rest. Few players will make it to the end of a 20-minute session (spanning four in-game years), as family members often fall ill and die in their efforts to keep their heads above water.

Poverty Is Not a Game (*PING*) is a three-dimensional (3D) role-playing game about individual poverty wherein players guide a recently poverty-stricken teen boy or girl through the process of finding a job, getting an education, and maintaining a roof over his or her head in a big Belgian city. As one storyline takes around 45 minutes to complete, it is one of the longer games in our selection.

Last, *My Cotton Picking Life* (*MCPL*) explores the despairing monotony of being forced to pick cotton in a field in Uzbekistan. Picking one day's quota of cotton (50 kg) in the game would by our estimation take up to 6 hours of uninterrupted game play. Because the game is very repetitive and offers no incentives to keep going for that long, it is unlikely that many players play the game for more than a few minutes.

With the exception of *MCPL*, all the games covering this theme in this sample rely heavily on linguistic persuasion. All are trying to convey the situation their characters have found themselves in; for the first three games this takes not only a backstory but also explanations of how their actions change their situation, taking the players through a narrative that the players have authorial control over. *MCPL*, on the other hand, does not focus on any story of the characters; their situation is left vague while the displayed text addresses the general issue of forced labor in Uzbekistan. This game focuses a lot of its persuasive signs on visual representation. The character looks unhealthy and unhappy, his (literal) outlook bleak. In the other games about poverty, the visuals are often underplayed. *Survive125* offers only schematic icons and a single background image. *Ayiti* and *PING,* however, both styled their protagonists to best fit their target demographics. *Ayiti,* seemingly made for children, is visually and aurally gaudy despite the grave circumstances. Characters trot to and fro with cheerful tunes, and only when they get severely ill does their demeanor change to an unhappy one. *PING* shows 3D models in baggy pants and loose clothes, whereas portraits shown during dialogues show edgy haircuts and the odd piercing. Again, however, their state is not reflected in the way they look. The characters do not look tired, grimy, or even unhappy. This was likely done not to shock or scare away players. Because the developers of *PING*, *Survive125*, and *Ayiti* used such a "tell, don't show" approach, players can slowly get to grips with the situations detailed in the games. Last, haptic signs are not used to any serious degree for the first three games. However, *MCPL's* message that the work involved in picking cotton is an arduous and monotonous task is carried out through its reliance on players to constantly click buttons. The movement itself is dull, perfectly reflecting its task in its sheer futility while avoiding the intensity of the work and the fatigue it creates.

When looking on the level of systems, the haptic signs of *MCPL* also form the backbone of its procedural rhetoric. The game mimics the real-world work and instills the sense of hopelessness and lack of freedom through its monotonous gameplay. *Ayiti* also employs strong procedural rhetoric; the choices players make for their characters could keep the family afloat but restrict individual development, and driving characters to work hard to eke out enough money can push them to the brink of death. The balance that players must seek mirrors the struggles of families in Haiti and other poverty-stricken countries. *Survive125* also covers that balance, but abstracts control of actions to one decision per day. Whether players send their child to school or to fetch water has an impact on both their current and future lives. In this regard, the games are similar, but because of the level of abstraction in *Survive125,* the choices are more easily made than if players would have to force these actions as it is in *Ayiti. PING* is about poverty in a Western city. The systems to be reflected in the game are necessarily different. *PING* therefore focusses its game play on the bureaucratic rat-race that destitute Western citizens fall into. Running to catch appointments at employment offices as well as asking friends for a place to stay are part of this routine.

Although *PING* reflects these real-world trials and tribulations in their procedures, it is impossible to fail. Spending what little money the characters have on hamburgers does not incur a fail state. Leaving his or her boss waiting for an hour does not mean they are terminated. In other words, this game uses conflicting tactical persuasion, as its difficulty does not match the problems faced in the real world. *Ayiti* fares better at this as it is quite difficult to make it through one session. Although this outcome is not inevitable, the family bond easily disintegrates into a game screen lined with tombstones. In fact, the tactical scope of this game is such that walkthroughs have been made available online by other players, and optimal strategies have been the topic of discussion on several online spaces. *Survive125* finds the middle ground between these games as it is possible to fail, but players who choose carefully can easily 'survive' its 30-day run.

Evidently, the difficulty levels of these games are the result of their specific messages and target audiences. *Survive125*'s minimalist aesthetic is aimed at more adult players when compared with *Ayiti*'s cheery animations and melodies, which might mean *Survive125*'s players crave less game-like elements (such as challenge). This is why these games can have the same message of finding balance while being poor but have very different degrees of difficulty. *PING*'s purpose was split between informing and persuading (De Grove, Looy, Neys, & Jansz, 2012), which in this case meant that (young) players who were not proficient would still be able to learn the appropriate actions in preparation of their own lives. Last, *MCPL* approaches difficulty differently. Despite threats of harm from an off-screen aggressor, there is no fail state. Still, the size of its quota means it is also nearly impossible to win, and a button marked 'Alright, I've had enough' is visible while playing. In this way, the game pushes players to give up, to stop playing to prove the point that forcing children to pick this much cotton is reprehensible.

The theme of poverty and hardship is prevalent in persuasive games because people want to spread awareness of humanitarian crises in novel ways (see also *Darfur is Dying*, for instance). However, adding a social component to help spread awareness seemed to have only been an ancillary concern for these games. Overall, these games use few direct calls to action, apart from *MCPL*'s share buttons and *Survive125*'s options to post messages to Facebook. Some games outside of the current selection, such as *Darfur is Dying* (mtvU, 2009), do link to mobilization pages.

Lived Experience and Disorders

Games in the theme of lived experience and disorders are about personal stories. These games were made to reflect on what life is like for certain individuals, whether those individuals are insecure, repressed, or suffer from a neurological disorder. The games subsumed under this theme were *Depression Quest* (Quinn, 2013), *Power and Control* (Sain, 2011), *Dys4ia* (Auntie Pixelante, 2012), and *Auti-Sim* (Kay, 2013). Two of these games, *Depression Quest* and *Dys4ia*, are partly autobiographical, as their developers relay their experiences with depression and hormone replacement therapy (HRT), respectively. *Auti-Sim* is biographical, developed by a parent of an autistic child. They all engage the player in first-person accounts of salient events or experiences.

Depression Quest is a branching text narrative that integrates the level of depression as a modifier that limits players' options as it deepens. Because the unavailable responses are still visible, the few months of the protagonist's life (shown through mood pictures, soft music, and text) the game follows are noticeably affected by this affliction.

The second game, *Power and Control*, is a uniquely designed game about a young female who is in a relationship with an abusive male. Displayed on a stark pink background and aurally accompanied by a male voice and varying background score, words are used to represent objects, actions, or thoughts that the players can approach and touch or even avoid. All interactions in this game occur through the mouse cursor.

Dys4ia is the developer's account of the situations she dealt with while undergoing HRT. The game is played as a series of around 40 micro-game vignettes (reminiscent of Wario Ware games (Nintendo, 2014)), that all use one game play mechanic to display a situation, thought, or feeling.

Last, *Auti-Sim*'s title is a portmanteau of autism and simulation. The game itself is a 3D simulation of an autistic child walking through a playground filled with children. Approaching these children leads to social anxiety in the child, which is relayed through off-putting shrieking sounds while white noise blurs the screen. Players are driven to avoid the other children and seek out quieter areas, reflecting how difficult it typically is for individuals with this disorder to establish human contact.

Similar to the previous theme, three of the four games about personal experience rely heavily on linguistic persuasion, although they differ in their presentation style. *Depression Quest* offers a full narrative with fleshed out characters who react to each choice made, with every situation described in detailed text. *Power and Control*, on the other hand, presents single words that take the place of visual stimuli and behaviour. The interactivity these words allow often gives them meaning as they stand in for the protagonist's thoughts as well. *Dys4ia* presents the middle ground, with short sentences describing a situation or feeling. This shows how even in the relatively narrow genre of first-person experiential games, text can be used to either create a total picture, or adversely to shield players from what would surely be off-putting (not to mention costly to produce) images. In all three cases, it allows for easier identification with the protagonist as players' minds fill in the blanks left by the text.

Auti-Sim, as can be seen in Table 10.1, is the only game in this sample that does not in any way rely on in-game text for persuasive effect. Instead, its emphasis is on visual and aural presentation. The masking of the screen and piercing noises form a deterrent to players from seeking out contact with others. The sensorial bombardment stands in for inner turmoil in anticipation or as a result of interaction. The game thus attempts to spread beyond the confines of the audiovisual browser game to simulate an internal state of being. Similarly, *Depression Quest* projects white noise on the game's background to signify deepening depression. However, in this case, the noise is not used to deter players but to frame the current situation. *Dys4ia* uses visuals in a very different way, though towards the same purpose. Its visuals are metaphorical, often either supreme close-ups of body parts or abstracted top-down views of social events. As the treatment progresses and insecurities come and go, the protagonist's body is in turn shown as silhouettes of oddly shaped lumps or stereotypical male and female icons. The transition is also marked aurally through the developer's deep voice as it was used to create high-pitched sound effects.

Last, although *Power and Control* uses its words to great effect, the power of the game's signs comes from the physical mouse interactions. The cursor is at once a finger, a body, and a decision. Told to approach, stay on, or avoid some of the words, the game is lent a physical dimension as the player is forced to 'touch' disconcerting concepts. Because there are no visuals beyond the words, the game's constantly oppressive male voiceover enforces the brunt of the emotional engagement.

Of the three themes, lived experience and disorder persuasive games seem to rely the least on procedural rhetoric. *Depression Quest* crosses off unavailable (often assertive or positive) ways to deal with situations, explicitly showing players that what they would normally do is simply not an option for the protagonist. Moreover, this funnels the player, making it harder to 'choose' his or her way back from the depression. Despite the limitations, it remains possible for players to simply always choose the most positive option available to work their way up – which is in our model labelled as conflicting tactical persuasion. This means the unavailability system does not necessarily cause *Depression Quest* to have players think or act as if they were depressed. The game therefore relies primarily on affective persuasion (by drawing the player into its narrative and making it their own) to envelop the player in its message.

Looking at *Dys4ia*, procedural rhetoric is not only limited (in that its systems do not meaningfully reflect real-world processes), players can get a sense that because the game is a straightforward set of micro-games, undergoing HRT is also not really a struggle. Its many tiny mechanics can be interpreted to show that each situation protagonists find themselves in is unfamiliar and requires novel ways of dealing with a situation. However, as with *Depression Quest*, *Dys4ia*'s power lies in narrative and affective persuasion, showing the players what such an idiosyncratic process feels like in a personal way.

What is then different from the other themes is that the games about these personal experiences are not hard. The developers have prioritized the game's experience and story over providing a challenge. The lack of difficulty does not always help the game's messages (*Depression Quest, Dys4ia*), but in most cases these games do not need to hinder the player more than needed to tell their stories. Last, just like in the poverty and hardship theme, social persuasion is mostly absent. *Depression Quest* does underline the importance of social contact for this affliction, though, by linking players to sites where they can look for help.

Persuasive games are a fitting home for personal experiences. Players can try to match their thinking to that of the protagonist, trying to get a feel for what cannot easily be transferred through an audiovisual medium. Similarly, many commercial games are picking up on this trend (coinciding with a shift towards greater diversity) and portray lived experiences in critically acclaimed games (e.g. *Gone Home, Life is Strange, That Dragon, Cancer*) as gaming culture is slowly becoming more inclusive. Interestingly, these high-profile games tend to show the same pattern of branching or uncoverable narratives as the smaller nonprofit counterparts described in this chapter.

Violence and Politics

This theme includes three games that seek to address the use of violence in wars and civilian contexts. The violence these games contain is therefore meant to address violence in society on a broader level. The games are *September 12th* (Frasca, 2003b), *The Best Amendment* (Molleindustria, 2013), and *Endgame: Syria* (Rawlings, 2012a). Two of these games (*September 12th* and *The Best Amendment*) condemn it outright, whereas the third (*Endgame: Syria*) explores its apparent necessity and uses in combating dictatorships.

September 12th is a self-titled 'toy world' exploring aggressive tactics used against terrorists. On a single screen, the player can fire missiles at terrorists walking among civilians in a Middle Eastern country. The delay between a missile's launch and impact as well as its large blast radius means it is impossible to keep from killing civilians. Those that are caught in the blast are mourned by other civilians who subsequently turn into terrorists, presenting a perennial cycle of violence where more terrorists are 'created' than are killed.

The second game, *The Best Amendment*, is concerned with gun violence in the United States. In this top-down, twin-stick shooter, players are competing with their former selves. By shooting these prior versions, subsequent levels then have this same aggressive act in them, increasing the violence and danger until it becomes impossible to survive. The message this extolls is that the use of violence only fights fire with fire, adding more violence until the situation becomes untenable and the player character is killed.

The third game is *Endgame: Syria*. Coming from the same developer as *My Cotton Picking Life*, this game similarly tackles a contentious topic: the early years of the Syrian civil war. Players play tactical and aggressive cards in an abstracted card game environment (in the vein of *Magic: The Gathering*) to maintain support for the rebels, weaken the regime's forces as well as negotiate cease-fires and peace talks.

The way the games are presented is surprisingly varied. *September 12th* displays text only before the game starts, although that text sums up most of the game's message: "It has no ending. It has already begun. The rules are deadly simple. You can shoot. Or not. This is a simple model you can use to explore some aspects of the war on terror" (Frasca, 2003b). *The Best Amendment* intersperses its combat scenes by quoting and referencing famous pro-gun activists from the National Rifle Association (NRA). The text explicitly references a dichotomy of good and bad and immediately problematizes this: "Be the good guy with a gun! Stop the bad guys with guns! But will that make you a bad guy in the eyes of somebody else?" (Molleindustria, 2013). Both games offer thinly veiled critique through the use of certain phrases. *Endgame: Syria*, conversely, does not include many subversive or explicitly persuasive messages. Instead, players are given a lot of information on each possible action, detailing effects such actions have on the rebels, support for the regime as well as civilian life. Through the act of playing this game, players can therefore get a sense of how both parties have behaved in this conflict.

Visually and aurally, both *September 12th* and *Endgame: Syria* make use of stimuli without relying on them for their argument. Though *September 12th*'s cell-shaded visuals seem out of place, they are never cheery, and the sounds of explosions and mourning establish a bleak atmosphere that reflects the continuing tragedies in this region of the world. *Endgame: Syria*'s visual and aural cues are all icon-based and mostly designed to quickly relay necessary information. As with the games on poverty and hardship, these games eschew horrific images, masking them with menus filled with numerical information in the case of *Endgame: Syria* or abstracting them to small and simple sprites (*September 12th*). Conversely, *The Best Amendment* seems designed for shock value. Characters bleed after being shot, for instance. The player character is a conical white figure, invoking images of Ku Klux Klan (KKK) robes. This racist connotation is made explicit because the enemies the player shoots are black cones and the game's score consists of frantic banjo riffs. The game's author, Paolo Pedercini, indeed drew a comparison between the NRA and the KKK when asked about this interpretation (Webster, 2013).

All three games approach violence differently. *The Best Amendment* is fast-paced and becomes progressively more difficult. *September 12th*

is sedate because the terrorists do not pose a threat to players and the time delay between firing a rocket and hitting the target precludes a fast rate of fire. *Endgame: Syria* allows players to set the pace, valuing strategy over reaction times. For the first and third games, this difference is caused by the distinct messages of these games. *The Best Amendment* aims to satirize and subvert pro-gun ideology, with zesty, violent game play conveying its message. *Endgame: Syria* instead treats its subject matter more solemnly. It aims to provide a realistic view of the different actions one can take to fight a civil war – though it leaves out civilian-targeting atrocities such as chemical warfare. Its message is therefore more one of understanding and, perhaps, sympathising. *September 12th*'s succinct point is delivered mainly through the single game play loop of firing missiles and hitting innocents to 'create' new terrorists. The similarities of these games therefore come down to a shared focus on the game's systems to relay the message. *Endgame: Syria*, in contrast to the others, further adds a narrative element to these systems. Through constant battles and contact with outside organizations and nations, players not only manage their resources, but can also actively choose to minimize civilian casualties, for example. The story of the civil war this creates will be counterfactual, but it is meant to let players experience how decisions they would make would work out.

In opposition to the previous theme's focus on narrative over game play, all three violence-focused games offer some degree of tactical freedom. Although this is comparatively limited in *September 12th*, players are likely to try to wrestle with different times of firing and different locations before they give up. This entails getting to grips with the inevitability of collateral damage, but the game leaves enough leeway for first-time players to get the sense that it is possible to only hit terrorists. In *Endgame: Syria*, the luck-based drawing of cards as well as the multiple advantages and disadvantages each card offers lend the game surprising depth. Players can choose to play in different ways, and the game's relative difficulty means there is an incentive to play tactically. The design of both of these games is aimed at tactical persuasion, as the leeway and freedoms granted to players all further promote the messages they send. *The Best Amendment* is fun to play and surprisingly addictive, incentivising repeated attempts in pursuit of a high score. Indeed, the game is such an enjoyably frantic game that its message could easily be lost on players amid the carnage. In that way, the game's score counter is to the message's detriment as it might cause players to want to add violence in pursuit of the leader boards, meaning it can be played and enjoyed by exactly those individuals it should be persuading. These players might get the feeling that though violence only builds up, it does make for an interesting experience. This is likely not the message its creators have wanted to spread.

Conclusion and Discussion

Overall, with the exception of *Auti-Sim*, all of the games discussed in this chapter rely on linguistic persuasion. The appeal of communicating with players through text is obvious; it is an efficient (and comparatively cheap) way of reaching the audience to make a message explicit. Moreover, although all games also emphasize other persuasive dimensions, the addition of text in most cases does not disturb the flow of the game or its core message. From the current selection, it seems that most games therefore include text to bolster an otherwise less clear message.

All games in this selection also use procedural rhetoric, although not every game is successful in this regard. Table 10.1 supports the contention that when developers set out to make a persuasive game they develop it around either a core narrative (*PING*, *Depression Quest*, *Dys4ia*, *Endgame: Syria*) or around their principal game play elements (*Ayiti*, *MCPL*, *September 12th*, *The Best Amendment*). Developers want to (allow the player to) tell a powerful story or they rely on the game play elements to tell the story for them. Although this harkens back to the ludology/narratology debate (Frasca, 2003a), there is no indication that narrative-focused persuasive games have uninteresting game play or vice versa. Moreover, both routes seem to lead to concrete and interesting experiences that offer strong messages.

Apart from procedural, linguistic, and – in half of the cases – narrative persuasion, other persuasive strategies are used only in a few of the games. Visual persuasion especially is used sparingly. This is likely the result of the reduced budgets available to persuasive game developers. However, *PING*'s 3D graphics – signifying a more generous production – are not used to convey elements like negative emotions or griminess often associated with living in destitution. The other reason for this paucity is the desire for developers to shield their audience from shocking visuals. The likely argument behind this is that shocking players would scare them away or at the very least remove attention from the game's message. This also holds in the case of *PING* and *Ayiti* because of their younger target audiences. For games such as *Survive125* and *Depression Quest*, the clean and unthreatening presentation seems to cater to a target audience that takes the subject matter seriously and is playing to be informed, rather than entertained. On the other hand, the bold visual styles of *Dys4ia* and *The Best Amendment* make these games stand out. Overall, the way persuasive games are presented depends on their target audiences and specific persuasive goals.

Several persuasive games studied here are trying to break free from their constrictive medium (i.e. the browser window). *Power and Control* draws players into an oppressive situation. Using only written and spoken words, it aims to unsettle players and cause them to feel threatened and belittled. *Depression Quest* and *Auti-Sim* both apply visual signals to indicate negative states of feeling. Compared with noninteractive media, these games more easily elicit empathic responses from players, as they are given a role to play, uniting their goals with that of their protagonists at least for the duration of play (Juul, 2013). The games about lived experiences and disorders all try to invoke an affective dimension, keeping with the emphasis on personal stories. Interestingly, this does not necessarily coincide with a focus on narrative persuasion. *Auti-Sim* does away with it entirely, and *Power and Control* relies more heavily on moment-to-moment interactions between the protagonist and her abuser, only developing into a coherent story as it reaches a crescendo where the protagonist is deciding whether or not to leave her tormentor. However, in keeping with their browser-based nature, only one game (*PING*) of the 11 can be said to apply cinematic persuasion. For the others, there are no cut scenes, and the framing of each scene is often abstract, minimalist, or purely functional. In other words, the viewpoint and mise-en-scene are not used to express the games' messages. The games are certainly attempting to expand beyond their windows, but they do not adhere to the strategies of other media. Instead, they make use of the unique engagement afforded by the playful, interactive experience.

My Cotton Picking Life, *September 12th*, and *The Best Amendment* share another interesting structural element. These games were not designed to let players win and experience mastery, but rather the opposite; these games intend for their players to give up. *MCPL* features a button that reads 'Alright, I've had enough', before chastising players who click it by telling them not everyone is in a position to decline this work. *September 12th* initially seems like an easy game of target practice before it frustrates players with the inevitability of harming innocents. *The Best Amendment* shows that acting violently only adds violence, escalating a situation and leading to more harm. This supports the point made by Ruggiero and Becker (2015) that some games are not made to be winnable. In fact, these games want players to give up to get their message across. Players need to have a revelatory moment where it becomes clear that their actions are futile (*MCPL*) or only escalate the problem (*September 12th*, *The Best Amendment*) and that "the only winning move is not to play" (Badham, 1983).

De la Hera's model (2015) enabled us to differentiate between the linguistic and procedural persuasive dimensions that are emphasized in almost every game, and dimensions that are used sparingly. Moreover, although dimensions are almost always used in tandem in any particular game, each dimension can be emphasised on its own as well. For example, narrative persuasion does not necessarily need to coincide with affective persuasion, and visual and aural persuasion can be distinguished from sensorial persuasion. We consider the model to be a valuable tool for descriptive purposes, discerning different kinds of persuasive games.

Additionally, the model is a means to visualize gaps – unused persuasive dimensions– that could be filled by future persuasive games. The social dimension, for example, saw little emphasis in most of the games discussed here, despite the level of reflection discussing these games could encourage (for more, see De Grove, 2014).

In this chapter, we investigated the persuasive dimensions games use to spread their message. We based our conclusions on 11 persuasive games that are currently playable online. Although these games only represent a small portion of the rapidly expanding catalogue of this genre, they also show a broad reliance on the written word and procedural rhetoric as well as an interesting variety of strategies. For example, differences can be found in the time needed to finish these games. Some authors feel their message needs or deserves a certain time investment from their players, while others are satisfied with 60 seconds of the players' attention (e.g. *September 12th, Auti-Sim*). Persuasive games can be seen as separate from entertainment games or other serious games because they were not made to appeal to as large a crowd as possible. Persuasive games can be short, hard – even unwinnable – and developed with any budget. They do not need to entertain their players for the duration of lengthy, cinematic campaigns to give players their "money's worth". Persuasive games justify their length and production values only insofar as they help to propagate their messages. This economical consideration informs their designs and presents the freedom to make games that, for example, almost force players to stop playing to prove their point. Similarly, other authors make it impossible to lose the game in favor of letting players stick to the narrative (*Dys4ia*), which might cause players who do not feel challenged to lose interest. The results of our case based analysis lead us to the conclusion that persuasive games offer organizations and idealistic authors alike an outlet for novel persuasive communication that can use different dimensions. In this sense, persuasive games are indeed the digital pamphlets of the current media landscape.

Note

1 The preliminary overview of persuasive games generated by our intern Clarissa Spiekerman in the first half of 2014 enabled us to fine-tune the selection for the analysis in this chapter.

References

Alhabash, S., & Wise, K. (2012). Peacemaker: Changing students' attitudes toward Palestinians and Israelis through video game play. *International Journal of Communication*, 6, 356–380. http://doi.org/http://ijoc.org.

Auntie Pixelante. (2012). Dys4ia. Retrieved from http://auntiepixelante.com/?p=1515.

Badham, J. (1983). *WarGames*. United Artists.

Bang, M., Torstensson, C., & Katzeff, C. (2006). The PowerHouse: A persuasive computer game designed to raise awareness of domestic energy consumption. *Persuasive Technology, 3962,* 123–132.

Bogost, I. (2007). *Persuasive games.* Cambridge, MA: The MIT Press.

Cohen, E. L. (2014). What makes good games go viral? The role of technology use, efficacy, emotion and enjoyment in players' decision to share a prosocial digital game. *Computers in Human Behavior, 33,* 321–329. http://doi.org/10.1016/j.chb.2013.07.013.

Connolly, T. M., Boyle, E., MacArthur, E., Hainey, T., & Boyle, J. M. (2012). A systematic literature review of empirical evidence on computer games and serious games. *Computers & Education, 59*(2), 661–686. http://doi.org/10.1016/j.compedu.2012.03.004.

De Grove, F. (2014). Youth, friendship, and gaming: A network perspective. *Cyberpsychology, Behavior, and Social Networking, 17*(9), 603–608.

De Grove, F., Looy, J. Van, Neys, J., & Jansz, J. (2012). Playing in school or at home? An exploration of the effects of context on educational game experience. *Electronic Journal of E-Learning, 10*(2), 199–208.

De la Hera, T. (2015). A theoretical model for the study of persuasive communication through digital games. In J. M. Parreno, C. R. Mafe, & L. Scribner (Eds.), *Engaging consumers through branded entertainment and convergent media* (pp. 74–88). Hershey, PA: IGI Global. http://doi.org/10.4018/978-1-4666-8342-6.

Deleon, C. (2011). Quit smoking. Retrieved July 21, 2014, from http://www.kongregate.com/games/deleongames/quit-smoking.

Frasca, G. (2003a). Ludologists love stories, too: notes from a debate that never took place. In *Proceedings of Levelup 2003, DIGRA*.

Frasca, G. (2003b). September 12th. Retrieved from http://www.newsgaming.com/games/index12.htm.

Games for Change. (n.d.). Retrieved July 15, 2014, from http://www.gamesforchange.org/about/.

Global Kids. (2006). Ayiti: The cost of life. Retrieved from http://ayiti.globalkids.org/game/.

Granic, I., Lobel, A., & Engels, R. C. M. E. (2013). The benefits of playing video games. *American Psychologist, 69*(1), 66–78. http://doi.org/10.1037/a0034857.

iMinds. (2010). Poverty is not a game. Retrieved from http://www.povertyisnotagame.com/?lang=en.

Juul, J. (2013). *The art of failure: An essay on the pain of playing video games.* Cambridge, MA: MIT Press.

Kay, T. (2013). Auti-Sim. Retrieved from http://gamejolt.com/games/strategy-sim/auti-sim/12761/.

Live58. (2014). Survive125.

McGonigal, J. (2011). *Reality is broken.* London: Vintage.

Molleindustria. (2013). The best amendment. Retrieved from http://www.molleindustria.org/the-best-amendment/.

mtvU. (2009). Darfur is dying. Retrieved July 14, 2014, from http://www.darfurisdying.com/.

Neys, J., & Jansz, J. (2010). Political Internet games: Engaging an audience. *European Journal of Communication, 25*(3), 227–241. http://doi.org/10.1177/0267323110373456.

Neys, J., Jansz, J., & Tan, E. S. H. (2014). Exploring persistence in gaming: The role of self-determination and social identity. *Computers in Human Behavior*, *37*, 196–209. http://doi.org/10.1016/j.chb.2014.04.047.

Nintendo. (2014). WarioWare, Inc.: Mega Microgame$. Retrieved July 14, 2014, from http://www.nintendo.com/games/detail/qFjHcz5rwpwamwp3 VDPhpBcE0fRkfKkq.

O'Keefe, D. J. (2002). *Persuasion: Theory and research*. (2nd ed.). Thousand Oaks, CA: Sage Publications.

Peng, W., Lee, M., & Heeter, C. (2010). The effects of a serious game on role-taking and willingness to help. *Journal of Communication*, *60*, 723–742. http://doi.org/10.1111/j.1460-2466.2010.01511.x.

Perloff, R. (2014). *The dynamics of persuasion: Communication and attitudes in the twenty-first century* (5th ed.). New York: Routledge.

PETA. (n.d.). Bloody Burberry: The fur fighters. Retrieved from http://www.bloodyburberry.com/features/fur_fighters/.

Quinn, Z. (2013). Depression quest. Retrieved from http://www.depressionquest.com/.

Raessens, J. (2015). Playful identity politics: How refugee games affect the player's identity. In V. Frissen, S. Lammes, M. De Lange, J. De Mul, & J. Raessens (Eds.), *Playful identities: The ludification of digital media culture* (pp. 245–260). Amsterdam: Amsterdam University Press.

Rawlings, T. (2012a). Endgame: Syria. Retrieved July 21, 2014, from http://gamethenews.net/index.php/endgame-syria/.

Rawlings, T. (2012b). My cotton picking life. Retrieved from http://gamethenews.net/index.php/my-cotton-picking-life/.

Ruggiero, D., & Becker, K. (2015). *Games you can't win (working paper)*.

Sain, J. (2011). Power and control. Retrieved from http://jenniferann.org/2011-game-third-place.htm.

Webster, A. (2013). "The best amendment": NRA blowback spawns an irreverent game about guns. Retrieved July 14, 2014, from http://www.theverge.com/2013/3/19/4122824/the-best-amendment-an-unofficial-nra-game.

11 "Resist the Dictatorship of Malygos on Coldarra Island!"

Evidence of MMOG Culture in Taiwan's Sunflower Social Movement

Holin Lin and Chuen-Tsai Sun

As ludic social spaces that support player interactions in multiple dimensions, Massively Multiplayer Online Games (MMOGs) are distinctly different from other forms of social media such as *Facebook*, *Twitter*, and online blogs. Whereas *Twitter* has been used to support the creation, tagging, and sharing of reading content, with hashtags being created to promote or support social movements (Gleason, 2013), MMOGs, in comparison, facilitate game-like strategy deployment in a spatial occupation and defense situation that plays a critical role in the Sunflower Movement that occurred in the spring of 2014 in Taipei, Taiwan. In this chapter, we will describe how MMOG players experience 'bodily' interaction via their avatars, use versatile interactional materials to achieve various mission goals, and constantly interact with each other within what we will call *contentious cooperative frameworks*— not only on a daily basis, but over extended periods in communities that sometimes mostly consist of complete strangers. There is increasing evidence showing that MMOG gaming experiences exert profound influences on the online and offline social lives of players both microscopically (e.g. interpersonal interactions, see Boellstorff, 2015; Taylor, 2009; Williams et al., 2006) and macroscopically (e.g. collective actions, see Lin & Sun, 2011; Pearce, Boellstorff, & Nardi, 2009).

In this chapter, we will focus on the offline/macroscopic aspect, which consists of large-scale social connections and involvement in the physical world, using Taiwan's 2014 'Sunflower Movement' as a representative case to demonstrate how MMOG-associated experiences and social interaction patterns have the potential to play central roles in civil action. Specifically, we will show that during the protest, the real-time tools of *Facebook* and Google applications were used for information-sharing and other communication purposes as they have been in social actions in other countries, but more importantly, organizational and collaborative models and mobilization strategies were clearly influenced by the MMOG-playing experiences, literacies, and cultures of the protest participants.

From our analysis of movement socio-technological factors, we have identified four characteristics indicating familiarity with online game culture: game-like organization and collaboration; ease of collaboration with strangers; 'game tip' creation, usage, and distribution; and using game culture concepts to comprehend situations and to plan and take action. We also found that a significant number of movement organisers and participants had long affiliations with online games, providing them with skills that helped them sustain and expand the political action. We observed many instances of effortless transfer of skills and subculture knowledge acquired via gameplay when cooperating with strangers and when assigning and accepting tasks. Movement participants frequently used game metaphors and analogies that rendered complex political and economic issues accessible to other movement members and potential supporters. Spatial similarities between the blockade of the Taiwan Legislative Yuan and castle-siege activities that are common to MMOGs also illustrate the relevance of online gaming experiences to this particular physical world event. We should emphasise here that although the focus of our analysis is on this single event, our goal is to explain general connections between MMOG activities and social movement organization.

Sunflower Occupation Events – 18 March to 10 April 2014[1]

Although March 18 is officially considered the first day of the occupation, hundreds of university students were already camped outside the Taiwan Legislative Yuan to protest a Cross-Strait Service Trade Agreement (CSSTA) with China that was being considered at that time. Whereas the ruling Kuomingtang (KMT) party used the word 'debated', opposition lawmakers and many students believed that the agreement was being rushed through the legislature with insufficient opportunity for debate or public comment.

KMT members make a 30-second announcement declaring passage of the CSSTA, which triggers a loud reaction of protest among the camping students. Upon learning that the KMT had approved the agreement without proper discussion, students and members of the Democratic Front Against Cross-Strait Trade in Services Agreement (a nongovernmental organization alliance) and other public interest groups initiate a protest in front of the building that houses the Legislate Yuan. That evening, one group of protestors breaks through police barriers and enters the building via the Jinan South Road entrance. At the head of the group are two graduate students, Chen Wei-ting of National Tsing Hua University and Lin Fei-fan of National Taiwan University (NTU), plus members of a pan-university organization known as the Black Island Nation Youth Frontier. They hang banners and signs on and around the rostrum, declare the successful start of an occupation, use furniture to block all entrances to the legislative chamber, and make three demands: an apology from President Ma Ying-jeou, the resignation of Premier Jiang Yi-hua, and the removal of police forces.

One student, who identifies herself as JO1YNN, uses her iPod to send messages to CNN iReport (http://ireport.cnn.com/docs/DOC-1108633). The original protestors surrounding the building and others in different locations throughout Taiwan use *Facebook* and various Bulletin Board Services for mobilization purposes. Based on news coverage and information shared via *Facebook*, tens of thousands of students and citizens fill the streets surrounding the government center in Taipei to express their support for the movement. An open sunflower is chosen as a symbol to express strong opposition to the hidden review process. Students from more than 100 universities eventually join the movement. One NTU professor, Fan Yun, encourages 43 of her colleagues to hold their classes outside the Legislative Yuan, teaching on the topics of democracy, civil disobedience, and human rights. The occupying students establish rules encouraging nonviolence.

On March 23, President Ma Ying-jeou rejects the students' demand to reassess the service trade agreement in a manner where open debate can be monitored. In response to the five-day standoff, more than 200 students use pieces of cardboard and bed sheets to climb over barbed-wire barricades to enter the Executive Yuan, the Taiwanese equivalent of cabinet offices. The 40 police officers present cannot stop the students, but later that evening an estimated 1,500 police officers dressed in riot gear use water cannons to storm the building and remove the students, injuring many in the process. An estimated 1,000 students occupy the area in front of the building, with 6,000 students and citizens nearby. It takes six waves of riot police to gain control. Smartphone images of bloodstained students and citizens spread rapidly via social networks and mass media outlets. Some evicted civilians return to the Executive Yuan with the intention of reentering the building, but are forced to leave.

At 4:00 a.m., police forcefully remove media representatives from the area. Riot police continue to beat unarmed students, who continue to practice nonviolent resistance, and use water cannons at the front and side gates of the Executive Yuan. Crowds of protestors gather and confront the police outside the east and west gates. As civilians continue to gather, the police use water cannons for a third time, forcing the crowd back to Qingdao East Road. Many bloodied civilians tell the media that the police attacked peaceful protesters. Several videos of police brutality are streamed on the Internet.

On March 25, 11 Taiwanese citizens call for a crowd-funding project using the Flying V platform to purchase newspaper ads in the *Apple Daily Taiwan* and *New York Times* to spread awareness of the Sunflower

Movement. Under the slogan, "Why are they here?" the ads list reasons for protesting the behind-the-door CSSTA negotiations. The ads proclaim that while "blood has been shed, the future is too bright for us to abandon it [the movement]". The first $1.5 million New Taiwan dollars (approximately USD50,000) for the front-page *Apple Daily* ad is raised in 35 minutes. Within 3 hours, $6.7 million NT dollars are raised to purchase a full-page ad in the *New York Times*. A total of 3,621 people make contributions.

On the afternoon of March 30, 500,000 Taiwanese citizens put on black shirts and appear on the streets to attend a protest rally against the trade agreement and police crackdown. Black shirts are chosen as a symbol of the dark night preceding democratic sunlight in Taiwan.

On March 31, President Ma and the Executive Yuan once again reject the students' demands. However, KMT Policy Director Lin Hung-chih and KMT Legislator Chang Ching-chung apologise publically for the way that the legislation was handled. Lin also resigns from his position as KMT party whip, submitting his resignation to President Ma, who is the party chairman.

The following day, Chang An-le, a former gangster known as "White Wolf", leads a pro-CSSTA rally with hundreds of Taiwanese, and threatens to physically retake the building – in his words, "return the legislature" from the student occupiers. His group is blocked by 500 riot police well away from the building, and the counterprotest ends at 5:00 p.m.

On April 5, the occupying students renewed their demand that the government to give official responses to what they call the "People's Council Reports". Written by the students, the reports contain information about the CSSTA deliberations compiled from a variety of sources. Student leader Lin Fei-fan describes the reports as a comprehensive review of the CSSTA process emerging from group discussions by more than 1,000 citizens – what he calls an example of true participatory democracy of much higher quality than the legislative decision-making that preceded the Sunflower Movement. Scholars and experts give detailed explanations of the major differences between the student-citizen's and Executive Yuan's versions of a "Cross-strait Agreement Monitoring Act". Nineteen discussion groups are organised.

The following day, Legislative Speaker Wang Jin-pyng visits the students in the Legislative Yuan and promises to enact a law to monitor the process of cross-strait pacts before the legislature begins a new review of the CSSTA. The students consider this statement as a substantial sign of progress because it actually responds to what they consider their most important demand. They express expectations that the ruling and opposition parties will follow Wang's example and adhere to the constitutionally stated requirements of legislative self-discipline and supervision.

On April 7, the students announce their intention to leave the Chamber in three days. On the 21st day of the occupation, student leader Chen Wei-Ting declares that the movement has completed the initial stage of its mission, and that it has achieved substantial progress on all four of the students' primary demands. According to Chen, the students pledged to leave the chamber and travel throughout Taiwan to plant seeds for a new democratic movement that will ensure that legislators from all political parties on the island fulfill their promises to pass legislation for a cross-strait oversight mechanism, and to halt all CSSTA review activities until the monitoring legislation is passed. The students also call on opposition parties and their legislative caucuses to renew their promises to keep the ruling party in check, and to stop the Ma government from further damaging the country's political system. Last, they demand that the civilian version of the oversight mechanism bill be deliberated, and that the version proposed by the Executive Yuan be removed from the table.

On April 10, as promised, the student activists file out of the Legislative Yuan and distribute sunflowers to the cheering crowds, vowing to spread the movement throughout Taiwan. Before leaving the main Assembly Hall at 6:00 p.m., they proclaim that their departure does not mean that they are giving up their beliefs or their demands. According to student leader Lin Fei-fan, "This movement for democracy that began on March 18 is a continuation of Taiwan's history of resistance and quest for freedom that has been ongoing for more than 100 years. We will continue the story, and we will never back down or give up".

Theoretical Perspectives

Our analysis of the Sunflower Movement involves new media practices and interactional frames in social movements. Jenkins (2009) notes that daily practices based on new media platforms offer a set of cultural competencies and social skills for individuals to participate in their community lives, resulting in a new type of participatory culture. The Sunflower Movement is an example of how various dimensions of new media literacy can serve as technical and social foundations for large-scale action. The participants constantly navigated across media platforms to select and integrate information in various formats and to make sense of it. They created posts about their involvement on social networking sites, thereby motivating their friends to take to the streets and show support. They broadcast information on the progress of offensive/defensive actions in support of making collective yet distributed decisions and coordinating groups of people who had never met. They used live-streaming technology to attract international media attention to ongoing events. These practices exemplify a broad range of new media usage and social competencies associated with online gaming experience (Kowert, 2015), and the ways that they supported the movement in terms of communication and organization.

However, focussing solely on the use of communication technologies would overlook aspects of self-organised role-playing, distributed collective problem-solving, and collaboration among a large number of individuals who previously had never met in person. In terms of social mechanisms, MMOGs support social networking for connection and sharing, and provide cultural materials for collective immersion and creation. More importantly, in addition to the functionalities shared by popular online cultural communities, online gaming has contributed new cognitive frameworks for collective interaction that are now considered pervasive in both game and physical worlds. In particular, MMOGs provide a cognitive schema for the contentious collective interactions and contentious cooperative frameworks described previously (e.g. Gee, 2003; Steinkuehler, 2008). Such interactions include offensive and defensive positions taken by competitive parties as well as within-group negotiation and collaboration. These configurations have significant implications for real-world collective social and political action. In gaming worlds, MMOG players are used to participating in contentious situations in the dungeons, arenas, and battlefields that constitute the majority of online gaming activities. As they become skilled and level up, they become increasingly literate in terms of social space because of the value that they give to game-related social activities and associated social status. More importantly, they develop community role identities through ongoing practice, which in turn reinforces their collective cognitive framework. Thus, when something happens in the physical world that reminds them of similar game world situations, players have a sense of what kinds of corresponding actions and cooperation patterns are required.

Game cultures have crossed popular cultural boundaries to become central aspects of daily life for millions of players worldwide. Raessens (2014) describes the "ludic turn" in contemporary media studies – an indicator of the ways that individuals are adopting game world language, rules, and mechanisms to construct and interpret physical world phenomena. When describing failed actions in contentious group activities such as political campaigns, we now hear or read comments such as, "I'm not afraid of god-like enemies, but I'm really afraid of pig-like teammates". When political figures draw unexpected attention to provocative statements that they make, they are now often described as accidentally using 'multiple-target taunting' – a common MMOG tactic of attracting the attention of a mob to protect one's teammates from attack. Once, during a political debate when a political leader took criticism of a general political practice as a personal affront, we noticed that one reader in the comments section wrote that "the critic accidentally pulled the boss when combating with the mobs".

These examples reveal the shared cognitive schema or mental model that penetrates both game and physical worlds. Individuals who are gaming-literate are increasingly appropriating rich vocabulary and innovative interactional frames in their daily (especially social) activities. The Sunflower protesters are examples of ludic turns in varied social dimensions ranging from playful communication to playful real-world collective action. We noticed that when specific instances of political content were easily transformed into personalised gaming concepts, they served as triggers for quick reactions – for example, the decisions to surround and defend the Legislative Yuan–activated cognitive frameworks associated with castle sieges and tower defenses. Contentious cooperative frameworks linked with game cultures provide a rich supply of tools to be used in physical situations involving social movements, political conflicts, and election campaigns. Online games represent a form of social media; therefore, information regarding issues, knowledge, tools, and influences can be readily distributed via texts, tweets, YouTube mashups, bulletin board posts, and, most significantly, the game worlds themselves, in which online gamers have expertise. On the one hand, the young generation is more capable of taking advantage of new communication technologies, in other words, they are more technologically savvy; on the other hand, we believe online gaming experiences provide them with extra capacity for handling such situations.

When examined from the perspective of a social movement, the Sunflower protest also reveals the implicit yet constructive roles of online gaming technologies and gaming experience. Bennett and Segerberg (2012) note that traditional social movement organizations are now empowered by communication technologies and social networks to become technology-enabled networks, with traditional collective action frames evolving into personal action frames for collective or connective actions. This new structure enables micro-coordination and flexibility in terms of social movement assembly and dispatch. Further, it supports a decentralised organizational structure so that the mobilization capability of a core groups becomes less critical for social movement success.

Fun is another central element in online gaming that apparently is shared in new-style social movements. According to Steinkuehler (2008), games are examples of 'push technology', which encourages players to explore general technology such as computers, and online affinity groups that emerge around games function as push communities that inspire participants to involve in other communities in different contexts. Game-related technology and organization penetrate player social involvement in a pleasant way, which affects game social movement characteristics. As MMOGs instantiate notions of social construction, they also endow real-world social reform with competence and fun. In light of online gaming, collective action and social movement may no longer take the conventional rational game form of agreeable n-prisoner dilemmas (Hardin, 1971), in which free riders present a great uncertainty to threaten the success of the movement, but of innovative practices in the ludic culture, in which the participants identify themselves as players who should identify their separate roles and then have fun in the process.

Findings and Analysis: Technology Usage and Online Game Culture

Data were gathered from news media, online forums, online game dialogues, social media posts, and journal articles published during and after the mass action. The evidence strongly supports the idea that information technology in the form of *Facebook*, *Twitter*, instant messaging, and PTT (an online bulletin board favored by many Taiwanese youth) was a key factor in the success of the Sunflower Movement. These tools were used to update information, distribute press releases, refute false and potentially damaging rumors, discuss various issues, and announce spontaneous protest actions. Smartphones and tablets were used to broadcast planned protest sites and to record instances of excess force on the part of the police. Cellphone flashlights were central to the celebration at the end of the Sunflower action (Chao, 2014).

Looking beyond the communication technologies, one finds roots of the movement's success in online gaming culture – an observation that sharply contrasts with organizational and inspirational aspects of traditional social movements. We have identified four major characteristics of the movement that indicate familiarity with online game culture.

Game-like Organization and Collaboration

The Sunflower Movement clearly borrowed from the participants' game culture experiences for purposes of empowerment. The occupation and defense of the Legislative Yuan complex was similar to a castle siege mission. We found that core members of the movement, most belonging to an inter-campus organization known as the Black Island Youth Society, had considerable teamwork experience accumulated from their previous protest activities. They resembled the members of an elite player guild for newcomers to admire and follow. From our data, it appears that movement supporters recognised the occupation situation based on their new media literacy (especially that which is online game-related), and played their assumed roles. Together, they successfully transformed a game fan-like community into a successful, if short-lived, real-world political movement.

Our evidence indicates that movement members relied less on a hierarchical command structure and more on dynamic organizational structures and collaborative patterns that resemble those commonly used in MMOGs such as *World of Warcraft (WoW)*. In *WoW* and similar games, all players exist as independent units with specific skills who collaborate to overcome barriers and to execute group tasks such as raids, which are considered representative of MMOGs. Players choose roles (e.g. tanks, healers, damage deliverers) that they execute individually while reacting collectively to evolving situations. In other words, players share a 'functionality template' that can be reassembled and modified for different missions. Their responsibilities include identifying the current situation, establishing their roles, and communicating with related parties according to their shared mental model. In this process, there is no need to wait for hierarchical orders to take action, and no need to report to designated commanders to modify strategies.

In one Sunflower Movement example, a group of students determined that their best action was to block a small lane near the legislative complex to hinder the movement of the police. Before this action, group members were complete strangers to each other. Their spontaneous action did not require material supplies, nor did it receive any attention from the media. We heard of numerous similar small-group actions like this one throughout the occupation.

Collaboration with Strangers

The recent development of random team-formation mechanisms in MMOGs encourages players to participate in shared mental models in support of efficient networking. The core Sunflower Movement event resembled a MMOG castle siege in that participants had to work with a large number of strangers toward a shared goal. To negotiate and coordinate with new acquaintances, movement participants were required to have knowledge of how to use multiple communication channels. Those familiar with game play were accustomed to performing multiple concurrent tasks in an efficient manner. Such experiences with organization ecology benefited the movement's many teams, including multilingual press liaisons and specialists in social media, research, technology support, logistics, and security, among others. There is evidence indicating that this organizational model resists misinformation: because information is more openly distributed, it is easy to verify via multiple channels, thus reducing the risk of rumors being spread.

When calling for support in a dungeon or on a battlefield, players must have confidence that teammates, even unknown strangers, will provide support via roles that they automatically recognise and fulfill. Such dynamic deployment and adjustment among strangers occurred multiple times during the legislative chamber occupation, and we believe that this could only have taken place because participants shared a mental model from their experiences with digital technology, especially MMOGs.

Game Tip Creation, Usage, and Distribution

Successful social movements must attract new participants and distribute information regarding past and current experiences. One MMOG-rooted practice that we observed in the Sunflower Movement was player-created tips for newcomers. Two major challenges encountered by the students were understanding and interpreting the detailed and technical nature of the legislation they were protesting, and convincing the stability-loving Taiwanese public that their occupation was both constitutionally legitimate and nonviolent.

Towards these goals, the students created a large number of text articles, slideshows, and tool kits for distribution via the web—an activity that any MMOG player would recognise. MMOGs are complex systems with few or no stated goals, rules, or official manuals or guidebooks. Instead, experienced players create walkthroughs and treasure maps, and provide graphic- or video-based tips to less experienced players on topics such as leveling-up, and distribute them via game forums. This practice empowers beginners in a much more efficient manner than formal instruction from official game managers. Two examples of these kinds of tool kits are shown in Figure 11.3, one listing the key factors of the service trade agreement and its hidden effects on various social sectors, the other an FAQ about occupation activities, giving participants and supporters evidence-based arguments that they could use with the media, opponents, or relatives. That these tips were provided by volunteers reflects a common gamer community practice, therefore participants quickly became aware of the tool kits and where to find them.

Using Game Culture to Understand Situations and to Take Action

Sunflower Movement activists and supporters also demonstrated their knowledge of MMOG game culture linguistically, especially in the use of game-related metaphors in their communications. These observations serve as evidence of how games have become part of the cognitive schema of adolescents and young adults for interpreting real-world events as well as for strategising, taking action, and persuading friends to join their activities. Examples of game-based metaphors include 'endless monsters' (associated with the *Hit the Gopher* game interface) to describe political issues and politicians; 'evil boss' to describe government in general; and analogies for unfair deals from popular games such as *League of Legends* and *Tower of Saviors* to describe aspects of the legislation they were protesting.

In one instance, a player used the public channel in *WoW* to criticise Sunflower Movement participants as 'Taliban.' This comment was immediately followed by multiple responses, including one call to "resist

Malygos' dictatorship on Coldarra Island!" The reference is to Taiwan as an island country: Malygos is the name of a *WoW* boss in the form of a blue dragon, and the color blue is linked with Taiwan's ruling KMT party. It is a comment that only the current generation of Taiwanese gamers could appreciate.

Conclusion: The Interplay Between Participatory Culture and Social Movement

During the Sunflower Movement, we witnessed many examples of the current digital generation's participatory culture, leading us to conclude that MMOGs played a critical role in preparing collective action frames for participants who were largely strangers to each other, but whose situated identities resulted from online gaming literacy. If the social movement is positioned in a larger cultural context, online gaming experiences clearly provided participants with cultural resources for interaction, thus supporting their efforts to recruit 'familiar strangers' to become teammates. Various tips were provided for social movement newbies to help them quickly understand the details of the primary motivation and to take part in self-organised actions. These practices are especially effective in spatial strategic situations and for executing tasks tied to short-term goals. According to our evidence, individual gaming experiences have become new frames for cultural cognition.

Our Sunflower Movement observations confirm Benford and Snow's (2000) assertion that in contrast to the commonly used approaches of resource mobilization and political opportunity, framing is a more relevant and/or useful concept for analysing contemporary social movement dynamics. Our micro-perspective, based on Goffman's (1974) interactional frames concept, supports an analysis of how movement participants with general online gaming literacy perceive themselves and their situations while negotiating their identities in public encounters within settings that in some ways resemble those found in MMOGs. Thus, when the spatial arrangement of a confrontational situation resembles a dungeon or battlefield, it may trigger connections between gaming experience and civil action. It is likely that the gaming literacies of Sunflower Movement participants prepared them with terminology, tools, and cultural repertoires that supported their ability to recognise roles and interactional frames, and to act accordingly.

As noted in a 2008 Pew report, young players who take part in game-related social interactions tend to be more engaged in civic and political affairs (Lenhart et al., 2008). During data collection for this and other research projects, we have found that online MMOG players regularly comment about current issues on game-related public channels—evidence of political awareness as well as the potential for participation in collective actions. Further, daily cooperative practices in MMOGs support player education in terms of quickly and flexibly collaborating with strangers – a development that supports the autonomous unfolding of new political and social actions such as the Sunflower Movement that are characterised by spatial occupation and two-party confrontations. This phenomenon contrasts sharply with traditional movements, which are heavily dependent upon preorganization on the part of core political groups.

Further, Sunflower Movement evidence and observations also support a broader perspective for analysing and understanding online gaming practices and culture, shifting the focus away from individual entertainment and toward community involvement in both physical and virtual worlds. Most contemporary MMOG players do not consider their time investments and participation in game communities as examples of social displacement that conflicts with their physical social lives, but as equally valuable and mutually penetrative as their offline activities. Social movement practices, empowered and constrained by participatory culture, offer a new and rich platform for layered investigations of an increasingly ludified society.

Note

1 A Chinese-language chronology of the Sunflower events is available at http://infographic.appledaily.com.tw/project/2014032701.

References

Benford, R.D. & Snow, D.A. (2000). Framing processes and social movements: An overview and assessment. *Annual Review of Sociology*, 26, 611–639.

Bennett, W. L. and Segerberg, A. (2012). The logic of connective action: Digital media and the personalization of contentious politics. *Information, Communication & Society*, 15(5): 739–768.

Boellstorff, T. (2015). *Coming of age in Second Life: An anthropologist explores the virtually human*. Princeton University Press.

Chao, V. (2014). How technology revolutionized Taiwan's Sunflower Movement: Facebook and Google, the favored tools of dissidents, are now shaping Taiwan's relationship with China. *The Diplomat*, April 15, 2014. Retrieved from http://thediplomat.com/2014/04/how-technology-revolutionized-taiwans-sunflower-movement/.

Gee, J. P. (2003). *What videogames have to teach us about learning and literacy*. New York: Palgrave Macmillan.

Gleason B. (2013). #Occupy Wall Street: Exploring informal learning about a social movement on Twitter. *American Behavioral Scientist*, 57, 966–982.

Goffman, E. (1974). *Frame analysis: An essay on the organization of experience*. London: Harper and Row.

Hardin, R. (1971). Collective action as an agreeable n-prisoners' dilemma. *Science*, 76, 472–481.

Jenkins, H. (2009). *Confronting the challenges of participatory culture: Media education for the 21st century*. Cambridge: MIT Press.

Kowert, R. (2015). *Video games and social competence.* New York: Routledge.

Lenhart, A., Kahne, J., Middaugh, E., Macgill, A.R., Evans, C. & Vitak, J. (2008). Teens, video games, and civics: Teens' gaming experiences are diverse and include significant social interaction and civic engagement. Pew Internet & American Life Project.

Lin, H. & Sun. (2011). A cyber diaspora in game world: Contact experience and identity negotiation among chinese and local players on Taiwanese World of Warcraft servers. *Digital Games Research Association (DiGRA) Conference,* Utrecht, the Netherlands.

Pearce, C., Boellstorff, T. & Nardi B. A. (2009). *Communities of play: Emergent cultures in multiplayer games and virtual worlds.* Cambridge, MA: MIT Press.

Raessens, J. (2014). The ludification of culture. In Fuchs et al. (eds), *Rethinking gamification,* 91–114. Meson Press.

Steinkuehler, C. A. (2008). Cognition and literacy in massively multiplayer online games. In D. Leu, J. Coiro, C. Lankshear, and K. Knobel (Eds.), *Handbook of research on new literacies.* Mahwah, NJ: Erlbaum.

Taylor, T. L. (2009). *Play between worlds: Exploring online game culture.* Cambridge, MA: MIT Press.

Williams, D., Ducheneaut, N., Xiong, L., Zhang, Y., Yee, N., & Nickell, E. (2006). From tree house to barracks the social life of guilds in World of Warcraft. *Games and Culture, 1*(4), 338–361.

12 Between Drudgery and "Promesse du Bonheur"

Games and Gamification

Mathias Fuchs

Gamification receives the most enthusiastic praises of leading to a "pleasure revolution" (Schell, 2011) and is at the same time dismissed as "bullshit" by others (Bogost, 2011). It seems that the appreciation of the process of turning extraludic activities into play is valued controversially and that the range of hopes and fears connected to the phenomenon range from extremely negative to utmost beneficial. This difference in opinion can be traced back to the classical positions in regard to games and play. Games can be valued in two different ways: Following Bataille (1975), we would hope that play could be a flight line from the servitude of the capital-labour relationship. Following Adorno (1970) and Benjamin (1939), however, we might discover that the escape from the drudgery of the worker leads to an equally alienating drudgery of the player. I argue that gamification might be seen as a form of ideology, but that games and gamification also hold the potential for change. Ever since the notion of gamification was introduced widely (Deterding, Dixon, Khaled, & Nacke, 2011; Reilhac, 2010; Schell, 2011), scholars have suggested that it is the mechanism of choice to turn playful activities into activities with an impact. This article analyses the controversial dialectics of self-contained play for play's sake and the ubiquitous notion of gamification as a purpose-driven activity that might actually trigger and shape social change.

Good Gamification

Similar to the cure-alls of medieval charlatans, the panacea of gamification was said to have an unlimited range of possible application areas and unrestricted trust and loyalty by the consumers: Gamification can "combine big data with the latest understanding of human motivation" (Paharia, 2013); "make living eco-friendly a lot more interesting" (Sexton, 2013); "can help children learn in the classroom, help build and maintain muscle memory, fight against some of the effects of aging, and distract from pain and depression" (Ramos, 2013); "When we're playing games, we're not suffering" (McGonigal, 2012b). These promises contain a *promesse du bonheur*, a prospect for better living, and the suggestion that gaming can definitely change individual lives and most probably change social life. But as long as there is no evidence for such change to have happened as a result of gaming, the promises might only conceal that games can neither change the individual nor society as a whole. It is difficult to falsify any of the announced effects of gamification because the inherent logic of the *apparatus* of gamification is consistent. Gamification has turned into one of the systems that Foucault described as:

> a thoroughly heterogeneous ensemble consisting of discourses, institutions, [...] administrative measures, scientific statements, philosophical, moral and philanthropic propositions–in short, the said as much as the unsaid (1977, p. 194).

Gamification as a *dispositif* or *apparatus* supports the current power-structure: Gamification is used as an administrative measure, it is talked about on blogs and in books like this one, it is used and misused by journalists, and it is applied to work as the rationale for propositions that contain a *promesse du bonheur* (wealth, health, end of suffering, reduction of the effects of aging) like religious salvation once did.

The notion of gamification was introduced widely in the 2010s (Deterding, Dixon, Khaled & Nacke, 2011; McGonigal, 2011; Schell, 2011; Zichermann & Cunningham, 2011) to suggest that marketing, design, health, and work might be seen as some kind of free play or leisure activity. A process that has been named by Joost Raessens the "ludification of culture" (2006) prepared us to consider activities as play that our parents and grandparents would never have thought of as play. Traditionally, three pillars of gamification would clearly have to be considered 'serious': health, work and economic exchange. During the timespan of one generation, this seems to have changed. Thirty years ago, nobody would have suspected that these fields could be mistaken for fun. Conversational language, proverbs, status of characters in novels and film, and pathos formulas within cultural artefacts would solidify what predecessor generations felt to be common sense and nondisputable. At least three assumptions were felt to be rock-solid and unquestionable.

Health, to start with, was a serious matter. People have been taking about a 'serious' condition. The patients asked the doctor: "Is it serious?" It took a quite a few years of ludification to arrive at a situation where popular new media could publish headlines such as "Fun ways to Cure Cancer" (Scott, 2013). Our parents would have been shocked and most probably argued that you do not make fun with such things as health. (Knock on Wood!)

Second, work was an aspect of life that could not be mingled with fun. "All work and no play makes Jack a dull boy," is constructed upon the firm opposition of work and play. The saying has been documented in print as early as 1659 in James Howell's *Paroimiographia* (Howell, 1659,

p. 12). Obviously considered to be of a commutative nature, the Irish novelist Maria Edgeworth added a line to the proverb:

All work and no play makes Jack a dull boy.
All play and no work makes Jack a mere toy.

Only children were allowed to confuse work and play or tools and toys and only they can say: "I am working very hard now", when they move their *Bob the Builder* dolls or their *Playmobil* characters on their playroom floors. Nowadays, proper grownups pretend that they play, when they work (Figure 12.1). Google employees have slides connecting their offices to prove that working for Google is mere play.

A poster in the streets of Berlin announcing shared office spaces for rent carries the slogan: "In ev'ry work that must be done, there is an element of fun". Obviously inspired by Mary Poppins the landlords of the rental space rely on some kind of magic that will turn work into play. The magic trick that makes the potential customers believe in this is called gamification. Zygmunt Bauman argues that playfulness in our ludic culture is no longer confined to childhood, but has become a lifelong attitude: "The mark of postmodern adulthood is the willingness to embrace the game whole-heartedly, as children do" (Bauman, 1995, p. 99). This very willingness to subscribe to playfulness as a guiding principle for most different activities has been diagnosed by Johan Huizinga as a character flaw that treats serious things as games and games as serious things. Huizinga blames what he calls "puerilism" for this "contamination" of play (Huizinga, 1936). In *The Shadow of Tomorrow*, Huizinga describes puerilism as

> [...] the evil of our time. For nowadays play in many cases never ends and hence it is not true play. A far-reaching contamination of play and serious activity has taken place. The two spheres are getting mixed. In the activities of an outwardly serious nature hides an element of play. Recognised play, on the other hand, is no longer able to maintain its true play-character as a result of being taken too seriously and being technically over-organized.
>
> (Huizinga, 1936, p. 177)

It seems that "the evil" of Huizinga's time has returned. The spheres of play and serious activity are mixed, blended and jumbled up. We even have an apologetic term to describe the paradoxical confusion: gamification. The second decade of the 21st century praises gamification and serious games as the key to wealth, health, and pleasure. Jess Schell goes as far as putting it into an anthropologic framework that has survival, followed by efficiency, and then followed again by fun: "We are moving from a time when life was all about survival to a time when it was about

Figure 12.1 Poster announcing co-working spaces in the streets of Berlin.

efficiency into a new era where gamification design is largely about what is pleasureable" (Schell, 2011). Such high hopes are in stark contrast to Huizinga's concerns about a dangerous and widespread phenomenon of puerilism. He warns of an

> attitude of a community whose behaviour is more immature than the state of its intellectual and critical faculties would warrant, which instead of making the boy into the man adapts to that of the adolescent age.
>
> (Huizinga, 1936, p. 170)

The Dutch philosopher and anthropologist may sound extremely pessimistic here, and the account he gives about U.S. politics and professional sports (sic!) just underlines what he thinks is wrong with society, but he obviously did not want his writings to abandon all hope; on page nine of the *Shadow of Tomorrow,* he states: "It is possible that these pages will lead many to think of me as a pessimist. I have but this to answer: I am an optimist" (Huizinga, 1936, p. 9). Different from the blind optimism of contemporary gamification evangelists, Huizinga did not see any benefits in turning a society into a society of eternal adolescents. His hope was rather directed towards a recovery of the 'sacred' boundary separating work from play. There is no evidence for such a separation being desirable today. By the turn of the century Jeremy Rifkin argues: "Play is becoming as important in the cultural economy as work was in the industrial economy" (Rifkin, 2000, p. 263).

A third premise that was guarded by the believe system of our parents' generation, was a strict separation between monetary transactions and ludic activities. Today, play turns out to be the number one ray of hope for the possibility of economic growth. Postindustrial society believes in monetary transactions being playful and relies upon exploiting the potential of such new forms of playfulness. Extremely hazardous economic transactions of so called 'big players' such as Northern Rock, Bank of Scotland, Lloyds, and Lehmann Brothers made it evident that gambling with huge financial resources was part of the daily banking business, the notion of "casino capitalism" (Strange, 1986) demystified the alleged seriousness of Wall Street and the finance sector. Gambler-stockbrokers turned out to be the new superheroes with enormous income and massive bonuses and the new super villains, who ruined thousands of clients, companies, and complete national economies in a fraction of a second. Other than the obsessive players of Dostoyevsky's novels, these gamblers were real and did not jeopardise their own fortune and future, but those of others. The gamification of the finance sector served as legitimisation for irrational risk-taking in economic transactions. According to Kuhnen and Knutson:

> The relationship between affect and risk taking that we propose here suggests a possible explanation for asset bubbles and crashes. Positive returns in financial markets may induce a positive affective state and make investors more willing to invest in stocks, and more confident that they have chosen the right portfolio, which will lead to increased buying pressure and future positive returns.

To spell out the concrete events Kuhnen and Knutson refer to, it is the "relationship between affect and risk taking" that can be made responsible for the real estate crash and the financial crisis of 2002. It is however, also possible that this very correlation can be used to stabilise micro-economies or private households. Apps that increase the efficiency of savings work with gamification mechanics, and software like *SaveUp* or *Punch the Pig* encourage their users to account carefully for their finances, make regular savings and stop irrational spending.

If play is good for our health, our working conditions and for our financial well-being, why should it not be possible to play our complete selves? Self-tracking and self-observation became the fashionable way of improving oneself. Whereas "technologies of the self" (Foucault, 1988) were centred around the care of oneself and used meditation and "gymnasia" (sports) in antiquity, modern technologies of the self were optimisation technologies that could be called "work on the self". Mark Butler argues that we have now reached a point that when playing with ourselves replaces the before mentioned care of the self and the work with the selves (Butler, 2014). Jennifer Whitson identifies the playfulness in monitoring our bodies and emotions for the purpose of self-improvement:

> There is already a game being played within everyday metering. Every time we imagine an action with multiple future outcomes, this becomes a game (see Malaby, 2007). For example, every time we prepare to step on a weigh scale, we play a game with ourselves: Will I be heavier? Have I lost weight? Have I hit my goal of losing two pounds? We frame our experiences in narratives of success and failure, and develop strategies for attaining victory (or evoke rituals such as the shucking out of clothes that may taint our results and praying for divine intervention).
>
> (Whitson, 2013, p. 169)

Once these games become formalised and implemented on digital devices, play turns into an activity that gamifies aspects of our daily life. The reason for playing this kind of mini-games is a mix of curiosity, boredom, and a promise of trophies and prices one is expected to be given. The gifts can rarely be monetised directly. They are either add-ons to the games played or they are access rights to services that one never did want to gain in the first place. My personal collection of gifts include a night in a five-star hotel in Dubai (if I get there at my own expenses), an upgrade from class C rental car to a class B rental car in Funchal (Madeira), a pair of men's slippers, and a free ticket for a friend to go to a *Star Wars* movie (if I was so desperate as to go there myself and pay for it). The give-aways of gamification are like the presents you get from distant relatives at Christmas times. Worse than the teapots from old aunts, gamification prices always serve the benefits of someone else (airlines that offer flights to Dubai or Madeira, an apartment store, a cinema that shows *Star Wars* movies). The presents are commodities in disguise. They are given away to get something back.

Free Gifts for All

A gift in a gamification context is never "le don" as Marcel Mauss conceived it emphatically (1923/24). The gamified *homo ludens* is just an advancement of the *homo economicus*. Marcel Mauss' gift and even more so George Bataille's excessive gift held a promise for the possibility to escape the cage of traditional economic reasoning. Mauss expresses his hope in the conclusions section of *Le Don*:

> Fortunately, everything is still not wholly categorised in terms of buying and selling. Things still have sentimental as well as venal value, assuming values merely of this kind exist. We possess more than a tradesman morality.
>
> (Mauss, 1990, p. 83)

But he is also sceptical about the possibility to escape the reciprocality of the gift and quotes an old Maori proverb, which is indicative of most of his ethnographic observations:

> Ko Maru kai atu
> Ko maru kai mai
> ka ngohe ngohe.
> 'Give as much as you take, all shall be very well.'
>
> (Mauss, 1990, p. 91)

Mauss was tempted, yet still hesitant to identify or predict a social configuration that would allow for an anti-utilitarian mechanism of gift-making beyond the limits of reciprocality. Pierre Bourdieu, Jacques Derrida, Alain Caillé, and the *Mouvement Anti-Utilitariste dans les Sciences Sociales* (M.A.U.S.S.) went a step further in this regard (Strehle, 2009, p. 129). It is not hard to see whose groundwork it was that prepared the theories of M.A.U.S.S. Influenced by the very same author, Bataille developed his utopian model of an economy beyond reciprocal exchange. Bataille was hoping for a Copernican revolution that turns an economy of scarcity into one of excess: "Changing from the perspectives of *restrictive* economy to those of *general* economy actually accomplishes a Copernican transformation: a reversal of thinking—and of ethics" (1991, p. 25). Bataille identifies the gift, excessive play, and sexuality as areas where this 'general economy' can already be observed nowadays. The French philosopher thinks of playing games in the wider sense as a nucleus of emancipation.

One hundred and forty years earlier, Karl Marx already played with the possibility that labour could escape the state of alienation and drudgery that it needs to have under capitalist relations of production. In *Excerpts from James Mill's Book "Élémens d' économie politique"*,

Marx sketches an utopian mode of economic relations that is not based on reciprocality of equivalent value exchange. "Let's assume we would have produced as humans. My work would be free expression of life and life's craving. It would therefore also be the enjoyment of living" (Marx, 1981, p. 462).

In such a situation, giving would be part of the craving and every gift would be a deliberate present. The reason to give would then not be to exchange and get back, but to just give. Samuel Strehle analyses this proposal from the viewpoint of human history:

> I give for the reason of giving, not of receiving. The communist liberation of man from his 'prehistory', the leap of mankind from the realm of necessity into the realm of freedom is essentially the liberation from reciprocality.[1]
>
> (Strehle, 2009, p. 144)

Theoreticians like Marx, Bataille, and, to some degree, Mauss were desperate to identify an element in society that would have the potential to disrupt or to even break open this cage of necessities effected by the system. Marcel Mauss (1923/24) believed that a fundamental quality of human interaction should exist outside the rationality of exchange and of monetary interest. Giving away without any expectation for payback allows us to act in a way that is non-alienated and differs considerably from the exchange of commodities with the aim of profit making. George Bataille's (1975) perspective on economic structure used the concept of the gift developed by Maus to support his affirmation of the possibility of human sovereignty within economic systems. For Georges Bataille, play was one of the conceivable frameworks that foster a type of sacrifice that resembles a gift. The game in a Huizingian (1938) sense of a free activity was therefore interpreted as opposed to alienated work. *Gaming* and *labour* would be diametrically opposed, and the 'sacred' within play was a source of hope to escape the master-slave dialectic of capital-labour relationships. Bataille did not phrase it in this way, but his theory suggests that gaming could change society in a positive way.

Bad Gamification

The question at stake here is, whether games actually change our society in such a way that work turns into play or whether it is just an ideological misconception that makes us think the former could be the case. There are good reasons to think of gamification as ideology. Gamification is intended to raise the profits of companies, and is said to do so at a staggering rate. Gabe Zichermann, one of leading industry consultants estimates that "Gamification techniques can increase productivity of employees by 40%" (Zichermann, 2013). As this rise in productivity is achieved under prevailing economic settings, there is obviously nothing to gain for labour. The profits remain on the side of capital. The necessities of the system guarantee what Louis Althusser describes as the reproduction of production relations ensured by the wage system (Althusser, 1971). It is due to "ideological apparatuses" like the one we call gamification that relations of production are not questioned, but are reproduced to increase the profit rate.

It is not always apparent on the level of individual gamification projects to see how the seemingly well-intended efforts to save water, cure diseases or increase health are linked and embedded into the whole of the "ideological state apparatuses" (Althusser, 1971). The extension of play into all kinds of nongaming contexts leads to an overaccumulation of play. This is to say that play looses its liberating dynamics and turns into a phase that is characterised by quantitative increase of games and gaming up to the level of play congestion. A situation could arise where the system's capacity to cope with further increase of playfulness is exhausted. This might lead to a qualitative leap that turns diversity into totality and free play into total play. As a perversion of the original play drive that is sensuous, liberating and free, a mode of total gamification could be prefigured where games are the new normal and where games are the only normal. It can be observed already in our decade that games are given a general license to be the solution to any conceivable problem. In his famous statement "Games are the New Normal" (Gore, 2011), the former vice president Al Gore paved the way for a general pardon for the impact of games and for a license for games (and the games industry) to proceed and expand without limits. Exclusive normality leads to totality. "Total gamification" (Fuchs, 2015) would describe a situation where all human and technical resources have to be gamified. In regard to human resources, we are already facing a situation where the old and the young, men and women, various ethnic groups and a huge reserve army of minorities and niche population are drawn into the gaming arenas. The main games industries work with their brothers in arms of the indie games industry to incessantly recruit new audiences: the homeless, black teenage mums, those with depression or Alzheimer's. But also on a technical level, total gamification takes its toll. In his essay, *Gamification as the Post-Modern Phalanstère*, Flavio Escribano describes a sector of gamification that he calls "technological gamification" (Escribano, 2012, p. 206–207). This is a type of gamification that is triggered and driven by technological innovation. Escribano's concept is reminiscent of Huizinga's complaint about play "being technically over-organized" (Huizinga, 1936, p. 177).

Escribano describes how large-scale simulations, medical research, sports training, or military operations are run on games technology to benefit from its ease of use, low cost, efficiency, legal status, and design appeal. One of the examples of "technical gamification" Escribano unmasks as serious and evil business done with allegedly harmless play-tools is the case of former Iraq authorities having bought 4,000 PlayStation 2 consoles to evade the computer embargo imposed upon Iraq in 2000. "Intelligence agencies suspected the hardware of these consoles was to be used to create a computer capable of controlling the trajectory of missiles equipped with chemical warheads" (Escribano, 2012, p. 206).

Good-looking Bad Gamification

Are there conceivable situations, when gamification seems to be all right and still it is not right at all? When Jane McGonigal (2012a) promises the audience of the popular TED talks to increase the live expectancy of every single person in the room by 10 years, if they invested in playing more often, she is of course telling a lie. But her statement, which is firmly and intentionally integrated within the ideology of gamification, carries a philanthropic utopian promise that connotes with moral statements, quasiempirical data, and light philosophical speculation. Nobody cares whether one year, 10 years, 11 years, or no time at all of added lifetime results from her gamified self-control therapy. And nobody will ever know. This is the nature of ideological statements: Whether they are true or false does not really matter. What matters here is an ensemble of references ("I am a game designer"), of status symbols (TED talks), of power (research and development director of the Institute for the Future), commitment to rationality ("I have maths to prove this"), and an endearing naïveté that announces big changes to come with only minimal efforts to be undertaken.

It is for these mentioned reasons why we suggest to conceive of gamification as the latest form of ideology. When the evangelists of gamification tell us that work must be play, that our personalities will be playful, that the whole economy is a game, and that each and every activity from cradle to grave can be turned into a game, we encounter false consciousness that is socially necessary. Today, gamification is used to tell people that if reality is not satisfactory, then at least play might be so. McGonigal (2011) phrased this aptly in her popular proposal that "reality is broken". Replacing reality-based praxis with storytelling, gaming, self-motivation, or 'self-expansion escapism' (Kollar, 2013) is what Marx and Engels would have labelled as ideology. McGonigal's 'When we're playing games, we're not suffering' (McGonigal, 2012b) is the cynical statement of somebody who is definitely not suffering economically and has probably little reason and even less time to play games any longer.

There are two complementary reasons to rightly classify gamification as ideology:

1 Gamification is false consciousness: The proposition that game design elements can change the nature of labour and successfully cope with exploitation, "alienation" (Zichermann & Linder, 2013), or "suffering" (McGonigal, 2012b) is proven on the basis of subjective assessment or mere speculation and not based on empirical economic analysis.
2 Gamification is socially necessary: Concluding from market analysis and market predictions data that Saatchi & Saatchi, Gartner, and Ernst & Young offer, the industry needs to implement gamification in most of the sectors that drive our economy. It will, therefore, be mandatory for consumers and prosumers to embrace gamification as well. Gamification is not a choice; it is necessary for the political economy of this decade.

Ideology works best when it distorts reality in such a way that we do not notice the distortion because everything seems to be all right. Although in fact a mistaken identity and a unification of play and labour serve the needs of the economic system, the ideas of ideology make it appear natural. It makes the subordinate classes accept a state of alienation against which they would otherwise revolt. This state of alienation has also been referred to as 'false consciousness.' In the closing chapter of Alfred Sohn-Rethel's *Intellectual and Manual Labour* (1978), the author invokes the concept of "necessary false consciousness." This is a type of false consciousness that is not just faulty consciousness. Necessary false consciousness is rather a type of false consciousness that is logically correct. However cruel, meaningless, or destructive it might seem, it is necessary for the system in which we are working to keep working until we die, so that we will shop until we drop.

It might be useful at this point to ask why such a complex phenomenon like gamification has to be installed, made popular and disseminated widely to warrant for the stability of the relations of production. In traditional Marxist understanding an ideology generally refers to theory that is out of touch with material processes of history. In *The German Ideology,* Marx and Engels observe that the ruling ideas of an epoch "are nothing more than the ideal expression of the dominant material relationships, the dominant material relationships grasped as ideas" (Marx & Engels, 2004, p. 64). They are the "Illusion of the Epoch". If we consider gamification as a ruling idea of our times and society, very much like "morality, religion, metaphysics" (Marx & Engels 2004, p. 64) have been ruling ideas for an earlier time and society, then gamification seems to the people to define and design material reality. According to Marx and Engels, it is the other way round. People believe that gamification efforts would redesign the health system, would create now financial opportunities, and would reconfigure working conditions. But this is ideology: false consciousness. It is instead true – according to Marx – that the production relations and the ensemble of means of production create ideas – like gamification – that become dominant ideas. Louis Althusser's concept of the "ideological state apparatuses" advances from the classical concept of ideology as false consciousness. Althusser rejects the concept of ideology as a distorted representation of reality by which the dominant elite cynically exploits the working classes, as a simplification. For him ideology is much more than a set of instrumental lies. Althusser proposes that all consciousness is constituted by and necessarily inscribed within ideology. Neither the elite nor avant-garde under-class intelligentsia can develop "true consciousness". Ideology as "necessary false consciousness" is a superstructure with a high degree of autonomy. Gamification can be seen as a part of this immense superstructure. In this context gamification is a mechanism for producing certain social practices. Bonus systems in supermarkets, playful communication on *Facebook* and other social media platforms, hotel booking with multiple-star ranking (Schrape, 2014, p. 21–46) or academic research incentives in the form of board games (Fuchs, 2014) are such social practices. As a result of first suggesting and then producing ways of being they also circulate forms of understanding the 'real'. In this way, gamification has a productive role in ideology formation.

Conclusion

I hope to have demonstrated that the complexity of the gamification phenomenon asks for an assessment that is multilayered and goes beyond simplifying assumptions of gamification being either just good or exclusively bad. There are elements of necessity and falseness dialectically interwoven into gamification processes that make them less enjoyable than a "pleasure revolution" (Schell, 2011) and more complex than "bullshit" (Bogost, 2011). If we agree to analyse gamification as an ideological state apparatus we must understand that gamification has a productive role in the formation of our selves and of consciousness at large.

It would be too simple to stop at a point where Adorno criticised the "repetitiveness of gaming" as nothing but "an after-image of involuntary servitude" (1984, p. 401; Adorno, "Nachbild von unfreier Arbeit", 1970, p. 371). One would also have to advance from Walter Benjamin's observation that the gamer's actions resemble those of the proletarian worker as they perform what is derived of all meaning: "drudgery of the player" ("Fron des Spielers", 1939, p. 72–73). Gamification has meaning and produces meaning in its role as ideology. An important transformation taking place in society and being reflected and promoted by gamification is the subsumption of play under the relations of production.

Aware of that Jürgen Habermas wrote his ultimate antigamification statement in the 1950s, when he told us in a somewhat melancholic mood: "And where it ever had existed, the unity of work and play dissolved" (1958/59, p. 220). Habermas is here the voice of the Frankfurt Critical School but also the voice of a materialist and Marxist view on the relation of labour and play. It is not by chance, therefore, that Habermas shares the belief promoted by Benjamin and Adorno that labour and play are two different things that certainly have an influence on each other, but that never can be harmonised as one.

Ultimately, the attempt to harmonise play and labour is ideology. Gamification that has at its core the suggestion that work can be fun is therefore caught in the trap of a self-contained ideological system that is in synch with the development of the relations of production of our society. 'Work is Play' might sound spectacular and enjoyable, but it is untrue because of its nature as necessary false consciousness.

Note

1 transl. MF, orig.: "Das Geben selbst wird zum Bedürfnis und jede Gabe in gewissem Sinne zur Simmel'schen 'ersten Gabe', ja zum Geschenk aus freien Stücken. Ich gebe, um zu geben, nicht um zu erhalten. Der kommunistische Ausgang des Menschen aus der bloßen 'Vorgeschichte', der 'Sprung der Menschheit aus dem Reich der Notwendigkeit in das Reich der Freiheit' ist in seiner Essenz der Ausbruch aus der Reziprozität."

References

Adorno, T. W. (1995 = 1970, engl. 1984) *Ästhetische Theorie*. Frankfurt/M: Suhrkamp.

Althusser, L. (1971) Ideology and ideological state apparatuses. In *Lenin and Philosophy and other Essays*. London: NLB, pp. 121–176.

Bataille, G. (1991) *The accursed share: Volume I*. New York: Zone Books.

Bataille, G. (1975) *Das theoretische Werk I: Die Aufhebung der Ökonomie (Der Begriff der Verausgabung—Der verfemte Teil—Kommunismus und Stalinismus)*. München: Rogner & Bernhard.

Bauman, Z. (1995) *Life in fragments: Essays in postmodern morality*. Hoboken, NJ: Wiley-Blackwell.

Benjamin, W. (1939) Über einige Motive bei Baudelaire. *Zeitschrift für Sozialforschung*, 8 (1), pp. 50–91.

Bogost, I. (2011) Gamification is bullshit! My position statement at the Wharton Gamification Symposium. *Ian Bogost Blog*, August 8. Retrieved from http://www.bogost.com/blog/gamification_is_bullshit.shtml.

Butler, M. (2014) *Das Spiel mit sich (Kink, Drugs & Hip-Hop). Populäre Techniken des Selbst zu Beginn des 21. Jahrhunderts*. Berlin: Kulturverlag Kadmos.

Deterding, S., Dixon, D. Khaled, R. & Nacke, L. (2011) "Gamification: Toward a definition", *Proceedings of the CHI (Conference on Human Factors in Computing Systems)*, Vancouver, BC. Retrieved from http://gamification-research.org/chi2011/papers/. Accessed 20 March 2014, pp. 1–4.

Escribano, F. (2012) Gamification as the post-modern phalanstère. In: P. Zackariasson & T. L. Wilson (Eds.), *The video game industry*. London: Routledge.

Foucault, M. (1977) "The confession of the flesh. Interview in C. Gordon" (1980). *Power/knowledge selected interviews and other writings*. New York: Pantheon Books, pp. 194–228.

Foucault, M.(1988) *Technologies of the Self*. L. H. Martin, H. Gutman, & P. H. Hutton (Eds.). Amherst, MA: University of Massachusetts Press.

Fuchs, M. (2014). Gamification as 21st century ideology. *Journal of Games and Virtual Worlds, 6*(2 June), 143–157.

Fuchs, M. (2015) Total gamification. In M. Fuchs (Ed.), *Diversity of pay*. Lüneburg: meson press.

Gore, A. (2011) Keynote Lecture at the 8th Annual Games for Change Festival in New York. Gamasutra, 20 June. Retrieved from http://www.gamasutra.com/view/news/35310/G4C_Al_Gore_Says_Games_Have_Clearly_Arrived_As_A_Mass_Medium.php. Accessed 29 October 2016.

Habermas, J. (1968, original text 1958) Soziologische Notizen zum Verhältnis von Arbeit und Freizeit. In H. Giesecke (Ed.), *Freizeit und Konsumerziehung*, Göttingen: Vandenhoeck & Ruprecht, pp. 105–122.

Howell, J. (1659) *Paroimiographia proverbs, or, old sayed savves & adages in English (or the Saxon toung), Italian, French, and Spanish, whereunto the British for their great antiquity and weight are added ...* collected by J.H., Esqr.

Huizinga, J. (1936) *In the shadow of tomorrow*. New York: W. W. Norton, & Company, Inc. Publishers.

Kollar, P. (2013) Jane McGonigal on the good and bad of video game escapism. *Polygon*, March 28, 2013. Retrieved online http://www.polygon.com/2013/3/28/4159254/jane-mcgonigal-video-game-escapism. Accessed 15 December 2013.

Kuhnen, C., & Knutson, B. (2011) The influence of affect on beliefs, preferences, and financial decisions. *Journal of Financial and Quantitative Analysis, 46*(3) (June), 605–626.

Malaby, Thomas. (2007). Beyond play: A new approach to games. *Games and Culture, 2*(2) (April), 95–113.

Mauss, M. (1990 = French original 1923/24) *The Gift. The forms and reason of exchange in archaic societies*, W.D. Halls (trans.), London: Routledge.

Marx, K. and Engels, F. (2004 = German Original 1844) *The German ideology*. New York: International Publishers.

Marx, K. (1981). *Auszüge aus James Mills Buch "Élémens d' économie politique"*. In: K. Marx & F. Engels, Marx-Engels-Werke (MEW), Ergänzungsband I. (pp. 463–465). Berlin: Dietz.

McGonigal, J. (2011) *Reality is broken. Why games make us better and how they can change the world*. New York: The Penguin Press.

McGonigal, J. (2012a) The game that can give you 10 extra years of life, *TED*, June 2012, Retrieved from http://www.ted.com/talks/jane_mcgonigal_the_game_that_can_give_you_10_extra_years_of_life.html. Accessed 20 March 2014.

McGonigal, J. (2012b) When we're playing games, we're not suffering. Retrieved from http://www.avantgame.com/. Accessed 12 March 2014.

Paharia, R. (2013) *Loyalty 3.0: How to revolutionize customer and employee engagement with big data and gamification.* New York: McGraw-Hill Professional.

Raessens, J. (2006) Playful identities, or the ludification of culture. *Games and Culture, 1*(1), 52–57.

Ramos, J. (2013) Gaming console or health care control panel? *Allied Health World, 11* (June). Retrieved from http://www.alliedhealthworld.com/blog/category/uncategorized/gaming-console-or-health-care-control-panel.html. Accessed 15 December 2013.

Reilhac, M. (2010) The gameification of life Retrieved from http://de.slideshare.net/tishna/the-gameification-of-life. Accessed 15 December 2013.

Rifkin, J. (2000) *The age of access. The new culture of hypercapitalism, where all of life is a paid-for experience.* New York: Jeremy P. Tarcher/Putnam.

Schell, J. (2011) The pleasure revolution: Why games will lead the way. Retrieved from https://www.youtube.com/watch?v=4PkUgCiHuH8. Accessed 15 December 2013.

Schrape, N. (2014) Gamification and governmentality. In: M. Fuchs, S. Fizek, P. Ruffino, & N. Schrape (Eds.), *Rethinking gamification.* Lüneburg: meson press.

Scott, H. (2013) Amazon, Facebook, and Google design fun way to cure cancer. *iTech Post*, 1 March 2013. Retrieved from http://www.itechpost.com/articles/5935/20130301/amazon-facebook-google-design-game-cure-cancer-research-uk.htm. Accessed 20 March 2014.

Sohn-Rethel, A. (1970) *Geistige und körperliche Arbeit. Zur Theorie gesellschaftlicher Synthesis.* Frankfurt am Main: Suhrkamp.

Sohn-Rethel, A. (1978) *Intellectual and manual labour.* Atlantic Highlands, NJ: Humanities Press.

Sexton, C. (2013) Life's a game. Be prepared to play with gamification, *Happy Valley Communications.* Retrieved from http://www.happyvalleycommunications.com/lifes-a-game-be-prepared-to-play-with-gamification/. Accessed 12 March 2014.

Strange, S. (1986) *Casino capitalism.* Oxford: Blackwell Publishers.

Strehle, S. (2009) *Jenseits des Tausches. Karl Marx und die Soziologie der Gabe.* Freiburg im Breisgau: Berliner Journal für Soziologie.

Whitson, J. R. (2013) Gaming the quantified self. *Surveillance & Society, 11*(1/2): 163–176.

Zichermann, G., & Cunningham, C. (2011). *Gamification by design: Implementing game mechanics in web and mobile apps.* O'Reilly Media, Inc.

List of Contributors

Joceran Borderie, PhD, is a social psychologist and game designer. His fields of expertise include cooperation, optimal experience states, team coaching, and game design. His research explores the intersection of social psychology and game design to further our understanding of cooperative gameplay in video games and enhance e-sports teams' efficiency. He also has more than 15 years of experience working on game-world building and story writing.

Andy Boyan, PhD, received his doctorate in Communication from Michigan State University (USA), where his research focussed on educational outcomes of interactions with game mechanics. He is currently working on a project examining communication as a complex phenomenon, and uniting this with digital game studies in conversation and social networks as well as in model matching a digital game learning hypothesis. He also serves on the executive board of the Game Studies Division on the National Communication Association.

Johannes Breuer, PhD, works as a postdoctoral researcher in the media and communication psychology group at the University of Cologne (Germany) and the project "Redefining Tie Strength" at the Knowledge Media Research Center in Tübingen (Germany). Previously, he was involved in the research project "The social fabric of virtual life: A longitudinal multi-method study on the social foundations of online gaming". He received his doctorate in psychology from the University of Cologne (Germany) with a thesis on video games, aggression, and learning. His research interests include the uses and effects of digital games, learning with new media, and the methods of media effects research.

Frederik De Grove, PhD, holds a Master's degree in Communication Sciences from Ghent University. In December 2014, he successfully defended his doctorate, which explored the game-related practices in the everyday life of young people. In his thesis, special attention was directed towards the relation between agency and structure and how to approach it methodologically and empirically. As a postdoctoral researcher, his interests include the interplay between digital media forms and communicative structures, the lifecycle of virtual communities and interest groups, social network analysis, and digital methods. In general, he is passionate about new media, methodology, and data analysis for the social sciences.

Teresa de la Hera, PhD, is a postdoctoral researcher and lecturer in New Media and Digital Culture at the Department of Media and Culture Studies at Utrecht University, where she is a core member of the Center for the Study of Digital Games and Play. She started her academic career in Spain in 2005 where she conducted research in the fields of new media and persuasive games. In 2011, she moved to the Netherlands where she obtained an International Ph.D. Fellowship to finish her doctorate: "Persuasive Structures in Advergames" at Utrecht University. Her thesis was awarded in 2014 as the Best Academic Work in the Field of Audiovisual Communication written by a Spanish Scholar by the Spanish Consell de l'Audiovisual de Catalunya. She is working on the Netherlands Organisation for Scientific Research–funded research project "Persuasive Gaming in Context" in which she explores the persuasive potential of digital games. She is also coordinator of the research domain Games for Inclusion of the Focus Area Game Research at Utrecht University.

Cherylann Edwards is a digital games researcher and a doctoral student within the School of Humanities at Griffith University in Australia. Her research interests include negotiating conflict within virtual gaming environments and the history of gaming through the experience of older gamers. Her doctoral research explores how multigenerational families can use the medium of video games to perform family togetherness from the perspective of the older gamer. Cherylann has been a gamer for more than 40 years. She enjoys most genres of games, but prefers massive online multiplayer online role-playing games, which she plays regularly with her children and grandchildren. She is looking forward to the next expansion of *World of Warcraft.*

Jesse Fox, PhD, is an assistant professor in the School of Communication at The Ohio State University and Director of the VECTOR (Virtual Environment, Communication Technology, & Online Research) Lab. Some of her research interests include video games, virtual environments, social media, and issues surrounding sex and gender in online spaces. Her work has appeared in journals such as *Journal of Communication, Communication Research,* and *New Media & Society.*

Mathias Fuchs, PhD, is an artist, musician, and media scholar. He pioneered in the artistic use of computer games and exhibited work at ISEA, SIGGRAPH, transmediale, PSi #11, futuresonic, EAST, and the Greenwich Millennium Dome. He was senior lecturer at the

University of Salford/UK from 2002 to 2012. In October 2012, he became a professor at Leuphana University in Lüneburg and is currently a professor at the Institute of Culture and Aesthetics of Media (ICAM) at Leuphana University in Lüneburg.

Qi Hao, PhD, is an assistant professor in the Department of Electrical and Computer Engineering at the University of Alabama Tuscaloosa.

Ruud S. Jacobs, MSc, is a doctoral candidate at the Erasmus Research Centre for Media, Communication, and Culture (ERMeCC) at the Erasmus University Rotterdam in the Netherlands. His doctoral project is focussed on the validation of persuasive games: games developed with the primary intention to persuade. His work is part of the Netherlands Organisation for Scientific Research–funded research project 'Persuasive Gaming in Context'. Apart from finding proof for attitudinal effects of persuasive games, he is interested in the psychology of entertainment media. His other tasks at Erasmus University Rotterdam include managing the ERMeCC Digital Research Lab and lecturing courses on statistics and quantitative methods (among others) in the International Bachelor Communication and Media.

Jeroen Jansz, PhD, holds the Chair of Communication and Media in the Department of Media & Communication at Erasmus University Rotterdam. He is a member of ERMeCC, the Erasmus Research Centre for Media, Communication, and Culture. His research is about the reception of new media. The appeal of digital games is a long-standing research interest. Currently, he and his coworkers are conducting a large-scale project on persuasive gaming: see http://persuasivegaming.nl; for his publications, see http://jeroenjansz.nl/. He is cofounder of the Game Studies Division in the International Communication Association, a member of PEGI's expert group (Pan European Game Information), and president of NeFCA, the Netherlands Flanders Communication Association.

Kendra Knight, PhD, earned her doctorate in Human Communication at Arizona State University. She serves as assistant professor of Communication Studies at DePaul University in Chicago, IL, USA. Her research examines a range of interpersonal communication processes (conflict, avoidance, repair), usually within romantic or close dyads but also between zero-history dyads. Her current work focusses on the negotiation of school/work and love among U.S. emerging adults.

Rachel Kowert, PhD, received her doctorate in psychology from the University of York (UK), where her research focussed on the relationships between social competence and online video game involvement. She recently completed a 2-year research post working on the EU-funded project SOFOGA – The Social Fabric of Virtual Life: A Longitudinal multimethod study on the social foundations of online gaming. She currently serves on the board of DiGRA (Digital Games Research Association) and the International Communication Association (ICA) Game Studies special interest group. For more information about Rachel, and her research, visit www.rkowert.com.

Annakaisa Kultima, PhD, is a game researcher that has been studying game design since 2006 at the University of Tampere Game Research Lab, Finland. Her research has been focussing on the role of creativity in game development contextualising it to a wider fabric of the game industry ecosystem and the everyday life of the game creators. She has been running several design research projects concentrating on the changing trends of the industry including hybrid play, the casual turn, and innovation in games and playful media. She teaches game research, design research, and game design at the University of Tampere and gives visiting lectures all over the world.

Benny Liebold, PhD, is a researcher in the Institute for Media Research at Chemnitz University of Technology. His research focusses on the cognitive and emotional processing of virtual environments with an emphasis on the role of emotions in human-computer interaction, presence, game studies, and media effects in general, such as skill transfer and aggressive behaviour.

Holin Lin, PhD, is professor of Sociology, National Taiwan University. Her major research interests include digital game studies, Internet and society, and gender studies. Since the late 1990s, she has been working on the interrelation between cultural practice, social relation, and economic action in massively multiplayer online communities. Her work focusses on several aspects: (1) the social dynamics of online gaming communities including norm and deviance negotiation, risk-management and cooperation with strangers, and altruistic game-tip sharing behaviours; (2) family relations mediated through video game technology, by analysing the phenomenon of adult children's giving Wii as a gift for parents to perform filial piety; (3) physical context of playing video games and its implications, including gendered gaming experience in different physical spaces and the role of onlookers in defining gaming situation; (4) the changing relations between the "magic circle" of gameplay and real-world economy as well as the blurring of work and leisure, labor and play, including the real money trading as a new form of cyber workers and the identity negotiation among Internet-hobbyist game workers; and (5) the underground culture of playing on private game servers (rouge servers) as a way of achieving more customised gaming experiences. Her most recent research explores the spatial implication of multiplayer online game worlds as new places for cross-border interaction in which physically distanced individuals "live together" on daily life basis.

André Marchand, PhD, is an assistant professor at the Marketing Center Muenster, University of Muenster, Germany. His research focusses on digitalization in marketing. Furthermore, he is interested in strategic media marketing, consumer behaviour in the digital era, and innovation management. He is also enthusiastic about the video games industry, especially about massive online multiplayer games. Previously, he also worked as a strategic business analyst for several enterprises. His work has been published in leading international marketing journals such as the *Journal of Marketing* and *International Journal of Research in Marketing.*

Frans Mäyrä, PhD, is professor of Information Studies and Interactive Media, with specialization in digital culture and game studies in the University of Tampere, Finland. He is heading the University of Tampere Game Research Lab, and has taught and studied digital culture and games from the early 1990s. His research interests include game cultures, meaning making through playful interaction, online social play, borderlines, identity, as well as transmedial fantasy and science fiction.

Nicolas Michinov, PhD, is a professor of Social Psychology at the University of Rennes 2 (France). He was director of a technological research team until 2008, and currently leads a social psychology research team. As a researcher in social psychology, he studies the interpersonal and intergroup processes involved in collaborative working and learning, both in face-to-face and online environments. His interests include social comparison, transactive memory, electronic brainstorming, and social identity, aiming to determine their influence on outcomes such as affect and academic performance. He is also involved in the development of new (online) research methods for the study of group processes, and in the pedagogical design of web-based learning environments (social learning, social gaming, etc.).

Daniel Pietschmann, PhD, is a postdoctoral researcher at the Institute for Media Research at Chemnitz University of Technology and a graduate of the interdisciplinary graduate program "Crossworlds: Connecting virtual and real social worlds" of the German Science Foundation. He holds a doctorate in empirical communication studies and wrote his thesis about the effects of sensorimotor interfaces on User Experience in video games and Virtual Reality. Most of his recent work focusses on Natural User Interfaces, immersion/presence, and skill transfer processes from video games to the physical world. Daniel's further research interests include psychological and physical aspects of experiencing digital media in general, TV studies, and transmedia storytelling.

Janne Paavilainen, MSc, is a games researcher at the Game Research Lab, University of Tampere, Finland. For the past decade, Janne has been involved in research projects focussing on mobile, casual, and social gaming. Janne's research interests are in game usability, playability, and player experience. Recently, he has studied the relationship of free-to-play revenue model, service design, and player experiences in social network games while finishing his doctoral dissertation on *Facebook* games.

Thorsten Quandt, PhD, holds the chair of Interactive Media and Online Communication at the University of Münster (Germany) and is a distinguished scientist with extensive experience in digital games research, both nationally and internationally. Quandt is a proficient teacher in the field of digital games studies and the principle investigator of the EU-funded project SOFOGA. He is an ECREA (European Communication Research and Education Association) board member and the founding chair of ECREA's temporary working group on Digital Games Research. Formerly, he served as an officer in the ICA (International Communication Association).

John L. Sherry, PhD, is an associate professor in the Department of Communication and a faculty member in the Cognitive Science program at Michigan State University. He is the founder and former chair of the Game Studies Special Interest Group of the International Communication Association. His expertise is in the use of media for education, using cognitive information processing approaches to understand the way that players interact with video games and other media.

Jaakko Stenros, PhD, is a game and play researcher at the Game Research Lab (University of Tampere). He has published five books and more than 50 articles and reports and has taught game studies and Internet studies for almost a decade. Stenros is a popular lecturer in and outside academia on topics ranging from the design of fictional stories for real-world environments to approaching gamification through the prism of playfulness. He is currently working on understanding and documenting adult play and uncovering the aesthetics of social play, but his research interests include norm-defying play, role-playing games, pervasive games, and playfulness. His work has received many awards, most recently a prize for the best dissertation of the year at the University of Tampere. Stenros has also collaborated with artists and designers to create ludic experiences. He lives in Helsinki, Finland.

Chuen-Tsai Sun, PhD, is adjunct professor of Computer Science and Education at National Chiao Tung University, Taiwan. He is currently engaged in research and teaching in the areas of digital games, digital learning, social network analysis, and artificial intelligence. His work on game study consists of: (1) player behaviour and motivation in massively multiplayer online games, including players' altruistic and deviant behaviours, networking strategies, identity negotiation, and self-regulation, as well as the roles of games onlookers, and player guild dynamics; (2) game design and its impacts on gameplay, including game spatial structures and task deployment, game reward systems, private game servers, and freemium business model; and (3) effects of commercial video games and digital scaffolds on players' cognitive elaboration and problem-solving behaviours. He coauthored with Holin Lin the Massively Multiplayer Online Role-Playing Games (MMORPGs) entry on International Encyclopedia of Digital Communication and Society.

Wai Yen Tang, PhD, holds a doctorate in Communication at The Ohio State University. His research interests include video games' influence on aggressive and prosocial behaviours and the social psychology of video game players in online environments. His dissertation and recent works examine the causal factors of sexual harassment within online video games and its consequences.

Jan Van Looy, PhD, is assistant professor at the research group for Media and ICT (iMinds-MICT), Ghent University, Belgium. In 2006, he finished his doctorate on the shaping of digital games, which was published as Understanding Computer Game Culture (2010). In 2007–2008, he worked as a Postdoctoral Fellow at HUMLab, University of Umeå, Sweden. Since September 2008, he has been working, first as postdoctoral researcher and then as an assistant professor at Ghent University. There, he and his team conduct multidisciplinary user research into digital gaming and immersive media. Past publications have dealt with the effects of stereoscopic three-dimensional media, omnidirectional video experience, measuring player identification; antecedents of gamer identity; effects of stereotype threat on game experience, teacher adoption of digital games in the classroom, and effectiveness of serious games for language learning, awareness raising, mental calculus and personal empowerment and social inclusion. Current research interests of the Gaming and Immersive Media Lab (www.mict.be/gaming) include brain correlates of flow experience, psychophysiological effects of gender stereotype threat, methodology for serious game effectiveness research, player persistence in exergames, high dynamic range video, and augmented reality quality of experience.

Georg Valtin, PhD, is currently working as a researcher at the professorship of Media Psychology at the Chemnitz University of Technology. As a former editor of gaming magazines like *PC Games* and *GameStar*, he has a thorough understanding and deep expertise of computer games. His main research interests include social and psychological effects of computer games, psychophysiological measurement of cognitive activities and emotional reactions, as well as prosocial and moral behaviour in the context of media usage. Furthermore, he is involved in the development and testing of new instruments, measures and research methods for the study of audiovisual media in general.

Jasmien Vervaeke, MSc, obtained her degree in Experimental and Theoretical Psychology in July 2013 at Ghent University. Since August 2013, she worked as a junior researcher at iMinds-MICT-UGent and conducted experimental research into the quality of experience of stereoscopic three-dimensional, multiviewpoint images, 360° videos and augmented reality, amongst others. She is currently a doctoral student for the Psychopathology and Affective Neuroscience Lab of the Faculty of Psychology and Educational Sciences at Ghent University where she is developing a gamified tool that is aimed at diagnosing and training cognitive control impairments in remitted depressed patients, in order to prevent them from having a relapse, in consultation with iMinds-MICT-UGent where she currently is an affiliate member.

Index

booth babes 124

Candy Crush Saga 18, 60
casual game(s) 17, 18–9, 21
casualization 5, 83–4, 86, 88–92;
    casual revolution 18
colocated 47–9, 58, 72, 97–8
Computer Mediated Communication
    (CMC) 67, 70–8, 118
cooperation 33, 83–5, 88–9, 91, 99
cultivation 20, 140–1, 144
"culture of masculinity" 139

Darfur is Dying 153, 156, 161
Day, F. 122
Depression Quest 157, 161–4, 167
Dungeons and Dragons 82

Entertainment Software Rating
    Board (ESRB) 102
Everquest 84–5, 89

Facebook 16–8, 21, 23, 26–7, 161,
    172, 174, 179, 196; *Facebook*
    games 3, 11–2, 15–22, 23, 25, 27
Farmville 3, 16, 23
Flow Theory 33

group flow 39
game design 12, 16, 18–21, 24–5,
    35, 44, 82, 154
gamer 3, 6, 11, 15, 18, 19, 85, 115–6,
    143; gamer culture 2, 6, 83, 85, 141
gamer identity *see* social identity
    120, 143
gaming capital 14, 22, 25
gaming community 137, 181
Grand Theft Auto (GTA) 97, 140
grounded theory 50, 54–5

Huizinga, J. 187–9
human computer interaction (HCI)
    12, 27

League of Legends 3, 35–6, 128, 181
Local Area Network (LAN) 15,
    53–4, 123

Marx, K. 191–2, 194–6
Massively Multiplayer Online Game
    (MMOG) 7, 67–9, 71, 77–8, 172–3,
    177, 180–3
Massively Multiplayer Online Role
    Playing Game (MMORPG) 5,
    82–93, 98
misogyny 141, 143, 145

online disinhibition effect 117
online games 15, 67, 73, 77, 92,
    116–8, 126, 143, 172–3, 178, 207;
    online gaming 5, 86, 117, 141–2,
    145, 173, 176–9, 182–3

PacMan 15
Piaget, J. 13
player communities 6, 11–2, 14, 23,
    85, 87, 91, 137, 141–5
Playful Experiences (PLEX)
    Framework 21

Sarkeesian, A. 123, 142
Sexism 6, 115–6, 122–8, 137, 141–5;
    benevolent sexism 119, 141; hostile
    sexism 117–9, 121, 123, 143
sexual harassment 116–9, 121, 124–8,
    141, 143, 145
social dominance orientation (SDO)
    118–9, 143
social identity 143

Social Identity Model of
   Deindivduation Effects
   (SIDE) 117–8
social network games *see Facebook
   games*
social play 3, 13, 21–3, 26–7, 46,
   48–50, 53, 55, 57–8, 60–1, 92
*Star Wars: The Old Republic
   (SWTOR)* 87, 89–91

Tennis for Two 14, 98
"third place" 85
Tomb Raider 47, 139
toxic gamer culture 6, 141

upward spiral 89

World of Warcraft (WoW) 4–5, 47, 54,
   70–9, 83–91, 122, 142, 179, 181–2

For Product Safety Concerns and Information please contact our EU
representative GPSR@taylorandfrancis.com
Taylor & Francis Verlag GmbH, Kaufingerstraße 24, 80331 München, Germany